Study Guide

with Programmed Units and Learning Objectives
for Hilgard, Atkinson, and Atkinson's
Introduction to Psychology
Seventh Edition

Rita L. Atkinson

John C. Ruch
Mills College

 Harcourt Brace Jovanovich, Inc.

New York   San Diego   Chicago   San Francisco   Atlanta

Cover: details from Morris Louis, *Aleph Series I:* 1960, Private Collection. Photograph courtesy André Emmerich Gallery.

Chapter opening art: Elizabeth Wiener

Tables on pages 160 and 161 from Reese, E.P., Howard, J., and Reese, T.W., *Human Behavior: Analysis and Application.* Dubuque, Iowa: William C. Brown, 1978. Used by permission of the publisher.

Art on page 207 by Geri Davis.

ISBN: 0-15-543670-8

Library of Congress Catalog Card Number: 78-71165

Printed in the United States of America

Contents

Each chapter in this *Guide* consists of Learning Objectives, a Programmed Unit, Terms and Concepts, a Self-Quiz, and Individual and/or Group Exercises.

To the Instructor

The *Study Guide* is designed to assist students in mastering the content of the introductory course. In the preparation of the *Study Guide,* consideration was given to four major difficulties students often encounter: First, they may be uncertain about what to learn from each chapter—how to distinguish crucial material from less important details. Second, they may fail to learn the meanings of specific psychological concepts and terms. Third, they may have no satisfactory way of knowing how well they have mastered the material until after an examination (which often is too late). Fourth, they frequently find it difficult to understand or appreciate the role that research plays in psychology.

The five sections of each chapter in this *Study Guide* have been designed to help students in each of these areas. The first section is a list of *learning objectives* to help students focus on what they should learn from the chapter. Next is a *programmed unit,* which gives students a preliminary acquaintance with some of the terms and ideas covered in the chapter. Students should work on this unit *before* reading the corresponding text chapter. Next is a list of the important *terms and concepts* in the chapter. After reading the programmed unit and the text, students should be able to provide brief identifications for each of these. Items missed then become an object for further study. Next is a multiple-choice *self-quiz,* which provides students with an opportunity to practice taking exams and, at the same time, points out their areas of weakness. Finally, there are *individual and class exercises,* which give students a closer look at one or more of the concepts discussed in the chapter, a chance to explore some interesting aspects of human behavior, and a feeling for the way information is derived from research. A few of the exercises must be done in class, but most have been planned so that students can carry them out on their own if the instructor does not want to take class time. The usual procedure is for each student to collect data, which he or she can then analyze or bring to class; each student's data can then be combined with those of other students for analysis and discussion.

To the Student: How to Use This Guide

The *Study Guide* is designed to help you in several ways: It tells you what you should learn from each chapter; it introduces the concepts and terms you will encounter in the text; it provides examination questions that will enable you to determine just how much you have learned; and, finally, it suggests exercises that will give you an understanding of the interests of the psychologist and, in most cases, a look at psychological research methods.

Each chapter in the *Study Guide* parallels one in the text, and there are five sections for each chapter. The first section of each chapter in the *Study Guide* lists the *learning objectives*—the ideas and facts you should learn from the chapter. Look them over before you start to read the chapter. You may want to refer back to each objective after you have covered the appropriate section in the text. Or you may prefer to complete the chapter and then see if you have mastered all the objectives. In any event, the learning objectives cover the important ideas in each chapter; they include topics you will probably be expected to know on an examination.

The second section of each chapter uses a technique of learning called *programmed instruction,* a method of self-instruction. This technique, based on certain principles of learning explained in Chapter 7 of your text, aids in the understanding and mastery of material.

These programmed units are intended as *previews* of the corresponding chapters in your textbook. From each programmed unit you will acquire an acquaintance with *some* of the key ideas and concepts presented in the text; as a result, you should be able to read the text chapter with increased understanding. Although the programmed units are meant to be completed before you read the text, they also may be profitably used later as a review before examinations.

A word of warning: The programmed units cannot serve as a substitute for the text chapters. They do not treat all the important ideas presented in the text—for the programmed units to do so would require a book many times the size of this one. Even the ideas they do cover are treated in much greater detail in the text. If you work through a programmed unit, however, and then go on to study the text, you will master the text treatment more easily than if you had not gone through the programmed material.

The programmed unit consists of a series of short steps called "frames." Each frame requires you to make a *response*—either by filling in a blank or by circling one of two words. To the left of the frame, on the same line as the blank, is the correct response.

Use a paper or cardboard strip to cover the answer column to the left of the program. After you have written your answer in the appropriate blank in the frame, move the strip down only far enough to reveal the correct answer. If you have made a mistake, cross out your answer and write the correct one above it.

Once you have completed the programmed unit, read the corresponding chapter in the text. After you study the text chapter, turn to the *terms and concepts* section of the *Study Guide* and see how many you can identify correctly. If you have trouble, consult the appropriate section of the chapter or look in the glossary. The list of terms and concepts may seem long for some chapters, but if you learn them all you will have a good grasp of the material that is likely to appear on an examination.

Next, turn to the *self-quiz* section of the *Study Guide* and answer all the questions. Check your answers against the answer key; for questions on which you made an error go back to the text and review the appropriate material.

The final section of each *Study Guide* chapter presents one or more *exercises* designed to illustrate various aspects of psychological research. A few of the demonstrations require special equipment and must be presented by the instructor in class, but most are designed so that you can carry them out on your own. Sometimes you may be asked to do an exercise on your own but to bring the data to class so that the data from all students may be combined for analysis and discussion. The exercises in the *Study Guide* are designed to give you a better understanding of scientific methodology, some interesting insights into human behavior, and a feeling for how psychologists investigate the types of problem presented in the chapters.

To summarize: There are five sections in each chapter of the *Study Guide:* learning objectives, programmed unit, terms and concepts, self-quiz, and individual or class exercise(s). First look over the learning objectives and complete the programmed unit for a chapter, then read the chapter, and then proceed to the terms and concepts for identification, the self-quiz, and the exercise(s). These sections are designed to help you understand the concepts in the text, to allow you to evaluate your learning, and, finally, to introduce you to the methods of psychology. It is important to remember, however, that the *Study Guide* is designed as a supplement, not a substitute, for the text. Used properly, the *Study Guide* will enhance your comprehension of the text's contents.

1

The Nature of Psychology

LEARNING OBJECTIVES

1-1.   Be able to name and define the five approaches to psychology used in the text. Know what characterizes each, and how each approach differs from the other four.

1-2.   Be able to state the definition of psychology given in the text. Be familiar with the several ways in which it has been defined and how the definition has changed over time.

1-3.   Be familiar with the different fields of specialization within psychology.

1-4.   Understand the interrelationships between basic and applied research and between the behavioral and social sciences. Be able to specify how psychology fits into each of these relationships.

1-5.   Know what distinguishes the experimental method from other methods of observation. Be able to define, and to differentiate between, an independent variable and a dependent variable.

1-6.   Be familiar with the observational, survey, test, and case-history methods as they are used in psychology. Understand when and why each is used and the advantages and disadvantages of each.

1-7.   Know what is involved in the designing of an experiment. Be able to define, and to differentiate between, an experimental group and a control group. Understand what is meant by a multivariate design and why it would be used.

1-8.   Understand the use of a mean in experimental design, including the use of tests of the significance of a difference between means.

1-9.   Know when correlation is an alternative to experimentation and understand its advantages and disadvantages.

1-10.   Know the meaning of differences in the size and arithmetic sign of a coefficient of correlation. Be able to show, with an example, why correlation cannot define cause and effect.

psychology
(or people)

1. *Psychology* studies people from a number of different viewpoints. This book will cover five approaches to the study of _____ .

2. The *neurobiological approach* attempts to relate a person's actions to events taking place within the *nervous system*. If you measure the activity of nerve cells in different parts of the brain when a person is angry, you would be studying emotion from

neurobiological

the neuro_____ approach.

nervous

3. The neurobiological approach to psychology studies the relation between a person's thoughts or actions and events taking place within the _____ system.

4. A study relating changes in the nerve cell structure to the learning of a new task is

neurobiological

an example of the _____ approach to psychology.

nervous

5. Instead of studying events occurring in the _____ system, we can focus on the individual's *behavior*.

6. Behavior refers to those activities of an organism that can be *observed*. When we

behavior

observe a child laughing or talking, we are observing _____ .

observed

7. Behavior refers to any action of an organism that can be _____ .

8. If we measure the neural hormones secreted when a person is angry, we are using

neurobiological

the _____ approach to study emotion. If, instead, we count the number of times the person strikes his or her fist on the table when

behavioral

angry, we are using the _____ approach.

observable
internal

9. The *behavioral approach* focuses on (*observable/internal*) events; the neurobiological approach studies (*observable/internal*) events.

10. Some behaviorists do study events occurring within the body, provided they can be objectively measured. But a strict behavioral approach, called *stimulus-response* (S-R) *psychology,* focuses on the *stimuli* that elicit behavioral *responses* and is not concerned with what goes on inside the organism. Stimulus-response psychologists

responses

study stimuli and _____ rather than internal events.

11. An experimenter studying how quickly a person can press a lever in response to the

stimulus-response

onset of a tone would probably be a _____-_____ psychologist.

12. Strict stimulus-response psychologists are not concerned with the mental processes that intervene between hearing a tone (the stimulus) and pressing a lever (the

response

response). They are interested only in the stimulus and the _____ . *Cognitive* psychologists, on the other hand, study the way the mind *processes* sensory information.

13. A psychologist who studies how the mind processes incoming information is called

cognitive

a _____ psychologist. *Cognition* refers to those mental processes by which sensory information is transformed in various ways, coded and stored in memory, and retrieved for later use.

14. As you read this sentence your mind transforms the stimuli of "marks on paper" into visual images and compares those images with others stored in memory to arrive at meaning. The events that intervene between stimulus input and your response are

cognition

what we mean by _____ . Perceiving, remembering, and thinking

processes

are all cognitive _____ .

thinking

15. Cognitive processes include perceiving, remembering, and _____ .

cognitive process

Perceiving is a _____ _____ , and so is remembering.

16. Cognitive psychologists are usually interested in *conscious* mental processes, such as

remembering

perceiving, _____ , and thinking, rather than *unconscious*
processes. Conscious processes are mental events of which we are *aware*. Percep-

conscious

tions, memories, emotions, and dreams are all _____ processes of
which we are aware.

17. Conscious processes are those internal psychological events of which we are

aware

fully _____ . If you are angry and are aware that you are angry,

conscious

this is a _____ process.

18. Some internal events are unconscious; these are emotions, repressed memories, and desires of which we are not aware. Internal psychological events of which we are

unconscious

unaware are called _____ processes.

19. If you are angry at your mother but are not aware of this anger, then it is an

unconscious

_____ process.

unaware
(or not aware)

20. The *psychoanalytic approach,* developed by Sigmund Freud, assumes that much of
our behavior is influenced by unconscious processes of which we are _____ .

21. Freud believed that many of the forbidden or punished impulses of childhood are

unconscious

driven out of awareness and become _____ . He assumed that
such unconscious impulses are expressed indirectly in dreams, slips of speech, and
other forms of behavior.

22. The assumption that many of an individual's impulses are unconscious is basic to

psychoanalytic

the _____ approach.

23. Freud believed that unconscious impulses are usually concerned with *sex* or *aggres-*

aggressive
consciousness
(or awareness)

sion. Sexual and _____ impulses are those most often punished in
children, and thus those most apt to be banished from _____ .

24. A fifth approach to the study of psychology focuses on the individual's *subjective experience,* the individual's own perception and interpretation of events. This approach is called *phenomenological* because it looks at events, or phenomena,

individual

through the eyes of the _____ .

subjective

25. The phenomenological approach is concerned with _____ experience rather than behavior. On her first day at school a little girl sits in the corner
crying. If you note the frequency and loudness of her sobs, you are using the

behavioral

_____ approach. If, instead, you ask her to describe how she

phenomenological

views the situation, what it means to her, you are using the _____
approach.

subjective

. The phenomenological approach focuses on the individual's _____

experience

_____ . Some phenomenological theories are also called *humanistic* because they emphasize those "human" qualities that distinguish people from
animals—primarily their *free will* and their drive toward *self-actualization.*

. Humanistic theories reject the idea that we are mechanically controlled either by
external stimuli or by unconscious impulses. We are responsible for our own actions

will

and thus are said to have free _____ .

. The psychological approach that focuses on the individual's subjective experience is

phenomenological

called _____ . Within this approach are theories

humanistic

that emphasize self-actualization and free will; they are called _____ .
Self-actualization refers to our need to develop our potential to the fullest.

self-

29. Our natural tendency to actualize our potential to the fullest is called _____

actualization

_____ .

30. For review, identify each of the following approaches to the psychological study of
people.

neurobiological

a. Relates actions to events in the brain and nervous system. _____

behavioral (or
stimulus-response)

b. Relates stimuli to observed responses. _____

cognitive

c. Focuses on the way the mind processes information. _____

psychoanalytic

d. Emphasizes unconscious processes. _____

phenomenological
(or humanistic)

e. Emphasizes subjective experience, free will, and self-actualization.

_____

31. Because there are so many different approaches to the study of psychology, it is
difficult to define the field precisely. For our purposes we will define psychology as
the science that studies behavior and mental processes. Behavior refers to any action

observed

of the organism that can be _____ . Mental processes are internal

are not

events that (*are/are not*) directly observable.

behavior

32. Psychology is defined as the science that studies _____ and mental

conscious

processes. If we are aware of our mental processes, they are _____ .

awareness

Unconscious mental processes are not available to one's _____ .

mental processes   **33.** Psychology is the science that studies behavior and _____ _____, both conscious and unconscious.

34. The aim of the science of psychology is to discover *relationships among variables*. A *variable* is something that changes, something that can take on different values. "To vary" means "to change"; therefore a quality that is subject to change is called a

variable   _____ .

is   **35.** A person's rate of breathing in different situations (*is/is not*) likely to change.

variable   Breathing rate is thus a _____ .

36. Many experiments in psychology study more than one variable. If we wished to dis-

two   cover the effect of fear upon breathing rate, we would have _____ (*number*) vari-

relationship   ables in the study. We would be trying to discover the rel_____

rate, fear   between the variables of breathing _____ and _____ .

37. *Time* is a variable in many experiments. A psychologist who wants to determine the effect of the passage of time on forgetting might ask several subjects to memorize the same set of materials and then have them recall the materials after varying intervals of time. In this case the variable whose effect the psychologist was trying to

time   discover would be _____ .

38. The psychologist studying the rate of forgetting by varying the passage of time is able to manipulate the time variable by deciding when he or she will test the subject's memory. A variable that is directly controlled or *manipulated* by the experimenter is called an *independent variable*. Time, in the experiment we have been

independent   describing, is an _____ variable.

39. We call such a variable independent because its value does not depend on the values

manipulated   of any other variable. Instead, it is controlled or _____ by the experimenter.

40. The experimenter can control or manipulate time in an experiment but cannot directly control or manipulate forgetting. If the experimenter finds, however, that forgetting is affected by the passage of time, it can be assumed that forgetting is *dependent* on time. If time is called an independent variable, then forgetting can be

dependent   called a(n) _____variable.

41. The independent variable is the variable manipulated by the experimenter. The variable whose value may vary as a result of changes in the independent variable is the

dependent   _____ variable. In other words, the value of the dependent variable is dependent on the value of the independent variable.

42. If we want to discover the effects of marijuana on sexual behavior, marijuana will

independent   be the _____ variable and sexual behavior will be the dependent variable.

43. If we are concerned with the effect of age on the accuracy of visual perception, age of the subject is the independent variable and the accuracy of perception is the

dependent _____ variable.

44. If an experimenter varies the temperature in a classroom to determine its effect on

independent examination grades, the temperature level is the _____ vari-

dependent able and the examination grades of the students constitute the _____
variable.

45. In a laboratory experiment the variable the experimenter manipulates, the

independent _____ variable, can be varied with precision. Similarly, the

dependent variable that is a consquence of the subject's behavior, the _____
variable, can be carefully measured. Other variables that the investigator does not
want to influence the outcome of the experiment can be *controlled.*

46. For example, if we want to study the effect of sleep loss on learning ability, we can
select subjects of the same age and intelligence, provide them with the same diet
and living conditions, and then see how their performance on a learning task (such

sleep as memorizing a poem) varies with the amount of _____ they are permitted.
In this situation, variables that we do not want to influence the results (such as age,

controlled intelligence, and diet) are con_____ . We can thus be fairly confi-

dependent dent that differences in scores on the learning task, the _____

independent variable, result from different amounts of sleep, the _____
variable.

control 47. Laboratory experiments thus enable us to _____ variables that we do
not wish to influence our results, as well as provide the means for careful manipula-

independent tion of the _____ variable and precise measurement of the

dependent _____ variable.

48. But it is not possible to study all types of behavior in the laboratory. *Observation* in
a natural setting is another method psychologists use to study behavior. Suppose we
want to know how a child's aggressiveness on the school playground is related to his
or her behavior at home. If the mother's answers to a questionnaire indicate that
the child is quite "aggressive" at home, will the child also exhibit aggressive behavior
on the playground? We cannot answer this question in the laboratory, where vari-

controlled ables can be precisely _____ . Instead we must determine how

observations the ratings provided by the mother correspond to _____
made by trained observers who record notes on the child's behavior on the playground.

49. The relationship between home behavior and playground behavior in this case (*is/

is not *is not*) determined by manipulating aggressive behavior at home and studying the
results on the playground; instead we observe both variables as they occur in nature
and then look for a *relationship* between them.

50. With observational methods we must find some method of determining the

relationship _____ between the two variables. The relationship between

| manipulate (or control) | two variables in situations in which we cannot experimentally _____ the variables is determined by *correlation*. |

51. Suppose we want to know whether "cooperativeness" is a personality characteristic that persists throughout life. Will a child who exhibits cooperative behavior in nursery school be judged cooperative as an adult? In this case we cannot use the experimental method to answer the question. Instead we use the method of

correlation   cor_____ to determine the relationship between some measure of

cooperative   cooperative behavior in childhood and another measure of _____ behavior in adulthood.

cooperative   **52.** As a measure of _____ behavior in childhood we might use judgments by nursery school teachers, who rate each child according to the degree he or she cooperates in play as opposed to being aggressive or withdrawn. As a

measure   _____ of cooperative behavior in adulthood we could look at the same individuals when they are in college and note how their dormitory mates rate them on a scale of cooperativeness.

measures (or variables)   **53.** The figure below shows the relationship between these two _____ for ten different young men. A rating of 1 indicates very uncooperative behavior,

cooperative   while a rating of 12 indicates extremely _____ behavior. Note

2   that John received a rating of 2 in nursery school and the same rating of __ in col-

uncooperative   lege. Thus we would say that John's behavior has been consistently (*cooperative/ uncooperative*) over the years.

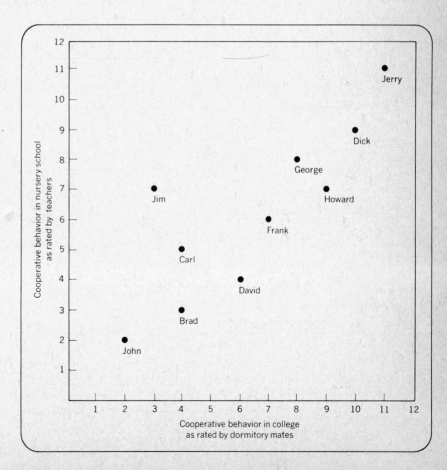

cooperative

54. Jerry received a rating of _____ in nursery school and also in college. His behavior appears to be consistently (*cooperative/uncooperative*).

7, less

Jim

55. What can we say about Jim and Howard? They both received the same rating of __ in nursery school, but in adulthood Jim is rated as (*more/less*) cooperative than Howard. Both boys changed over the years, but the change was greater for _____ .

ratings

correlation

56. The other subjects show some discrepancy between ratings in childhood and _____ in adulthood. But their ratings are similar enough to indicate a close relationship, or cor_____ , between cooperative behavior in childhood and cooperative behavior in adulthood.

correlation

57. If the c_____ between child and adult behavior were perfect, then all the ratings would fall on a straight *diagonal* line when plotted on the graph; each person would have received the same rating in adulthood as he did in

childhood

_____ .

correlation

58. If there were no relationship, or _____ , between adult and child cooperative behavior, then the scores would be scattered randomly all over the graph.

59. Since the scores in this hypothetical experiment fall very close to a straight

diagonal

_____ line, we can conclude that there is a close relationship, a high

correlation

_____ , between child and adult behavior.

60. The actual measure in a correlational study is the *coefficient of correlation,* signified by the lower-case letter *r*, which expresses the degree of relationship. If there had been a perfect correlation between cooperation in childhood and adulthood in

coefficient

the above study, then we would have a correlation coef_____ of $r = +1.00$.

61. The plus sign signifies that the relationship is *positive,* that a child who is cooperative will tend to be cooperative as an adult. A positive coefficient of

correlation

_____ , or *r,* indicates a positive relationship between the two

increase

variables; an increase in one variable is associated with an _____ in the other.

62. If, on the other hand, children who were cooperative in nursery school always turned out to be uncooperative adults, we would have a perfect *negative correlation.*

correlation

A negative _____ of $r = -1.00$ indicates that one variable

variable

increases as the other _____ decreases.

63. Life expectancy decreases as the amount a person smokes increases. This is an ex-

negative

ample of a (*positive/negative*) correlation.

64. Life expectancy increases as the adequacy of one's diet increases. This is an example

positive

of a _____ correlation.

positive

negative

65. A correlation of +1.00 signifies a perfect (*positive/negative*) relationship between two variables. A correlation of −1.00 indicates a perfect _____ relationship.

coefficient

r = .00

66. A correlation _____ of r = .00 signifies no relationship at all. If we tried to determine the relationship between hair color and grades in college, we would expect a correlation of (*r = 1.00/r = .00/r = −1.00*).

67. A correlation between r = .00 and either +1.00 or −1.00 indicates an imperfect

correlation

relationship. The more closely the _____ approaches 1.00, either plus or minus, the greater the degree of relationship, either positive or negative. In our study on cooperativeness, for example, we might expect a correlation

r

positive, is not

in the neighborhood of ___ = +.86 between childhood and adult behavior. There is a (*positive/negative*) relationship between the two variables, which (*is/is not*) perfect.

68. Cause-and-effect relationships cannot always be inferred from high negative or high positive correlations. In laboratory experiments we can manipulate the

independent

dependent

cannot

_____ variable and measure precisely its effect upon the _____ variable. In correlational studies we can only note that two variables vary together. We (*can/cannot*) say for certain that one variable *causes* the other.

69. For example, there is a high positive correlation between the softness of the asphalt in city streets during the summer and the infant mortality rate. We do not assume that some poisonous vapor from the soft asphalt causes infants to die. Instead we

heat (or a synonym)

attribute the relationship to a third variable—probably _____ .

70. Correlation implies the existence of a positive or negative relationship between two

causes

variables. It does not necessarily mean that one _____ the other.

71. Now let's review. Psychology is concerned with the study of behavior and mental activity. By "behavior" we refer to those activities of an organism that can be

observed

_____ by another person.

72. Mental activity includes internal events, such as emotions and memories, which we

conscious

unconscious

are aware of and can report; these are called _____ processes. Internal events of which we are not aware are called _____ processes.

activity

73. In studying behavior and mental _____ psychologists often measure quantities that are subject to change. Any quantity subject to change is called a

variable

_____ .

independent

74. The variable under the control of the experimeter is called the _____ variable; by manipulating this variable the experimenter can observe its effects upon

behavior

the b_____ of the subject.

75. The variable that the experimenter observes and that depends upon the value of the independent, dependent   _____ variable is called the _____

variable.

independent   **76.** In laboratory experiments we find careful manipulation of the _____

measurement   variable, precise _____ of the dependent variable, and

control   _____ over variables that we do not wish to influence the experiment.

77. In situations in which we cannot control the variables but simply make observations,

correlation   we use the method of _____ to determine the relationship

variables   between the _____ .

r   **78.** The coefficient of correlation, which is signified by the letter ___, tells us whether

relationship   there is a rel_____ between the variables, and whether the

positive, negative   relationship is _____ or _____ . It does not necessarily

causes   imply that one variable _____ the other.

A reminder: This programmed unit is intended as an introduction to, not a substitute for, Chapter 1 of the text. If you have mastered the terms presented here, you will draw more meaning from the text itself. But you will find that the text presents more ideas, and goes deeper into the ideas presented here, than it is possible to do in this programmed unit.

TERMS AND CONCEPTS

neurobiological approach _____

_____

_____

_____

behavioral approach _____

_____

_____

_____

S-R psychology _____

_____

_____

_____

cognitive approach *The way the mind prosses info.*

_____

_____

_____

psychoanalytic approach *Uncontous prosses*

_____

_____

_____

_____

unconscious processes _____

_____

_____

_____

phenomenological/humanistic approach _____

_____

_____

_____

developmental explanations* _____

_____

_____

_____

interactive explanations* _____

_____

_____

psychology _____

_____

_____

_____

experimental psychologist _____

_____

_____

_____

physiological psychologist _____

_____

_____

_____

developmental psychologist _____

_____

_____

_____

social psychologist _____

_____

_____

_____

personality psychologist _____

_____

_____

_____

clinical psychologist _____

_____

_____

_____

counseling psychologist _____

_____

_____

_____

school psychologist_____

_____

_____

*Indicates terms used in Critical Discussions

educational psychologist _____

_____

_____

_____

industrial psychologist _____

_____

_____

_____

engineering psychologist _____

_____

_____

_____

basic research _____

_____

_____

_____

applied research _____

_____

_____

_____

experimental method _____

_____

_____

_____

independent variable _____

_____

_____

_____

dependent variable _____

_____

_____

_____

observational method _____

_____

_____

_____

survey method _____

_____

_____

_____

test method _____

_____

_____

_____

case history _____

_____

_____

_____

longitudinal study _____

_____

_____

_____

experimental design _____

_____

_____

_____

experimental group _____

_____

_____

_____

control group _____

_____

_____

_____

mean _____

_____

_____

_____

correlation_____

_____

_____

_____

C

1. Different methods in psychology serve different purposes. For example, the _____ method may be used prior to the experimental method, as an introduction to the problem.
   a. observational
   b. test
   c. case history
   d. longitudinal

A

2. In order to study experimentally the simultaneous effects of several variables, you would use
   a. a graphical representation
   b. a multivariate design
   c. a coefficient of correlation
   d. the test method

3. In the early 1900s, John B. Watson
   a. introduced the "introspection" technique
   b. maintained that behaviorism was futile
   c. advanced a position later known as behaviorism
   d. advocated examining carefully a person's mental experiences and activities

4. Psychologists may be usefully categorized by
   a. the type of problems they are interested in
   b. their approach to problems that interest them
   c. the type of organization that employs them
   d. all of the above

5. A coefficient of correlation
   a. can be used only when experimental control is possible
   b. can be used with large masses of data
   c. is usually a good indication of cause-effect relationships
   d. all of the above

6. A psychoanalytic conception of people
   a. is somewhat pessimistic
   b. is widely accepted by psychologists
   c. is based on experimental studies
   d. emphasizes their differences from animals

7. A plan to vary a single dependent variable, while noting the effects on a single independent variable, is
   a. nonsense
   b. a simple "experimental desgn"
   c. likely to yield results which can be graphically represented as a curve
   d. both b and c

8. A correlation of +.70
   a. will always be statistically significant
   b. is twice as great as +.35
   c. is twice as great as +.50
   d. both a and c

9. A strict S-R psychologist would
   a. firmly oppose taking a "black box" approach
   b. not consider an individual's conscious experiences
   c. make inferences about mental activity from verbal reports of conscious experiences
   d. both a and c

10. The mean is
   a. the arithmetic average
   b. the sum of the measures divided by the number of measures
   c. the most common statistic used in psychology
   d. all of the above

11. A humanistic psychologist probably
   a. believes that people are driven by the same instincts as animals
   b. would be concerned primarily with an individual's subjective experience
   c. would see people as acted on by forces outside their control
   d. all of the above

12. In studying the influence of sleep on learning
   a. the amount of learning is the independent variable
   b. the amount of sleep is the dependent variable
   c. the amount of sleep is the independent variable
   d. sleep "is a function of" learning

13. The experimental method
   a. requires the use of a laboratory
   b. seeks relationships among variables
   c. always requires precision apparatus
   d. all of the above

14. Cognitive psychology
   a. argues that the mind is active rather than passive
   b. developed partly in reaction to S-R psychology
   c. can be considered analogous to a computer
   d. all of the above

_____ 15. For controlling aggression, either a _____ or a _____ might suggest changing aspects of the environment.
  a. behaviorist, humanist
  b. psychoanalyst, humanist
  c. cognitive psychologist, neurobiologist
  d. neurobiologist, behaviorist

_____ 16. The control group
  a. is a comparable group tested in a different experiment
  b. refers to the people running an experiment
  c. does not receive the variable being studied
  d. none of the above

_____ 17. Would-be psychologists primarily concerned with satisfying their own curiosity should try to get into
  a. applied research
  b. the social sciences
  c. basic research
  d. Masters and Johnson's laboratory

_____ 18. Psychology has been defined by psychologists as the
  a. study of behavior
  b. science that studies behavior and mental processes
  c. study of mental activity
  d. all of the above

_____ 19. To say that a difference between two numbers is statistically "significant" is to say that it is
  a. trustworthy
  b. important
  c. of practical significance
  d. all of the above

_____ 20. A neurobiological concept of human beings
  a. relates people's actions to events in their brains and nervous systems
  b. is at present the best basis for understanding human psychological make-up
  c. offers at present only a remote possibility of a comprehensive theory of human behavior
  d. both a and c

KEY TO SELF-QUIZ

Page numbers refer to the textbook page on which the answer is found.

1. a p. 18	6. a p. 8	11. b p. 8	16. c p. 20
2. b p. 21	7. a p. 17	12. c p. 17	17. c p. 15
3. c p. 5	8. c p. 22	13. b p. 16	18. d p. 11
4. d p. 12	9. b p. 6	14. d p. 6	19. a p. 21
5. b p. 21	10. d p. 21	15. a p. 10	20. d p. 5

INDIVIDUAL EXERCISES

PUBLISHED PSYCHOLOGICAL RESEARCH

One way to get an idea of what psychologists do is to look at their publications. Go the library and ask where the psychological journals are located. They may be placed together in one area of the current periodical room, or they may be arranged alphabetically with the other periodicals. There are a large number of psychological journals published in the United States and in many other countries. Some, like the *Journal of Experimental Psychology,* the *Journal of Comparative and Physiological Psychology,* and *Developmental Psychology,* publish primarily research reports. Others, like the *Journal of Abnormal Psychology,* the *Journal of Personality* and *Social Psychology,* the *Journal of Applied Psychology,* and the *Journal of Educational Psychology,* publish both theoretical and research papers. *The Psychological Review* presents original theoretical papers; *The Psychological Bulletin* publishes articles reviewing and evaluating areas of research. *The American Psychologist* publishes the official papers of the American Psychological Association, as well as articles of general interest to psychologists. *Contemporary Psychology* reviews current books in the field. These are some of the general research publications in psychology; many other publications are devoted to more specific interests, for example, *Perception and Psychophysics* and *Psychotherapy: Theory, Research, and Practice.*

In addition to these professional psychological journals, several other publications present articles of interest to psychologists. *Human Behavior* and *Psychology Today* offer brief research summaries and longer articles by and about psychologists but written for a nonprofessional audience.

Other publications that deal with a variety of scientific topics also include articles on psychology. New and important findings frequently appear in the prestigious but often difficult journal *Science. American Scientist, Scientific American,* and *Smithsonian* offer general but more readable articles, often beautifully illustrated. A recently created journal, originally named *The Zetetic,* now called simply

The Skeptical Inquirer, seeks to present a carefully documented scientific view of a wide range of paranormal claims, from ESP and UFOs to plant perception and psychic archeology.

Glancing at the index and scanning a few articles in several of these journals will give you an idea of the range of problems studied by psychologists, as well as the way in which psychological research is conducted and reported. If you are seeking particular information—whether for personal interest or for an assignment—there are numerous abstracting systems, which both index and summarize all the articles published in hundreds of journals. The professional psychology journals will be found in *Psychological Abstracts,* while related material will be in *Sociological Abstracts* or *Educational Index.* The *Reader's Guide to Periodical Literature* indexes general publications. Your librarian can help you learn to use these systems. (For further suggestions see *Writing the Psychology Paper* by R. J. Sternberg.)

THE SCIENTIFIC METHOD

Introduction

The status of psychology as a science depends on its use of the experimental method. An experiment involves observation of some aspect of behavior (dependent variable) while one factor (independent variable) is systematically changed under certain specified conditions (controlled variables). In the experimental method all the factors producing a given result, except the one whose effects are being examined, are held constant. Before an experiment is performed, the experimenter generally states a hypothesis describing the process that he or she believes underlies the behavior under investigation.

Although the experimental method provides the most reliable source of scientific information and is the preferred method of science, difficulties are encountered even in simple experiments. Many experiments appear to have satisfied the fundamental requirement of controlling relevant variables). In the experimental method all the factors producing reveals the presence of overlooked, uncontrolled variables that may invalidate the results.

This simple experiment will provide you with an opportunity to criticize procedure and to become somewhat more familiar with the scientific method.

Procedure

The results of a fictitious experimental study are given in Tables 1 and 2. Read carefully the experimental problem, the hypothesis, the procedures used, the results obtained, and the conclusions drawn. Then, using the concluding questions as an aid, make an analysis of the experiment.

1. EXPERIMENTAL PROBLEM: To investigate the effects of drinking coffee (which contains caffeine) on the achievement of college students on a final examination in general psychology.

2. HYPOTHESIS: Two cups of black coffee taken immediately before a task requiring mental exertion increase a student's academic efficiency.

3. PROCEDURE: Two groups of subjects were used. Group 1 consisted of 200 freshmen who were matched in age, intelligence, sex, and grade-point average with the 200 freshmen in group 2. Subjects in both groups were enrolled in the elementary course in psychology. All subjects in group 1 drank two cups of black coffee immediately before taking the final examination. All subjects in group 2 were instructed not to take any stimulants during the day the final examination was to be taken. For purposes of analysis, the grades of the students of both groups were converted into the following numerical equivalents (grade points): A = 4; B = 3; C = 2; D = 1; and F = 0. The average grade-point score for each of the two groups was then computed on this basis.

4. RESULTS: The results of the experiment are summarized in the tables. Table 1 indicates the number and percentage of students in each group obtaining each of the five letter grades on the final exam in general psychology. Table 2 gives the average grade-point scores of the two groups.

These results indicate that the students in group 1 did consistently better than the students in group 2.

TABLE 1				
	Group 1 (drank coffee)		Group 2 (did not drink coffee)	
Grade	Number	Percent	Number	Percent
A	30	15	14	7
B	46	23	24	12
C	80	40	112	56
D	36	18	40	20
F	8	4	10	5

TABLE 2	
Group	Average grade-point score
1 (coffee drinkers)	2.25
2 (noncoffee drinkers)	1.96

5. CONCLUSIONS: Comparison of the final examination grades earned in general psychology by two groups of college students (a stimulant-taking group and a non–stimulant-taking group) indicates that taking a mild stimulant, such as two cups of black coffee, immediately before an examination increases the academic efficiency and achievement of freshmen college students in a general psychology course.

Questions for Discussion

1. What is the dependent variable in this experiment?

2. What is the independent variable in this experiment?

3. What were some of the controlled variables in this experiment?

4. What are some of the limitations of the experiment?

5. Why is this procedure superior to a simple correlation that would seem to imply the same finding? Suppose, for example, you were told that coffee drinking showed a high and statistically significant correlation with exam grades. What could you conclude?

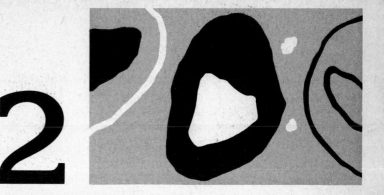

2
Biological Basis of Behavior

LEARNING OBJECTIVES

2-1. Be able to identify the major components of a neuron. Know the difference between afferent and efferent neurons and between neurons and nerves. Understand the major events of neural transmission.

2-2. Be able to identify the main features of a synapse and to describe synaptic transmission. Understand the difference between excitatory and inhibitory synapses.

2-3. Be able to name, and to diagram the relationships between, the major components of the nervous system. Be able to explain the functioning of a spinal reflex.

2-4. Know what structures comprise each of the three concentric layers of the human brain. Be able to describe, in general, the functions of these structures.

2-5. Be able to define and describe the cerebral cortex. Be able to describe its major areas and know approximately where each is located.

2-6. Be familiar with the right/left differences typically found in humans. Know what functions are usually controlled by each of the two hemispheres.

2-7. Be able to describe, in general, the differing structure and function of the two divisions of the autonomic nervous system. Understand the general principle of antagonistic functioning and the exceptions to it.

2-8. Be familiar with the major endocrine glands and their hormones. Understand the interrelationships between the endocrine system and the autonomic nervous system.

2-9. Be able to define and differentiate between genes and chromosomes. Understand what is meant by dominant, recessive, and sex-linked genes. Be familiar with the several chromosomal-abnormality syndromes discussed in the text.

2-10. Understand the multiple contributions to human traits, including polygenic transmission and environmental interaction. Be familiar with the use of selective breeding and twin studies.

1. All behavior depends on the integration of bodily processes by the *nervous system*.

    system   The basic unit of the nervous _____ is the *neuron,* or nerve cell, which is
                diagramed below. The human nervous system contains many billions of these

    neurons   nerve cells, or _____ .

2. The neuron has three main parts: the *cell body,* the *dendrites,* and the *axon.* As you

    body   can see from the diagram, the wide part of the neuron is its cell _____ .

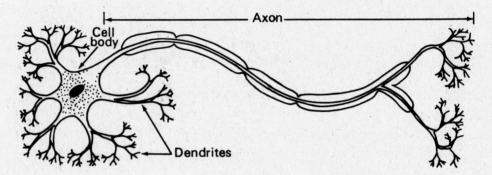

3. The short, branching fibers at one end of the neuron are the *dendrites.* The den-

    cell   drites and the _____ body receive messages from other neurons.

    dendrites   4. A neuron receives messages by way of its cell body or its _____.
                These messages are then transmitted to other neurons by way of the *axon.*

    dendrites   5. Messages are received by the cell body or the _____ of a neuron

    axon   and transmitted by the _____ .

    receiving   6. The dendrites are the (*receiving/transmitting*) end of the neuron and the axon is the
    transmitting   (*receiving/transmitting*) end.

    synapse   7. The junction between the axon of one neuron and the cell body or dendrites of the
                next neuron is called a *synapse.* This junction, or _____ , is not a direct
                connection. There is a slight gap across which the message must be transmitted.

    synapse   8. Neural transmission across this gap, or sy_____ , is usually by means of a
                chemical intermediary. The axon of one neuron releases a chemical, called a *neuro-*

    neuron   *transmitter,* into the synapse, stimulating the dendrites of the next _____ .

9. Neural transmission at the synapse is in one direction only. The axon sends the mes-

    synapse   sage and the dendrites receive it. The signal is transmitted across the _____

    axon, dendrites from the _____ of the first neuron to the _____or cell
                body of the next neuron.

10. The chemical intermediary that transmits the signal across the synapse is called a

    neurotransmitter _____ .

cell body	**11.** To review: The three main parts of the neuron are the _____ _____ ; the
dendrites, axon	_____, which receive(s) messages; and the _____, which
synapse	transmit(s) messages across the _____ .

12. While all neurons have these general features, they vary in size and shape, depending on the particular function they perform. Neurons that carry messages to the brain or spinal cord about what is going on in the environment or within the body are

neurons   called *afferent* _____ .

13. Afferent neurons carry messages to the _____ or spinal cord about what is

brain

environment, body   going on in the _____ or within the _____ .

14. For example, neurons that inform the brain that your skin is being pierced by a

afferent   needle would be called _____neurons.

15. Afferent neurons receive their input from *receptors,* which are specialized cells in the sense organs, skin, muscles, and joints. Receptors detect changes in the environment and translate these events into messages that are transmitted, via

afferent, spinal   _____ neurons, to the brain and _____ cord.

16. Special cells in the inner ear translate sound waves into signals that are transmitted to the brain via afferent neurons in the auditory nerve. These cells would be called

receptors   re_____ .

changes   **17.** Receptors detect _____ in the environment or within the body and

afferent   signal the brain by means of _____neurons.

18. Specialized cells within the joints tell us about the position of our arms and legs.

receptors   These cells would also be called _____ .

brain, spinal   **19.** Afferent neurons carry messages to the _____ or _____

cord   _____ . *Efferent neurons* convey signals from the brain or spinal cord to the muscles that control our movements as well as to those that control some of the internal organs.

efferent   **20.** When your brain signals your hand to move, the message is carried by _____

efferent   neurons. Contraction of the heart muscles is also controlled by _____

neurons   _____ .

afferent   **21.** Information from the environment is carried to the brain by _____

efferent   neurons. Signals to action are transmitted by _____ neurons.

22. A convenient way to remember the difference between *af*ferent and *ef*ferent

efferent   neurons is to remember that the outgoing, or ef_____ , neurons make connections with *ef*fectors, that is, with the muscles that have an *ef*fect on the individual's response to the environment.

23. A *nerve* is a bundle of axons belonging to many neurons. The axons of hundreds of

nerve

neurons joined together form a _____ .

afferent   24. Some nerves are composed mainly of the axons of incoming, or _____ ,

efferent   neurons; some contain mainly outgoing, or _____ , neurons; and some

axons   are composed of _____ from both types of neurons.

25. The *central nervous system* is composed of the brain and the spinal cord. The spinal cord provides connections for simple reflexes (such as the knee jerk) and for the passage of messages to and from the brain. Together, the brain and spinal cord con-

central nervous system   stitute the _____ _____ _____ .

spinal cord   26. The central nervous system consists of the brain and the _____ _____ .

afferent   27. The   incoming,   or _____ ,   neurons   and   the   outgoing,   or

efferent   _____ ,   neurons form connections in the brain and spinal cord. Since these are the chief centers in which junctions between neurons occur, you might expect the brain and spinal cord to contain large numbers of such junctions,

synapses   or sy_____ .

28. Nerves leading from the brain and spinal cord to other parts of the body form the *peripheral nervous system.* Some of these nerves carry incoming messages from

receptors   specialized cells, called _____ , that detect changes in the environ-

nervous   ment. Others carry messages from the central_____ system to the muscles that control movement of the body.

29. Nerves connecting the brain and spinal cord with the sense receptors, skeletal muscles, and body surface are part of the peripheral nervous system; they form the

nervous   *somatic division* of the peripheral _____ system.

peripheral   30. Another part of the p_____ nervous system is the *autonomic system,* which includes nerves running to the *glands* and *smooth muscles* (those found in the stomach, intestines, and other internal organs). We would expect the nerves

autonomic   leading to the salivary glands to be part of the (*somatic/autonomic*) system.

peripheral   31. The somatic and autonomic systems together make up the _____

nervous system   _____ _____ . The brain and the spinal cord form the

central nervous system   _____ _____ _____ . The division into systems helps in anatomical discussions; in actuality, however, all parts of the nervous system function in a highly integrated manner.

brain   32. Let's review. The central nervous system consists of the _____ and the

spinal cord   _____ _____ . All nerves outside of the brain and spinal cord are

peripheral   grouped into the _____ nervous system, which has two divisions:

somatic   the _____ division consists of nerves running to and from sense organs,

autonomic   skeletal muscles, and the body surface; the _____ division consists of nerves running to the glands and smooth muscles.

Since the brain is the most important part of the nervous system, we will need to look at it in more detail. The illustration of the human brain on page 22 is an adaptation of the illustration you will find in the text. In this programmed unit you will begin to learn the names of the parts of the human brain. Note that the text illustration, in addition to listing the labels shown here, provides lists of the various functions of each part of the brain. (These functions are also described in the text.) You will not learn all these functions from this programmed unit, but you will become acquainted with some of them. Now look at the illustration and go on to the next question. Refer to the illustration as necessary.

33. As the spinal cord enters the brain it enlarges to form the *brain stem* (not labeled on the illustration). The lower portion of the brain, connecting with the spinal cord,

brain stem   is the _____ _____ .

34. An important structure within the brain stem is the *medulla*. The medulla regulates breathing and controls some of the reflexes that help us maintain an upright pos-

medulla   ture. Some very basic life processes are regulated by the _____ .

35. Attached to the rear of the brain stem, just above the medulla, is a convoluted structure known as the *cerebellum;* it regulates intricate motor coordination. The complex movements involved in such activities as walking, dancing, speaking, and

cerebellum   playing a musical instrument are controlled by the _____ .

36. Starting in the brain stem and extending upward is a system of neural circuits called

system   the *reticular system.* The reticular _____ controls our state of *arousal* or

reticular   *alertness.* When we change from sleep to wakefulness, nerves in the _____

system   _____ are involved.

alertness   37. The reticular system controls our state of arousal or _____ .

38. The convoluted structure to the rear of the brain stem that controls complex motor

cerebellum   skills is the _____ .

39. Now locate on the diagram a small but vital structure in the center of the brain called the *hypothalamus.* The hypothalamus plays an important role in *motivation* and *emotion.* It helps regulate hunger, thirst, and sex; it influences our feelings of pleasure, fear, and anger. When we experience pangs of hunger, the brain structure

hypothalamus   involved is the _____ .

motivation   40. The hypothalamus plays an important role in _____ and emotion.

41. By regulating hunger and thirst the hypothalamus attempts to maintain *homeostasis,* a level of functioning characteristic of the healthy organism. If the blood-sugar level gets too low, the hypothalamus signals the organism to start eating. Ingested food

homeostasis   raises the level of sugar in the blood, thus restoring homeo_____ .

42. The hypothalamus attempts to maintain the body in a state of normalcy or con-

homeostasis   stancy. This optimal level of functioning is called _____ .

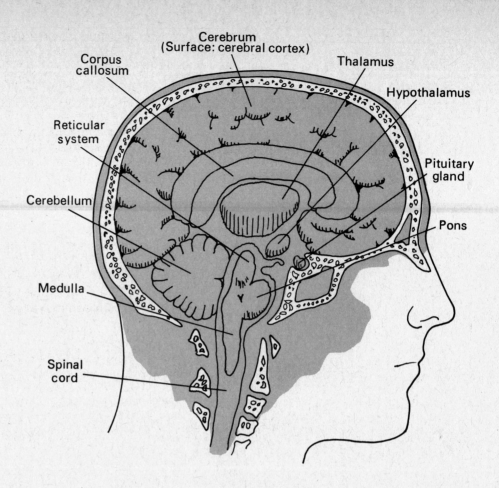

Cerebrum
(Surface: cerebral cortex)

Corpus callosum

Thalamus

Hypothalamus

Reticular system

Pituitary gland

Cerebellum

Pons

Medulla

Spinal cord

43. When the concentration of salt and certain other chemicals in the blood becomes too great, the hypothalamus signals the organism to start drinking water. Water intake dilutes the blood chemicals to the proper concentration. This is another

homeostasis   example of _____ .

44. The brain structure that maintains homeostasis and plays an important role in moti-

hypothalamus   vation and emotion is the _____ .

45. Now locate another part of the brain stem, the *thalamus*. This portion serves as a sensory relay station for impulses coming up from the spinal cord and down from the higher brain centers. In any activity that requires the coordination of informa-

thalamus   tion from several receptors, the (*hypothalamus/thalamus*) is likely to be involved.

spinal   46. The thalamus is a sensory relay station for impulses coming up from the _____

cord   _____ and down from the higher brain centers.

47. For a review of the brain areas discussed so far, identify the structures involved in each of the following functions.

cerebellum   a. Controls body coordination, as in walking or dancing. _____

                  b. Maintains homeostasis and plays important role in motivation and emotion.

hypothalamus   _____

thalamus   c. Serves as a sensory relay station. _____

reticular

system

medulla

d. Controls state of arousal, as from sleep to wakefulness. _____

_____

e. Regulates basic body processes such as breathing and postural reflexes.

_____

48. The large mass of brain tissue that surrounds the brain-stem structures is the *cerebrum*—the most highly developed portion of the human brain. The surface of the cerebrum is highly wrinkled, or convoluted. The fact that this surface, known as the *cerebral cortex,* has so many wrinkles, or convolutions, means that the total

greater

surface area is much (*greater/smaller*) than it would be if the surface of the cerebrum were smooth.

49. Since the cerebral cortex, or surface, of the cerebrum is so large, it provides room for many interconnections of neurons. Thus the cerebral cortex makes it possible for us to learn, remember, think, and carry on many of the activities that distinguish us from the lower animals. You might expect the cerebral cortex of a fish to

less

be (*more/less*) wrinkled, or convoluted, than that of a human being.

cerebrum, cerebral

50. The _____, with its wrinkled surface, the _____ cortex, is the part of the human brain that makes possible thinking and reasoning.

51. A top view of the brain, as distinguished from the side view shown here, would show that the cerebrum is divided into two halves, or hemispheres. (Your text will make this clear.) Now locate the *corpus callosum,* which contains fibers connecting the two cerebral hemispheres. The two cerebral hemispheres are connected by the

corpus callosum

_____ _____ .

52. Now locate the *pituitary gland,* a small structure below the hypothalamus. The pituitary gland is *not* a part of the nervous system; it is an important *endocrine gland.* Endocrine glands secrete special chemical messengers, called *hormones,* into

endocrine

the bloodstream. The pituitary gland is one of the most important _____ glands.

hormones

53. The chemical messengers, or _____, secreted by the endocrine glands help the hypothalamus maintain its normal level of functioning, called

homeostasis

homeo _____ . They also play an important role in growth, sexual and maternal behavior, emotions, and reactions to stress.

pituitary

54. The endocrine gland located just below the hypothalamus is the _____ gland. It is often called the *"master gland"* because it secretes the largest number of

hormones

h _____ and also controls the secretion of several other endocrine

glands

_____ .

pituitary, master

55. The _____ gland is often referred to as the "_____ gland" because its influence on the body is so pervasive. One of the pituitary hormones controls the timing and amount of *body growth.*

56. If an individual develops into a giant, we can suspect that a malfunctioning of the

pituitary

_____ gland is involved. Other hormones secreted by the pituitary gland trigger the action of the sex glands, or *gonads,* which, in turn, influence *mating* and *reproductive behavior.*

margin answers (left column):

master gland

body, mating (or
reproductive)

gonads

endocrine

adrenal

glands

autonomic

nervous

autonomic

aware
(or conscious)

smooth

antagonistic

antagonistic

sympathetic

---

57. We can see why the pituitary gland is called the "_____ _____," since it influences such important functions as _____ growth and _____ behavior.

58. In addition to triggering the action of the sex glands, or _____, pituitary hormones also influence the secretion of the *adrenal glands.*

59. One adrenal gland is located just above each kidney. The adrenal glands secrete hormones into the bloodstream, as do other _____ glands. Two important hormones secreted by the adrenal glands are *epinephrine* (also known as adrenalin) and *norepinephrine* (noradrenalin).

60. Epinephrine and norepinephrine are secreted by the _____ glands. They act in a number of ways to prepare the organism for an emergency.

61. We noted earlier that the autonomic nervous system consists of nerves running to the smooth muscles (such as line the stomach and other internal organs) and the g_____. It should not be surprising to learn, therefore, that there is a close interrelationship between the endocrine glands and the_____ _____ system.

62. The secretion of the adrenal glands is regulated by the autonomic nervous system. The autonomic nervous system controls many activities that are "autonomous" or "self-regulating." The process of digestion, for example, goes on autonomously without any conscious willing on our part. Digestion is controlled by the (*autonomic/central*) nervous system.

63. The self-regulating activities controlled by the autonomic nervous system can go on while a person is asleep or unconscious, that is, without the individual being _____ of them.

64. The autonomic nervous system has two divisions: the *sympathetic* and the *parasympathetic* divisions. These two divisions are often opposite, or *antagonistic,* in their actions. Both divisions control the glands and the _____ muscles, but their actions are often an_____.

65. The sympathetic division of the autonomic nervous system operates to *dilate* the blood vessels of the heart, while the parasympathetic division operates to *constrict* these blood vessels. This is an illustration of the fact that the two divisions are often opposite, or _____, in their action.

66. The sympathetic division tends to be active in *excited* states, while the parasympathetic division tends to be more important in *quiescent* states, or those activities that conserve and protect bodily resources. If you observe that a man's heart rate has speeded up, that he is perspiring profusely, and that his pupils are dilated, you might expect that the _____division of the autonomic nervous system is playing a part in these responses.

67. Since the adrenal gland is dominant in excited states, it would be logical to con-

parasympathetic

clude that the _____ division has no connection to this gland.

68. The two divisions of the autonomic nervous system are the _____

sympathetic
parasympathetic (either order),
sympathetic
parasympathetic

and the _____ divisions. The _____ division tends to be active during excited states, whereas the _____ division tends to take over during quiescent states.

autonomic

69. The _____ nervous system has two divisions, the sympathetic and

antagonistic

parasympathetic divisions, which are often _____ in their action.

70. Let's review. The *autonomic nervous system* derives its name from the fact that

autonomous

many of its activities are _____ , or self-regulating, and occur

aware

without our being _____ of them. It has two divisions that are often

antagonistic, sympathetic

_____ in their action: the _____ divi-

parasympathetic (either order)
sympathetic
parasympathetic
quiescent

sion and the _____ division. The _____ division tends to be active in excited states, whereas the _____ division tends to take over during _____ states.

peripheral

71. The autonomic nervous system is one division of the (*central/peripheral*) nervous system. Its nerves are outside of the brain and spinal cord, which constitute the

central

(*central/peripheral*) nervous system. The other part of the peripheral nervous sys-

somatic

tem is the _____ system, which consists of nerves running to and from the sense receptors, body surface, and skeletal muscles. All these systems coordinate in a complex manner to provide for the smooth functioning of the organism.

72. Many of our *physical characteristics* are inherited from our parents. *Genetics,* the

characteristics

science of heredity, shows how physical ch_____ such as eye and hair color are transmitted from one generation to the next. Psychological characteristics—ability, temperament, and emotional stability—may also depend to some extent on heredity. As you might guess, the branch of genetics that studies the inheritance of psychological or behavioral characteristics is called *behavior*

genetics

g_____ .

73. Behavior genetics studies the degree to which psychological characteristics are

inherited (or hereditary)

_____ .

74. The *hereditary units* that individuals receive from their parents and transmit to their offspring are carried by microscopic particles known as *chromosomes,* found within each cell of the body. Each human body cell has 46 chromosomes. At conception the human being receives 23 chromosomes from the father's sperm and 23

chromosomes

_____ from the mother's ovum. These 46 chromosomes form 23 *pairs,* which are duplicated in every cell of the body as the individual develops.

chromosomes

75. A fertilized ovum contains 46 _____ , 23 of its own and 23 received from the sperm.

76. The chromosomes are duplicated in every cell of the body as the individual develops. Thus every body cell contains _____ chromosomes arranged in 23 _____.

46, pairs

77. The chromosomes carry the basic units of heredity, which are called *genes.* Each chromosome carries many of these hereditary units, or _____. Like chromosomes, the genes occur in pairs; one gene of each pair comes from the sperm chromosome and one gene from the ovum _____.

genes

chromosome

78. Chromosomes occur in pairs, and each chromosome contains many pairs of _____.

genes

79. In human beings each chromosome carries more than 1,000 genes. Since the fertilized ovum has _____ pairs of chromosomes, the number of genes is high enough to make it extremely unlikely that any two persons would have the same heredity. The exception would be individuals who develop from the same ovum; such individuals are called *monozygotic twins.*

23

80. Monozygotic twins develop from the same _____ . They are also called identical twins; since they share the same heredity, they are alike in many respects.

ovum

81. Fraternal or *dizygotic twins* develop from two separate ova fertilized by two separate sperm cells. Thus they (*do/do not*) share the same heredity and are no more alike than ordinary siblings.

do not

82. Because _____ twins have exactly the same heredity, differences between them are attributed largely to differences in environment.

monozygotic
(or identical)

83. Genetic studies frequently compare the similarities between monozygotic twins and those between dizygotic twins to determine the extent to which a psychological characteristic is influenced by heredity. For example, monozygotic twins are much more similar in intelligence test scores than dizygotic twins. This finding suggests that (*heredity/environment*) influences intelligence.

heredity

84. If one monozygotic twin develops a mental illness called schizophrenia, there is a 60 percent chance that the other twin will be schizophrenic. Among dizygotic twins there is only a 15 percent chance that if one twin is schizophrenic the other will be also. This indicates that there is a(n)_____ component in the susceptibility to some forms of schizophrenia.

hereditary
(or genetic)

TERMS AND CONCEPTS

neuron _____

_____

_____

_____

dendrite _____

_____

_____

_____

axon _____

_____

_____

_____

synapse _____

_____

_____

_____

terminal button _____

_____

_____

_____

afferent neuron _____

_____

_____

_____

efferent neuron _____

_____

_____

_____

nerve _____

_____

_____

_____

resting potential _____

_____

_____

action potential _____

_____

_____

_____

myelin sheath _____

_____

_____

_____

all-or-none principle _____

_____

_____

_____

graded potential _____

_____

_____

_____

neurotransmitter _____

_____

_____

_____

central nervous system _____

_____

_____

_____

peripheral nervous system _____

_____

_____

_____

somatic nervous system _____

_____

_____

_____

autonomic nervous system _____

_____

_____

interneuron _____

cerebral cortex _____

_____

_____

_____

_____

_____

cerebrum _____

motor area _____

_____

_____

_____

_____

central core _____

somatosensory area _____

_____

_____

_____

_____

_____

_____

cerebellum _____

association areas _____

_____

_____

_____

_____

thalamus _____

Broca's area _____

_____

_____

_____

_____

_____

_____

hypothalamus _____

corpus callosum _____

_____

_____

_____

_____

_____

_____

homeostasis _____

sympathetic division _____

_____

_____

_____

_____

reticular system _____

parasympathetic division _____

_____

_____

_____

_____

_____

_____

limbic system _____

endocrine gland _____

_____

_____

_____

_____

_____

_____

hormones _____

_____

_____

_____

pituitary gland _____

_____

_____

_____

adrenal glands _____

_____

_____

_____

behavior genetics _____

_____

_____

_____

chromosome _____

_____

_____

_____

gene _____

_____

_____

_____

dominant gene _____

_____

_____

_____

recessive gene _____

_____

_____

_____

sex-linked trait _____

_____

_____

_____

XYY syndrome _____

_____

_____

_____

polygenic trait _____

_____

_____

_____

selective breeding _____

_____

_____

_____

_____ 1. Which of the following is *not* one of the important types of cerebral cortex areas?
   a. visual area
   b. somatosensory area
   c. organization area
   d. language area

_____ 2. If you are a female with blue eyes, we know that
   a. your father had blue eyes
   b. one of your parents had blue eyes
   c. both of your parents had blue eyes
   d. none of the above

_____ 3. The human brain may be thought of as being composed of three concentric layers. Of these the _____ is on the outside, while the earlier evolutionary development, the

   _____ , is concealed within it.
   a. limbic system, central core
   b. cerebrum, limbic system
   c. limbic system, cerebrum
   d. cerebral hemispheres, cerebrum

_____ 4. The _____ gland has been called the "master gland" because it

   _____
   a. pituitary, controls the secretion of several other glands
   b. adrenal, produces the largest number of hormones
   c. pituitary, produces epinephrine
   d. adrenal, controls the secretion of several other glands

_____ 5. When a rat is raised in an "enriched" environment,
   a. it weighs more
   b. its rate of neural conduction becomes faster
   c. it develops a large and complex cerebellum
   d. it develops a heavier cerebral cortex

_____ 6. In sorting out the effects of environment and heredity, one ideally should study
   a. monozygotic twins
   b. dizygotic twins
   c. both of the above
   d. neither of the above

_____ 7. The minor, right hemisphere can usually comprehend language to the extent of

   a. responding to simple nouns by picking up the object
   b. responding to simple commands, for example, "wink" or "nod"
   c. producing simple sentences
   d. all of the above

_____ 8. The sympathetic and parasympathetic systems
   a. typically act in an antagonistic fashion
   b. are divisions of the autonomic nervous system
   c. may be involved in the same behavior via sequential action
   d. all of the above

_____ 9. Damage to the _____ results in jerky, uncoordinated movements, because of its central role in coordinating complex motor activity.
   a. cerebrum
   b. cerebellum
   c. medulla
   d. limbic system

_____ 10. Myelinated fibers do *not*
   a. utilize nodes
   b. have a uniformly thick sheath
   c. transmit impulses faster than unmyelinated ones
   d. represent a recent evolutionary development

_____ 11. When release of a neurotransmitter at a synapse produces a change in permeability in the direction of depolarization, the synapse is
   a. an excitatory one
   b. an inhibitory one
   c. becoming polarized
   d. in a refractory phase

_____ 12. The many large areas of the cerebral cortex not directly concerned with sensory or motor processes have been called
   a. projection areas
   b. organization areas
   c. association areas
   d. thinking areas

_____ 13. Homeostasis is maintained by the _____ , which also plays an important role in motivation.
   a. hypothalamus
   b. thalamus
   c. limbic system
   d. reticular system

14. In a test of a split-brain patient, if the name of an object is briefly flashed on the left half of the screen, he or she can
    a. say what the object is
    b. pick out the object from a pile of others
    c. write down what the object is
    d. all of the above

15. The simplest reflex may involve
    a. an efferent neuron and a motor fiber
    b. a connector neuron
    c. only afferent and efferent neurons
    d. a three-neuron reflex arc

16. The speech centers for left-handed people are
    a. usually in the left hemisphere
    b. usually in the right hemisphere
    c. typically in both hemispheres
    d. about evenly divided, with some left-handers having centers in the left hemisphere and some in the right hemisphere

17. Each neuron in the nervous system consists of three main parts: the _____, the _____, and the _____.
    a. glia, cell body, dendrites
    b. axon, nerve, cell body
    c. glia, axon, cell body
    d. dendrites, cell body, axon

18. The _____ nervous system includes both the _____ system and the _____ system.
    a. peripheral, central, autonomic
    b. somatic, autonomic, peripheral
    c. peripheral, autonomic, somatic
    d. autonomic, somatic, peripheral

19. A normal male child has received
    a. an X chromosome from his mother and a Y from his father
    b. a Y chromosome from each parent
    c. a Y chromosome from his mother and an X from his father
    d. an X chromosome from each parent

20. Synaptic transmission involves
    a. graded potentials
    b. a refractory phase
    c. an all-or-none principle
    d. all of the above

KEY TO SELF-QUIZ

1. c p.42	6. c p.58	11. a p.33	16. a p.46
2. d p.55	7. a p.49	12. c p.45	17. d p.30
3. b p.36	8. d p.51	13. a p.38	18. c p.35
4. a p.53	9. c p.38	14. b p.47	19. a p.56
5. d p.42	10. d p.42	15. c p.36	20. d p.32

INDIVIDUAL EXERCISE

REACTION TIME

Introduction

Every voluntary motor act takes time, not only to perform, once movement begins, but to initiate. Because we do not easily sense small time increments, we normally assume that a movement occurs as soon as we think about it. While this is an acceptable approximation for ordinary daily activity, it is an oversimplification when movements are judged with respect to small time intervals. We typically encounter such intervals in relation to rapidly moving objects: tennis balls, hockey pucks, and other objects outside us, or automobiles and airplanes, with us inside them. As various organizations concerned with automotive safety often tell us, a major portion of the distance needed to stop a car is covered between the time the stimulus for stopping occurs and the time when the brakes are applied. Although your braking may seem "immediate" to you, the time needed to register the stimulus, interpret it, decide on action, signal that action, and operate the muscles allows your car to cover a substantial distance.

The time between the onset of a stimulus and the subject's response is called the *reaction time*. Obviously we cannot have our readers running down hapless pedestrians in demonstrations of their reaction time. This exercise, however, is designed to demonstrate a similar phenomenon: movement past you while you take time to react. It provides you with a scientific approach and, for the less inhibited among you, a party trick.

Equipment Needed

Ruler (preferably a yardstick).

Procedure

While this exercise can be attempted by one person, it is really necessary for one person to test another.

1. Have your subject stand and hold out either hand with the thumb about an inch in front of the index finger and the fingers set to quickly squeeze together (see right photo). Hold the yardstick between the subject's fingers and thumb, and tell him or her to grasp the yardstick when you drop it. The subject is to watch your hand so that as soon as you release the yardstick,

he or she is prepared to grasp it. Both of you may be surprised to see that it drops several inches no matter how quickly the subject tries to react.

2. Make your procedure more precise by specifying the subject's finger-to-thumb gap each time and by starting with one of the inch markers of the yardstick opposite his or her middle finger so that you can measure the distance it falls.

3. An even better technique is to have your subject stand by a doorway, with his or her palm by the jamb and the fingertips curved loosely around the doorjamb (see

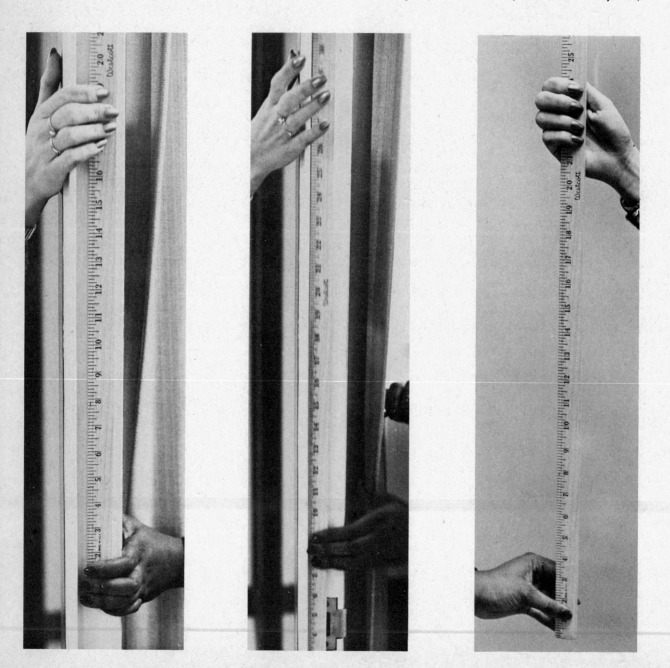

left photo). Begin with the yardstick held flat against the jamb and the zero mark beneath the subject's middle finger. This procedure helps assure a vertical fall of the yardstick and allows measurement directly from zero.

4. The number of inches the yardstick falls can be translated into seconds. For our purposes we can use the following equation for estimating the number of seconds it takes a falling body to move a certain distance:

$$seconds = \frac{\sqrt{inches}}{13.9}$$

A nine-inch fall thus represents a reaction time of

$$\frac{\sqrt{9}}{13.9} = \frac{3}{13.9} = .216 \text{ seconds}$$

Using the table below you can easily convert inches to reaction time in seconds.

Inches		Seconds
1	=	0.072
2	=	0.102
3	=	0.125
4	=	0.144
5	=	0.161
6	=	0.176
7	=	0.190
8	=	0.203
9	=	0.216
10	=	0.227

For greater precision, give five trials and use the average distance in calculating the reaction time.[1]

5. The basic procedure can now be used to study other variables. Some possibilities include comparing the

reaction times of males and females, right hands and left hands, subjects suffering from lack of sleep and normal subjects, and so forth.

6. Other important variables that can be examined involve attention and expectation. You might try varying the cues: sometimes say "Get ready," and other times drop the yardstick without warning. To note the effects of distractions, use a confederate or take advantage of naturally occurring distractions; your distracted subject may feel he or she is paying attention, yet miss the yardstick completely.

7. A different demonstration based on the same principle does not yield measurements but is nonetheless dramatic and may serve to impress your friends—provided you do it right. Suggest that you are going to drop a dollar bill through your friends' fingers and that anyone who can catch it may keep it. Armed with your research data, you can arrange the procedure so that no one is likely to do so. (If your subjects always took six inches or more to catch the yardstick and the bill is held halfway through your friends' fingers, you can see that you are pretty safe.) If you want to be sure, control not only the finger gap and the length of bill left to catch, but also take advantage of the distraction effect. Under these circumstances you should be able to use the same bill all evening.

Questions for Discussion

1. Why is it necessary that one person drop the ruler for another? Try catching the ruler yourself. Can you catch the ruler sooner than your subjects? Why? (Hint: your reflexes are *not* that fast!)

2. Is this a good test to compare reaction times for different individuals? Could the experimenter unintentionally bias the results? (Hint: if you wanted to make one person do better than another at the task, how could you use the variables noted earlier to ensure it?)

[1] Reaction-time data are usually presented in milliseconds (msec) rather than as fractions of a second (1,000 msec = 1 sec); thus .216 seconds would be 216 msec.

3

Psychological Development

1. Human development is determined by a continuous *interaction between heredity and environment.* The *biological predispositions* we inherit from our parents and the *experiences* provided by the environment in which we are raised both influence the way we develop. Our behavior at any stage in life results from the continuous

interaction

_____ between them.

heredity

2. Most of our abilities are not determined solely by environment or by h_____, but by the interaction between the two.

3. For example, all human infants are born with the ability to learn a spoken language. Other species are not so endowed. Thus, language ability is an inherited biological

predisposition

pre_____ .

4. The language the child learns to speak, however, will be that of the culture in which he or she is raised. Language development depends on both heredity and

environment (or experience)

_____ .

predispositions

5. The biological _____ with which we are born express themselves through the process of *maturation.* Maturation refers to innately determined sequences of growth or bodily changes that are relatively independent of learning or experience. If all members of the same species develop certain behavior at about the same time, without special training, we may suspect that the be-

maturation

havior is largely the result of _____ .

6. Some species of birds reared in isolation, so that they never hear the song characteristic of their species, are still able to reproduce it fairly well at the appropriate stage of development. Thus we can reasonably say that singing in these birds is controlled

maturation

largely by _____ rather than by learning.

7. When behavior depends more on physical *growth* processes than on *learning,* the

maturation

process controlling the behavior is said to be _____ .

8. Maturation refers to growth processes that produce behavior changes that are rela-

learning (or experience)

tively independent of _____ . If the behavior change is due to training

learning

or experience, the process is called _____ rather than maturation.

9. The development of the fetus within the mother's body, which follows a fixed time schedule, provides a clear picture of what we mean by maturation. Fetal behavior, such as turning and kicking, follows an orderly sequence depending on the growth

maturation

stage of the fetus; fetal behavior is thus a result of _____ .

10. Growth, of course, is not complete at birth. The physical skills of the infant after birth develop in such an orderly sequence (rolling over, sitting, standing, walking)

growth

that these behaviors appear to be the result of continuing _____ processes,

maturation

or _____ , rather than learning.

11. Maturation provides the readiness to learn, and most behavior depends on both learning and maturation. Children will learn to talk only after they have reached the

maturity (or synonym)

proper stage of _____ . The language they will speak is the one they

learning (or experience)

hear, thus indicating the role of _____ .

12. We noted earlier that human development is determined by a continuous interaction

heredity

between _____ and environment. We can state this principle more specifically by saying that behavior during the early years of development frequently

maturation, learning

reflects an interaction between m _____ and l _____ .

13. Physical skills, such as reaching for objects or walking, develop without special

maturation

training because they are primarily the result of _____ . But environmental conditions can affect the *rate of development.*

14. Infants raised in very restricted environments—confined in cribs for most of the day with little opportunity to move about freely—will learn to sit up, stand, and

rate

walk much later than normal. A restricted environment retards the _____ of development.

15. Infants provided with a colorful mobile suspended above their cribs will develop the eye-hand coordination necessary for reaching for an object earlier than infants who are kept in a bare crib with nothing to look at. A more stimulating or enriched

rate of development

environment accelerates the _____ _____ _____ .

16. Thus, although physical skills are primarily dependent on maturation, the rate at

environment

which they develop can be influenced by the quality of the _____ .

17. The development of many behaviors follows an *orderly sequence,* usually proceeding from *simple* behaviors to those that are *more complex.* Children learn to walk before they run, to speak words before they speak sentences, to count by rote before they understand the concept of numbers. Their behavior proceeds in an

sequence, complex

orderly _____ from simple to more _____ actions.

orderly

18. Some psychologists view this _____ sequence of development as a con-

learning (or experience)

tinuous process in which maturation interacts with _____ to produce a smooth and continuous change in behavior. Other psychologists see development as a series of *stages* through which individuals pass as they grow up.

19. When we talk about infancy, childhood, adolescence, and adulthood, we are talking

stages

broadly about successive _____ of development.

20. Psychologists have defined the concept of developmental stages more precisely. For example, the Swiss psychologist Piaget has proposed that children progress through a fixed sequence of stages in their *cognitive development.* The first stage, from birth

cognitive

to two years, is called the *sensorimotor stage* of _____ development.

sensorimotor

21. During the sensori_____ stage children do not use language or symbols but explore the environment by means of the senses and motor activity.

At first they can study objects only visually, but they soon learn to reach for and explore them with the fingers and mouth.

22. One of the many things the child learns during the sensorimotor _____ is that an *object* is *permanent;* that is, it continues to exist even when it is not present to the senses. The rattle does not disappear forever when hidden by a blanket but is a permanent _____ that will reappear when the child lifts the blanket.

stage

object

23. The concept of object permanence is achieved, according to Piaget, during the _____ stage of development, which occurs in the first _____ years of life.

sensorimotor

two

24. A later stage in cognitive _____ , called the *preoperational stage,* occurs between the ages of two and seven years. The child now possesses language and can begin to deal with problems by means of symbols and concepts. Objects become symbols that represent classes of things.

development

25. During the pre_____ stage, the child begins to use sym_____ to conceptualize the environment. The preoperational _____ covers the period from two to _____ years.

preoperational

symbols, stage

seven

26. One of the concepts developed toward the end of the pre_____ stage is that of *conservation.* The child learns that the amount of a substance does not change—that is, it is conserved—when the substance is divided into parts or placed in different-sized containers. If a four-year-old is shown two identical short jars containing what he or she acknowledges to be an equal amount of beans and watches while the contents of one jar are poured into a tall, cylindrical jar, the child will say that the tall jar contains more beans. The four-year-old (*has/has not*) attained the concept of conservation.

preoperational

has not

27. A six- or seven-year-old presented with the same situation will say that the contents of the short and tall jars are equal. The child has attained the concept of _____ .

conservation

28. If a child says that a ball of clay contains the same amount of material when it is rolled into a sausage shape as when it is a sphere, he or she has achieved the concept of _____ .

conservation

29. The development of the concept of conservation occurs during the _____ stage, which covers the ages of _____ to _____ . Later stages of cognitive development during which the child's thought processes gradually approach those of an adult are discussed in the text.

preoperational, two

seven

30. The infants' tendency to *seek closeness* to the individuals who care for them and to *feel more secure* in their presence is known as *attachment.* Babies at the crawling stage follow their mothers from room to room as they move about the house. This is an example of _____ .

attachment

31. A toddler clings to mother's skirt in an unfamiliar situation and cries when separated from her. This is another example of _____ .

attachment

32. It seems reasonable to assume that attachment to the mother, the tendency to seek

closeness, secure

_____ to her and feel more _____ in her presence, develops because she is the source of food and thus satisfies a basic need. But experiments with infant monkeys cast doubt on this assumption. If a monkey is raised from birth in a cage containing two artificial "mothers," one constructed of wire but with a nipple providing milk and the other covered with soft terry cloth but no milk supply, the monkey will spend most of its time clinging to the terry cloth "mother."

33. The infant monkey will show greater attachment to the cuddly, terry cloth

food
is not

"mother" despite the fact that she is not a source of _____ . These results indicate that attachment to the mother (_is/is not_) solely dependent on the fact that she provides food.

34. In human infants, attachment to the mother begins to appear around eight months and reaches a peak at about age two. If a toddler does not seem distressed when mother leaves him or her alone with a stranger, you can suspect that the child is

older

(_younger/older_) than two years.

two

35. Attachment to the mother reaches a peak at about age _____; from then on, the child becomes progressively more willing to be separated from the mother. But attachment to the parents and other family members still remains close during the preschool years. Because the parents are the dominant figures in children's lives, they serve as models, or _identification figures,_ for children to copy. When we say that children _identify_ with their parents, we mean that they assume many of the parents' values and patterns of behavior as their own.

36. When Sarah bathes and diapers her doll using the same mannerisms and tone of voice that her mother uses in caring for her baby brother, we may assume that

identifies

she _____ with her mother.

37. When Tommy staggers around in his father's fishing boots casting an imaginary line into the bathtub, we may assume that Tommy's father serves as an

identification

_____ figure.

38. When we say that a person is identifying with another person, we mean that whether

like (or a synonym)

the individual knows it or not, he or she is trying to become _____the other person.

39. One of the major areas of behavior in which children identify with their parents is

standards

in the acquisition of _sex-role standards_. Sex-role _____ refer to the ways of behaving that a culture considers appropriate for men and women.

role standards

40. Children acquire many of their sex-_____ _____ by identifying with the parent of the same sex. If a culture expects aggressive behavior

sex-role standard

from its male members, then aggression is a _____ - _____ _____ for men in that culture.

41. A girl acquires many of her sex-role standards by identifying with her mother; a boy

sex-role standards, identifying

acquires his _____-_____ _____ by _____ with his father.

same	**42.**	Sex-role identification develops as children perceive themselves as similar to the parent of the (*same/opposite*) sex.
	43.	If a girl's mother is aggressive and domineering and rejects the sex-role standards of her culture, we would expect the girl to have difficulty in developing the appropriate sex-role id_____ .
identification		
	44.	Many *personal characteristics,* however, are not sex typed. A sense of humor, personal warmth, and many moral values are shared by both men and women and may be learned from either parent. A girl may acquire her father's dry sense of humor,
personal		and a boy may learn consideration from his mother. These _____ characteristics are not sex typed.
sex-role	**45.**	Learning behavior that is appropriate to one's sex is called _____ - _____
characteristics		identification, but many personal _____ may be learned from either parent.
	46.	*Adolescence,* the transitional period from childhood to adulthood, is a period of
changes		development marked by *changes.* The most striking of these _____ are physical changes in the *sex characteristics* and *rate of growth* that culminate in *puberty.*
	47.	Mary is a typical twelve-year-old adolescent girl. We would expect her to experience
sex, rate		striking physical changes in _____ characteristics and in _____ of growth,
puberty		culminating in _____ .
	48.	Puberty, which is marked by menstruation in girls and the appearance of live sperm cells in the urine of boys, is reached at different ages by different youngsters. There
puberty (or maturity)		is a wide variation in the age at which boys and girls reach _____ .
	49.	In general, however, girls attain puberty two years earlier than boys. Thus, girls,
earlier		on the average, mature (*earlier/later*) than boys.
puberty	**50.**	Girls generally reach _____ before boys.
	51.	Boys and girls who mature markedly later than their classmates tend to have adjustment problems. Bob is a late maturer. He will probably have (*more/less*) difficulty
more		in adjusting than his early-maturing classmates.
puberty	**52.**	On reaching sexual maturity, or _____, adolescents are faced with decisions about sexual behavior. Since society's attitudes toward sexual activities are much more *permissive* today than in the past and guidelines for "appropriate" behavior are less clear, adolescents may experience *conflict.*
more	**53.**	Because current attitudes toward sexual behavior are (*more/less*) permissive than in the past, parental standards of sexual morality may differ markedly from the standards of the adolescent's peers. These differing values may be a source of
conflict		con_____ for the adolescent.
	54.	Surveys indicate that today's adolescents are engaging in sexual intercourse at an

earlier age than did their parents. These data undoubtedly reflect the fact that
permissive | society's attitudes concerning sex are now more _____ .

55. While adolescents and parents may agree on many of their values, they are most apt
sexual | to have different views about appropriate _____ behavior.

56. The adolescent, in addition to deciding on standards for sexual behavior, must
formulate *standards of conduct* for other areas of life. This is part of developing a
identity | sense of *personal identity.* A sense of personal _____ involves decid-
conduct | ing what is worth doing and formulating standards of _____ . It also
involves feelings about one's own competence.

personal | 57. A major task facing the adolescent is to develop a sense of _____
identity | _____ . We noted earlier that young children assume many of their
identify | parents' values as their own; that is, they _____ with their parents.

58. As children grow toward adolescence, the values of peers and of teachers and other
adults become increasingly important. When parental views differ markedly from
those of peers and other adults, the adolescent may have difficulty developing a
personal identity | sense of _____ _____ ; he or she may experience *role
confusion.*

confusion | 59. Role _____ means that the young person tries out one role after
another and has difficulty synthesizing the different roles into a single indentity.

60. Margaret's parents expect her to be docile and submissive to their values. Her
teachers encourage independent thinking and self-direction. Her friends tend to
role | rebel against any adult authority. Margaret will probably experience _____
confusion, personal identity | _____ in her search for _____ _____ .

inconsistent | 61. Role confusion is apt to occur when parental values are (*consistent/inconsistent*)
with the views of peers and other adults.

62. We have looked at some aspects of development from infancy through adolescence,
but development does not end with the attainment of physical maturity, or
puberty | _____ . It is a continuous process extending from birth to old age. Erik
Erikson has proposed a series of eight *psychosocial stages* to characterize develop-
psychosocial | ment throughout life. He calls them psycho_____ stages because
he believes that psychological development depends on the social relations established at various points in life.

cognitive (or intellectual) | 63. While Piaget's stages are concerned with _____ development,
psychosocial | Erikson's focus on problems of _____ development. For
example, Erikson claims that during the *first year of life* infants learn to *trust or
mistrust* other people, depending on how well their needs are attended to at a
period when they are helpless and totally dependent.

64. Infants' first social contacts occur while they are being fed. If the experience is

trust   pleasant and their needs are satisfied, they learn to associate mother with satisfaction and relaxation. They learn that they can tr_____ other people to satisfy their needs.

65. If, on the other hand, the feeding situation is unpleasant and hurried, so that the

mistrust   infants remain hungry and uncomfortable, they may learn to mis_____ others as a source of satisfaction. We can see how these experiences during the

first, trust   _____ year of life might well lead to a basic attitude of _____

mistrust (either order)   or _____ toward people later in life.

66. During the second year of life, children have their first real encounter with discipline and self-control, in connection with toilet training and in learning not to touch forbidden or dangerous objects as they begin walking. According to Erikson

psychosocial   the psycho_____ problem at this stage is one of *autonomy* versus *doubt.*

67. The psychosocial stage during the second year of life concerns autonomy and

doubt   _____. If parental discipline is warm but firm, children learn pride in controlling their own impulses. If the parents try to discipline by shaming the child and making the child feel that he or she does not live up to their expectations, the child

doubt   is likely to develop feelings of self-_____.

68. Erikson has proposed a number of later stages that are concerned with

psychosocial   _____ problems. You might expect that the major problem

identity   during the adolescent stage is developing one's personal _____ in relation to parents, peers, and other people important in one's life.

TERMS AND CONCEPTS

maturation _____

_____

_____

_____

developmental stages _____

_____

_____

_____

sensorimotor stage _____

_____

_____

_____

object permanence _____

_____

_____

_____

preoperational stage _____

_____

_____

_____

principle of conservation _____

_____

_____

_____

concrete operational stage _____

_____

_____

_____

formal operational stage _____

_____

_____

_____

attachment _____

_____

_____

_____

identification _____

_____

_____

_____

sex-role standards _____

_____

_____

_____

adolescent growth spurt _____

_____

_____

_____

secondary sex characteristics _____

_____

_____

_____

puberty _____

_____

_____

_____

role confusion _____

_____

_____

_____

psychosocial stages _____

_____

_____

_____

_____ 1. Maturation
    a. is influenced primarily by variations in the environment
    b. is relatively independent of experience
    c. depends on cultural influences
    d. ends by the age of twenty or twenty-five

_____ 2. Very young infants
    a. cannot differentiate sweet from sour or salt
    b. prefer sweetened cow's milk to human breast milk
    c. are unresponsive to tastes
    d. prefer their own mother's milk to another mother's

_____ 3. The concept of developmental stages
    a. implies that behaviors at a given stage are organized around a dominant theme
    b. concerns only cognitive development
    c. emphasizes the smoothness and continuity of development
    d. all of the above

_____ 4. It has been found that parents who are affectionate but not very controlling or demanding tend to have children who are
    a. especially mature
    b. unusually self-controlled
    c. both mature and self-controlled
    d. immature and lacking in self-control

_____ 5. Which is the most correct statement regarding early adolescent development?
    a. While girls mature earlier than boys throughout childhood and are taller and heavier in each grade, this difference is most noticeable after puberty.
    b. The beginning of growth of the secondary sex characteristics marks the onset of puberty.
    c. Puberty takes place over about two years, the years of the adolescent growth spurt.
    d. On the average, boys experience their growth spurt two years later than girls.

_____ 6. Piaget's concept of the _____ is demonstrated when a child systematically investigates the variables involved in the oscillation period of a pendulum.
    a. formal operational stage
    b. conservation of energy
    c. sensorimotor stage
    d. concrete operational stage

_____ 7. In developing a sense of identity, adolescents
    a. find parental values of increasing importance
    b. invariably reject earlier beliefs
    c. may experience role confusion
    d. all of the above

_____ 8. The sociable, well-liked child is theoretically most likely to have been the
    a. first born
    b. second born
    c. middle born
    d. last born

_____ 9. Erikson proposed eight stages of _____ development.
    a. psychosexual
    b. psychoanalytical
    c. psychosocial
    d. cognitive

_____ 10. The data now available, while limited, seem to show a definite change in adolescents' sexual behavior; adolescents are
    a. behaving more promiscuously
    b. more open in their discussion of sex, although their actual behavior differs little from that of their predecessors
    c. engaging in sexual activity at an earlier age than their parents
    d. beginning to have sex at the same age as earlier generations, but doing so with more partners

_____ 11. When young monkeys were reared with access only to artificial "mothers,"
    a. the females grew up to be unusually affectionate mothers
    b. they preferred the terry cloth "mothers"
    c. they used the wire "mothers" for security when exploring strange objects
    d. the females made poor mothers as adults, although their social relationships with peers were nearly normal

_____ 12. Studies of sex-role identification show that three-year-old boys
    a. do not yet show sex stereotypes in their preference for toys
    b. already prefer sex-appropriate toys
    c. prefer neutral toys to sex-categorized ones
    d. show a weak preference for feminine toys, although this is already beginning to reverse

13. According to the psychoanalytic view, identification with a parent provides a child with
   a. a source for feelings of strength and adequacy
   b. self-control and a conscience
   c. the appropriate sex role
   d. all of the above

14. A study of the effects of early stimulation on human infants' visually directed reaching showed that
   a. too much stimulation too soon may be upsetting
   b. the rate of development of this reaching response could not be significantly increased
   c. the enriched environment helped infants to discover their hands earlier than infants in a control group
   d. increasing the amount of handling was more effective than hanging elaborate ornaments over the cribs

15. Qualities such as sense of humor, friendliness, and integrity
   a. tend to come from the same-sex parent
   b. tend to come from the opposite-sex parent
   c. may come from either parent
   d. are most likely to come from peers

16. Recent research into the "generation gap" shows
   a. an increasing and nearly insurmountable gap between parents and children in most countries
   b. some distance between parents and children but much less than implied by the media
   c. a large gap between parents and children in the United States but a smaller gap in Denmark
   d. substantial differences between the United States and Denmark in amount of parent-child estrangement

17. According to Piaget, a child who can correctly predict that a ball of clay and a similar ball rolled out to a long sausage will balance on a scale must have achieved
   a. conservation of weight
   b. object permanence

c. conservation of mass
d. all of the above

18. Which of the following summarizes best the problems of development over a lifetime?
   a. Developmental problems continue throughout life, but are different at the different stages of life.
   b. Developmental problems are most severe for the adolescent and diminish thereafter, as people's lives become stable.
   c. Biological problems get more severe as people age, even though psychological development has stopped.
   d. Much of life has its problems, but middle adulthood does not, since vocational status is established, income is at its maximum, and family life is stabilized.

19. When mothers are insensitive or unresponsive during the first year, their babies
   a. come to depend more on others
   b. cry less often and generally pay less attention to adults
   c. show anxious attachment in the "strange situation"
   d. show significantly different patterns of mother-child interaction in daily routines

20. Child-rearing methods in the United States
   a. differ from one social group to another
   b. differ little from those in other countries
   c. have changed very little over the past 50 years
   d. are now pretty much the same from one social class to the next

KEY TO SELF-QUIZ

1. b p.65	6. a p.73	11. b p.77	16. b p.93
2. d p.67	7. c p.92	12. b p.85	17. d p.72
3. a p.66	8. b p.88	13. d p.84	18. a p.95
4. d p.83	9. c p.95	14. a p.69	19. c p.79
5. d p.89	10. c p.90	15. c p.85	20. a p.81

INDIVIDUAL EXERCISE

SEX ROLES

Psychologists have for many years investigated behaviors that differ by sex. Where once it was assumed that differ-

ences in male and female behavior reflected biological differences, the common assumption now is that most such differences (other than those directly related to reproduction) reflect cultural training. For many sex-differentiated behaviors, however, it is not readily apparent whether biological factors, cultural factors, or both, are involved. A report in the journal *Science* described one such behavior. Female college students carry their books differently than males do, reported the authors; the former cradle them in both arms, the latter hold them at their sides. While this particular behavior is not of earthshaking importance, it illustrates the complexity of trying to understand sex-differentiated behaviors.

What do you think? First of all, do you agree that book-carrying behavior is sex differentiated? Look around you, preferably following a defined procedure for sampling and scoring a reasonable number of subjects of both sexes. If you observe a sex difference in book-carrying behavior, what do you think is its cause? Remember, as you consider the problem, the kinds of variables involved: (1) physical variables such as arm length, arm strength, hip shape, or breast development; (2) cultural training, for example, modeling the carrying styles of adults; (3) other cultural variables that may differ by sex, such as clothing, size of typical books for classes taken more frequently by males or females. The problem is not as simple as it seems at first. To compare the authors' logic and conclusions with your own, consult the original report, which should be available in most libraries: Jenni, D. A., and Jenni, M. A. (1976) Carrying behavior in humans: Analysis of sex differences. *Science,* 194: 859–60.

INDIVIDUAL AND CLASS EXERCISE

BIRTH ORDER AND PERSONALITY CHARACTERISTICS

Introduction

Research has shown that some aspects of an individual's personality are related to order of birth. First-born or only children, in particular, tend to differ from other children. The text discusses several factors that make the first-born or only child's position in the family unique. This exercise will show whether personality differences among your acquaintances bear any relationship to birth order.

Procedure

In the spaces provided at the left of the data sheet (p. 47), write the names of ten people of your own sex whom you know quite well. Now rate each person on the personality traits listed at the bottom of the data sheet. Note that a rating of 1 means that the person possesses the trait to only a slight degree, while a rating of 5 indicates that he or she possesses the trait to a high degree. For example, a rating of 5 on the trait "aggression" indicates a very dominant, aggressive person; a rating of 1 would describe someone who is quite meek and unassertive. After deciding which number best describes the aggressive or nonaggressive nature of your first subject, enter this number in the first column next to his or her name. Now rate the subject according to the remaining three traits. Carry out the same procedure for each acquaintance. Try to avoid the common tendency of rating everyone toward the middle of the scale.

Treatment of Data

After you have rated each of your ten acquaintances on all four traits, find out their birth order (if you do not already know it) and turn to the data tabulation sheet on page 48. List the name of all first-born or only children in the appropriate column and enter their ratings for each trait. Do the same for those who were later born. Add the ratings for each trait and enter the total at the bottom of each column. Divide each total by the number of subjects in the column to find the average rating.

If this is to be done as a class exercise, bring this sheet with you to class. Your instructor will tabulate the average ratings obtained by each class member for the four traits.

Questions for Discussion

1. Is there any difference in the average ratings for first-born or only children as compared to those for the later born? If so, which traits are most affected by birth order?

2. How do the circumstances of the study limit interpretation of the results? That is, might different results have been obtained if the subjects had been selected from the population at large rather than from a group of college students?

3. What are some of the factors relevant to the individual's position in the family that might explain the results?

DATA SHEET

Name	Personality traits			
	Aggression	Conscientiousness	Intellectual ability	Sociability
1.				
2.				
3.				
4.				
5.				
6.				
7.				
8.				
9.				
10.				

Aggression	Conscientiousness	Intellectual ability	Sociability
1. Very meek	1. Careless in attention to responsibilities	1. In lower 10% of class	1. Withdrawn; a loner
2.	2.	2.	2.
3. Moderately aggressive	3. Moderately conscientious	3. Average	3. Moderately sociable
4.	4.	4.	4.
5. Very aggressive	5. Very conscientious	5. In upper 10% of class	5. Very outgoing and sociable

DATA TABULATION FOR BIRTH-ORDER STUDY

First-born or only child

Name	Aggression	Conscientiousness	Intellectual ability	Sociability
Total				
Average				

Later-born child

Name	Aggression	Conscientiousness	Intellectual ability	Sociability
Total				
Average				

4

Sensory Processes

1. All of our information about the world comes to us by way of stimuli impinging on

   sense

   our *sense organs.* Without our eyes, ears, nose, and other _____ organs, we would know nothing about the people, objects, and events that make up our world.

2. We gain information about the world in which we live by way of our _____

   sense

   organs

   _____ . But a certain *minimum* of sense-organ *stimulation* is required before any sensory experience will be evoked. The minimum physical energy necessary to activate a given sensory system is called the *absolute threshold.* To put it

   absolute

   another way, the _____ threshold is the intensity at which a stimulus becomes effective.

3. A spot of light in a dark room must reach some measurable intensity before an individual can distinguish it from darkness. In other words, the degree of intensity

   threshold

   necessary for the spot of light to be seen is its absolute _____ for that individual.

4. Likewise, a sound emitted in a soundproof room must reach a certain intensity before it can be heard. The intensity at which it can be heard by someone is its

   absolute

   _____ threshold.

5. In both the instances mentioned above, we see that a certain minimum of sense-organ stimulation is required before any sensory experience will be evoked. This

   absolute threshold

   minimum is called the _____ _____ .

6. A pin prick cannot be felt unless the pressure of the pin on the skin reaches a certain intensity. The intensity of pressure necessary for the pin prick to be felt is its

   absolute threshold

   _____ _____ .

7. We can see from these examples that whether the stimulus is light, sound, or touch,

   minimum, stimulation

   a certain _____ of sense-organ _____ is required before any sensory experience will be evoked. This minimum is called the

   absolute threshold

   _____ _____ .

8. There must also be a certain magnitude of difference between two stimuli before one can be distinguished from the other. The minimum amount of difference necessary to tell two stimuli apart is known as the *difference threshold.* Thus, two tones must differ to some degree before one is heard as higher than the other. The point

   difference

   at which they can be told apart is the _____ threshold.

9. The transition between no sensory experience and some sensory experience is the

   absolute

   _____ threshold; the transition between no difference and some

   difference

   difference in stimuli is the _____ threshold.

10. Thresholds *vary* from one person to the next and may even *fluctuate* over time within one individual. Therefore, we should think of a threshold measurement as a statistical average. If a psychologist were interested in measuring your

difference   dif_____ threshold for discriminating between two tones, he or she would probably not get identical results at each testing. Likewise, your threshold for discriminating between the two tones would probably not be the same as someone else's threshold.

vary   **11.** Thresholds not only _____ from one individual to the next but may even fluctuate within one individual from time to time.

12. Threshold measurement should be thought of as a statistical average. That is, for

fluctuate   the same person thresholds may _____ from one time to the next,

individual (or a synonym)   and thresholds also vary from one _____ to another.

absolute   **13.** The two kinds of thresholds we have discussed are the _____ threshold, which is the transition between no sensory experience and some sensory

difference   experience, and the _____ threshold, which is the transition between no difference and some difference in stimuli.

sense   **14.** The human eye is one of the most complex _____ organs. Note the drawing of the human eye and as you proceed, consider the location and functions of its different parts. To begin, locate the *cornea,* where light *enters* the eye.

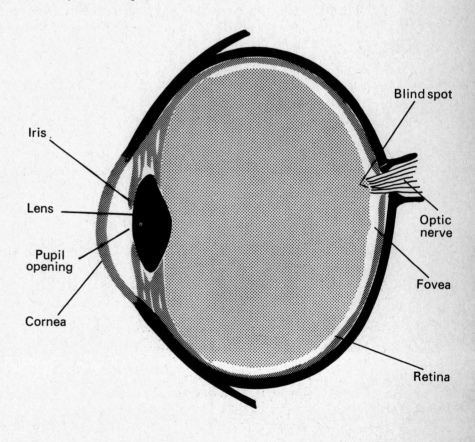

cornea   **15.** Light enters the eye through the _____; the amount of light is *regulated* by the size of the *pupil opening,* which is an opening in the *iris*.

enters   **16.** The cornea is the portion of the eye through which light _____; the

pupil   amount of light entering the eye is regulated by the size of the _____ opening.

cornea	**17.** After light has entered the eye through the _____ and its amount has been
pupil opening	regulated by the _____ _____, the *lens* then *focuses* the light on the receptor surface, the *retina*.
cornea	**18.** The parts of the human eye we have identified thus far are the c_____, the
pupil, iris	p_____, the i_____, and the lens, which focuses light on the retina.
enters	**19.** Light _____ the eye through the cornea; the amount of light is
regulated	_____ by the size of the pupil opening, which is an opening in the
focuses	iris. The lens then _____ the light on the receptor surface, the retina.
lens, retina	**20.** The _____ focuses the light on the receptor surface, the _____.
retina	**21.** The lens focuses the light on the_____, which is made up of a number of specialized cells. Two of these specialized types of cells (not shown in the drawing) are of particular interest. These are the *rods* and *cones,* which have different functions. (In the text you will find a diagram showing the rods and cones.)
	22. *Rods* and *cones* are specialized cells with *different* functions and are found in the
retina	_____.
different	**23.** Rods and cones, which have _____ functions, are found in the receptor surface, the retina.
rods, cones (either order)	**24.** Two specialized types of cells in the retina are _____ and _____.
	25. *Cones* are active primarily in *daylight* vision and permit us to see both *achromatic* colors (white, black, and the intermediate grays) and *chromatic* colors (red, green,
different	blue, and so on). The rods and cones are specialized cells with _____
retina	functions and are found in the _____ .
chromatic	**26.** The cones of the retina permit us to see white, black, and the intermediate grays (the achromatic colors), and red, green, blue, and the other _____ colors.
	27. The *rods,* in contrast to the cones, enable us to see only *achromatic* colors. The rods function mainly in vision under *reduced* illumination, as in twilight or *night vision.*
achromatic, chromatic (either order)	Cones enable us to see both _____ and _____ colors.
reduced	**28.** The cones function in normal daylight vision, whereas the rods function under _____ illumination, as in night vision.
achromatic	**29.** Rods enable us to see only _____ colors and function in vision
reduced	under _____ illumination.
daylight	**30.** Cones function in normal _____ vision, whereas the rods function in
night	_____ vision.

31. When you enter a dark room your eyes gradually become more sensitive to light, so that after a while you are able to see more than when you first entered. This experience is known as *dark adaptation.*

adaptation

32. The experience of dark _____ shows how the rods and cones differ in their functions. When you first enter a dark room, the cones in your retina become more sensitive to light. Stated another way, their absolute threshold is

lowered

(*raised/lowered*).

33. After about five minutes in the dark, the sensitivity of the cones has increased as much as it will. The rods, however, continue to adapt to the dark and become appreciably more sensitive for about half an hour. You can see better after twenty min-

rods

utes in the dark than after five minutes because of the functioning of the _____.

cone

34. The _____ cells no longer increase their sensitivity to light after a few minutes

daylight

in a dark room because they function best in normal _____ vision.

achromatic, chromatic
(either order)

Cones enable us to see both _____ and _____ colors.

rod, achromatic

35. The _____ cells function in night vision and enable us to see only _____ colors.

cones

36. In the experience of dark adaptation the _____ increase their sensitivity for

rods

the first few minutes, but the _____ become increasingly more sensitive over a longer period.

37. The most sensitive portion of the eye in normal *daylight* vision is a small area of the retina called the *fovea,* on which light that comes from the center of the visual field

cone

is focused. The fovea must contain _____ cells because these function in normal daylight vision.

fovea

38. The most sensitive portion of the eye in normal daylight vision is the _____; it contains *only cone* cells, which are packed closely together in a small area.

Rod

_____ cells are found only *outside* the fovea.

rod

39. The portion of the retina outside the fovea contains *both* _____ and cone cells.

rod, cone (either order), cone

40. Outside the fovea are _____ and _____ cells. Within the fovea are only _____

daylight

cells, which are closely packed together and function best in _____ vision.

41. Not far from the fovea, on the surface of the retina, is an insensitive area, the *blind spot,* where nerve fibers from the retinal cells come together in a bundle to form the *optic nerve,* which carries impulses from the eye to the brain. The area where

nerve

the optic _____ leaves the eye is called the blind spot because it contains neither rods nor cones.

fovea

42. The most sensitive portion of the eye in normal daylight vision is the _____,

blind

which contains only cone cells; the insensitive area is the _____ spot, where the nerve fibers from the cells of the retina come together in a bundle to form the

optic   _____ nerve.

43. Without looking at the earlier drawing you should be able to label the parts of the eye in the drawing presented here. Check your results with the labeled drawing of

cone

the eye. (Rod and cone cells are not shown, but you should remember that _____

fovea, rod

cells are concentrated in the _____, whereas both _____ and

cone (either order)

_____ cells are found outside the fovea.)

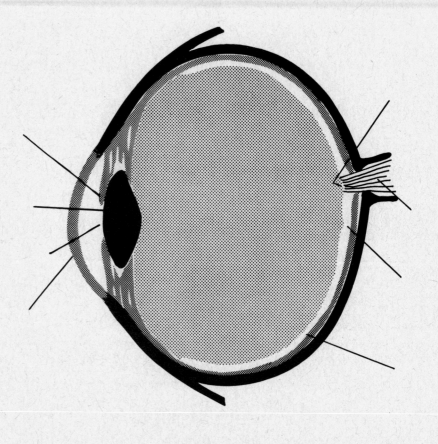

44. Let us now discuss color vision. You recall that red, blue, green, and so on, are

chromatic

_____ colors. We can produce the colors that are familiar to us in a *rainbow* by passing sunlight through a prism, which breaks it into a band of vari-colored light.

45. When sunlight is passed through a prism, it breaks into a band of varicolored light

rainbow

that is familiar to us in the _____. The colors correspond to *wavelengths,* the *red* end of the rainbow being produced by the *long* light waves, the *violet* end by the *short* light waves.

46. Sunlight sent through a prism produces a rainbow effect. This band of varicolored

wavelengths

light is called a *solar spectrum.* The colors correspond to _____ , the red end of the spectrum being produced by the long light waves and the violet

short

end by the _____ light waves.

47. The colors of the solar spectrum can be arranged in the form of a *color circle*. The

solar

_____ spectrum is bent back around itself to form a circle as shown below. The break in the color circle between red and violet contains colors that do not appear in the solar spectrum but can be produced by mixtures of other colors. The

color circle

colors *opposite* each other on the _____ _____ are called *complementaries.* Note that blue and yellow, red and green, are found opposite each other.

complementaries

They are _____ .

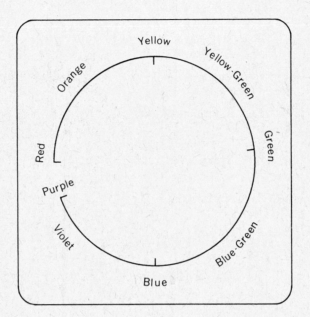

48. Blue and yellow, red and green, are complementaries, since they appear

opposite

_____ each other on the color circle. When complementary pairs of colors, such as yellow and blue, red and green, are mixed as *lights* (*not as pigments*), they cancel each other and result in neutral *gray. Spectral colors* (the colors of the

color circle

solar spectrum) must be opposite each other on the _____ _____ in order to be considered complementaries.

spectral

49. The s_____ colors resemble a rainbow. When they are opposite each

complementaries

other on a color circle, they are called _____ .

50. Blue-green and orange are a pair of complementary colors on a color circle. If mixed

gray

together as *lights,* the resulting color would be a neutral _____ .

51. Complementaries are spectral colors that are opposite each other on a color circle;

lights

when mixed together as _____ , they cancel each other and result in a neutral gray.

52. Some of the colors appear to be more elementary than others; that is, they appear to be composed of a single hue, which is a technical name for the quality of redness, blueness, greenness, and so on, that differentiates one color from another. These elementary colors are called *psychological primaries,* and usually four are named: *red, green, blue,* and *yellow.* Colors such as orange or purple are not psychological primaries   _____, since their components can be recognized—for instance, both red and yellow can be identified in orange.

psychological   53. The _____ primaries are red, green, blue, and yellow.

red, green, blue   54. The psychological primaries are _____, _____, _____, and

yellow (any order)   _____ .

                               55. Red, green, blue, and yellow appear to be more elementary than other colors and

psychological   are therefore called _____ primaries. Another set of primaries are called *color-mixture primaries;* these are any three widely spaced colors on the spectrum that can be used to provide all the other colors by *additive mixture.*

                               56. Any three widely spaced colors on the spectrum can be used to provide all the other

color-mixture   colors by additive mixture. These are called _____-_____ primaries.

                               57. Red, green, and blue are widely spaced colors on the spectrum that can be used to provide all the other colors by additive mixture. Therefore we call these colors

color-mixture   _____-_____ primaries.

red, green, blue   58. The psychological primaries are _____, _____, _____, and

yellow (any order), color-   _____ . The _____-_____ primaries are any three

mixture   widely spaced colors on the spectrum that can be used to provide all the other

mixture   colors by additive _____ .

                               59. The *negative afterimage* is an interesting phenomenon in color perception. If you stare at a red circle and then look at a plain gray surface, you will have the experience of seeing a green circle on it; that is, you experience a negative afterimage. The afterimage is called "negative" because green is the complementary color of red. You recall that blue and yellow are complementary colors. Were you to stare at a yellow circle and then look at a plain gray surface, you would have the experience

blue   of seeing a _____ circle on it.

                               60. If you stare at a green circle and then look at a plain gray surface, you are likely to

red, negative   see a _____ circle on it; that is, you experience a _____ afterimage.

negative afterimage   61. A _____ _____ is so named because after staring at a particular color, one usually sees its complementary color on a gray surface.

rods, cones (either order)   62. The light-sensitive receptors in the retina, the _____ and the _____, appear to be especially responsive to *changes in light intensity.* They will fire nervous impulses to the brain more rapidly when a light is turned on or turned off than they will in response to a steady light.

changes   63. The visual receptors are sensitive to _____ in light intensity.

                               64. If the eye is completely immobilized so that the light image impinging on the retina is unchanging, or *stabilized,* visual acuity decreases. This occurs because the visual

intensity   receptors respond primarily to changes in light _____ .

65. Vision is, of course, only one of several human senses. In everyday language, most

five, taste

smell (either order)

people speak of our having _____ senses: sight, hearing, _____ , _____ , and touch.

66. Students of psychology are expected to be more precise in defining the senses. As you will see shortly, the sense of touch is not one sensation but four. In addition, there are two special senses that provide information about body position and body movement and enable us to keep our balance. Therefore it is inaccurate to say that

senses

humans have only five _____ . (Hearing, and the senses dealing with body position and movement and balance, are treated in the text.)

67. Taste, smell, and the skin sensations are important in everyday life, but they do not provide us with the rich patterns and organization that vision and audition do. Vision and audition are spoken of as the "higher senses"; taste, smell, and the skin

lower

sensations are therefore thought of as the " _____ senses."

68. Psychologists have identified four primary taste qualities: *sweet, sour, salt,* and *bitter.* But most taste experience is brought about by a fusion of these qualities with other sense experiences. As you might guess, the "taste" of strong cheese is

smell

considerably affected by our sense of _____ .

taste, bitter

69. The four primary _____ qualities are *sweet, sour, salt,* and _____ . But taste is also affected by other senses. If you were blindfolded and your nostrils

smell

were pinched together so that you could not _____ , you would have trouble distinguishing between the taste of an apple and a raw potato.

sweet, sour, salt

70. The four taste qualities are _____ , _____ , _____ , and

bitter (any order), senses

_____ . Other _____ contribute to taste.

71. From an evolutionary point of view, the sense of *smell* is one of the most primitive

senses

and most important of the _____ . Smell has more direct neural pathways to the brain than any other sense.

smell

72. The sense of _____ has more direct neural pathways to the brain than any other sense. It plays a more important role in the life of the lower animals than in humans.

73. There are four *skin* sensations. That is, the familiar sense of touch is not one sensation but at least four: *pressure, pain, warm,* and *cold.* These sensations are felt

skin

through separate *sensitive spots* on the surface of the _____ .

cold

74. Touch is not one sensation but at least four: pressure, _____ , warm, and

pain (either order), sensitive

_____ . These sensations are registered through separate _____ spots on the surface of the skin.

75. The sensations provided by sensitive spots on the surface of the skin include

pressure, pain, warm

cold (any order)

_____ , _____ , _____ and _____ .

TERMS AND CONCEPTS

absolute threshold _____

_____

_____

_____

psychophysical function _____

_____

_____

difference threshold _____

_____

_____

just noticeable difference (j.n.d.) _____

_____

_____

Weber's law _____

_____

_____

ROC curve* _____

_____

_____

_____

pupil _____

_____

_____

lens _____

_____

_____

retina _____

_____

_____

rod _____

_____

_____

cone _____

_____

_____

fovea _____

_____

_____

blind spot _____

_____

_____

chromatic colors _____

_____

_____

dark adaptation _____

_____

_____

complementary colors _____

_____

_____

psychological primaries _____

_____

_____

*Indicates terms used in Critical Discussions

color-mixture primaries _____

_____

_____

_____

hue _____

_____

_____

_____

brightness _____

_____

_____

_____

saturation _____

_____

_____

_____

color solid _____

_____

_____

_____

trichromat _____

_____

_____

_____

dichromat _____

_____

_____

_____

monochromat _____

_____

_____

_____

negative afterimage _____

_____

_____

_____

opponent-process theory* _____

_____

_____

_____

recurrent inhibition _____

_____

_____

_____

stabilized retinal image _____

_____

_____

_____

pitch _____

_____

_____

_____

loudness _____

_____

_____

_____

decibel _____

_____

_____

_____

overtone _____

_____

_____

_____

timbre _____

_____

_____

_____

cochlea _____

_____

_____

_____

basilar membrane _____
_____
_____
_____

organ of Corti _____
_____
_____

place theory* _____
_____
_____
_____

frequency theory* _____
_____
_____
_____

volley principle* _____
_____
_____
_____

taste buds _____
_____
_____

kinesthesis _____
_____
_____

equilibratory senses _____
_____
_____
_____

semicircular canals _____
_____
_____

vestibular sacs _____
_____
_____
_____

_____ 1. If a subject can detect a difference in temperature of $1^\circ C$ at $20^\circ C$, how small a difference can he or she detect at $60^\circ C$, according to Weber's law?
  a. 1°
  b. 2°
  c. 3°
  d. 4°

_____ 2. One of the most primitive and most important of the senses, from an evolutionary viewpoint, is the sense of
  a. smell
  b. touch
  c. vision
  d. taste

_____ 3. The dimensions of tone that correspond to hue, brightness, and saturation of colors are
  a. pitch, loudness, and timbre
  b. loudness, pitch, and overtone
  c. timbre, pitch, and overtone
  d. pitch, frequency, and loudness

_____ 4. The _____ is the minimum physical energy necessary to activate a given sensory system.
  a. difference threshold
  b. absolute threshold
  c. psychophysical function
  d. stimulus intensity

_____ 5. Sound is a function of pressure changes in the air that can be represented as waves. In such a wave
  a. amplitude refers to the amount of compression and expansion of the air
  b. frequency is measured in the number of vibration cycles per minute
  c. amplitude is measured in Hertz
  d. frequency is shown by the amount by which the wave is displaced above or below the baseline

_____ 6. Some of the fibers from each eye cross over to the opposite brain hemisphere at the
  a. optic chiasma
  b. optic nerve
  c. blind spot
  d. fovea

_____ 7. Of the several layers of the retina, the light-sensing cells (rods and cones) are

  a. closest to the front of the eye
  b. the second layer from the front of the eye
  c. the second layer from the back of the eye
  d. closest to the back of the eye

_____ 8. Which of the following is *not* one of the relationships shown on the color solid?
  a. Hue is represented by points along the radius.
  b. Brightness ranges from white at the top to black at the bottom.
  c. Hue is represented by points around the circumference.
  d. Saturation varies from highly saturated on the outside to gray in the center.

_____ 9. Cones_____ while rods _____.
  a. sense only chromatic colors, sense only achromatic colors
  b. require more intense light, function under reduced light
  c. function mainly at night, are active only in daylight
  d. can be compared to black-and-white film, can be compared to color film

_____ 10. The _____ represent(s) the final stage in the process by which the ear turns air pressure changes into neural impulses.
  a. organ of Corti
  b. basilar membrane
  c. hair cells of the organ of Corti
  d. cochlea

_____ 11. Recurrent inhibition is important because it allows the organism to
  a. process visual information from each eye separately
  b. pay attention to the portions of the environment that are the most brightly lighted
  c. utilize multiple receptor cells, as in the horseshoe crab
  d. attend to the portions of the environment that are changing

_____ 12. When we are at rest, our sense of our body's position is provided by
  a. vestibular sacs
  b. otoliths
  c. hair cells
  d. all of the above

_____ 13. The _____ threshold is defined in

terms of the crucial amount of change in the physical stimulus, i.e., the _____.
a. absolute, crucial stimulus change
b. difference, barely detectable change
c. absolute, minimal stimulus difference
d. difference, just noticeable difference

_____ 14. Our skin provides us with a sensation of "hot" when
a. specific "hot" nerve-end structures in the skin are stimulated
b. "warm" and "cold" skin receptors are stimulated simultaneously
c. skin receptors for "warm" are stimulated beyond the intermediate threshold
d. "warm" and "pain" skin receptors are stimulated simultaneously

_____ 15. The sense of taste is an interesting one, in that
a. some animals cannot taste sweet at all
b. the human taste receptors continuously reproduce themselves
c. even individual human taste cells vary in their responsiveness to sweet, salt, sour, and bitter
d. all of the above

_____ 16. The person with normal color vision is called a
a. quadrochromat
b. trichromat
c. dichromat
d. monochromat

_____ 17. Feedback about the position of our body parts as we walk and climb is provided by the _____ sense.
a. equilibratory
b. vestibular
c. kinesthetic
d. otolithic

_____ 18. If an image is projected onto the retina in such a way that the same cells continue to be stimulated, the image begins to
a. seem unfamiliar
b. quiver and oscillate in small movements
c. fade and disappear
d. change color

_____ 19. Colored lights that are complementary
a. fall adjacent to each other on the color circle
b. yield a neutral gray when mixed
c. are the same colors as complementary paint pigments
d. do not exist in the spectrum but can be produced by mixing wavelengths

_____ 20. After a few minutes in a dark room we can see better than when we first entered because the
a. rods have adapted
b. rods and cones have adapted
c. cones have adapted
d. bipolar cells have adapted

KEY TO SELF-QUIZ

1. c p.105	6. a p.110	11. d p.116	16. b p.114
2. a p.123	7. d p.109	12. d p.125	17. c p.124
3. a p.120	8. a p.114	13. d p.105	18. c p.117
4. b p.104	9. b p.111	14. b p.124	19. b p.113
5. a p.119	10. c p.122	15. d p.123	20. c p.112

INDIVIDUAL EXERCISES

SEEING AND NOT SEEING

Introduction

There are several procedures that can help you experience aspects of your visual system not normally noticed. The text describes the eye in detail, but it is sometimes hard to relate that description to your own experience. Exercises such as the following, as well as those in the text, can help you really "see" what is happening.

A. Phosphenes

First note that your eyes are sensitive to more than light. If you apply gentle pressure to them, with the lids closed, you will "see" patterns of color, called "phosphenes." These result when the eye translates pressure into a visual experience.

B. Fundus

Next, consider that light, the usual stimulus for the eyes, has to travel through a series of eye tissues before it is registered by the rods and cones. Normally you do not see the portions of the eye through which the light must pass, because they remain in a fixed location with respect to the retina. As noted in the text, recurrent inhibition ensures that anything not moving with respect to the retina is not seen. The network of blood vessels in the eye, however, can sometimes be noticed as a pattern of fine flickering movement when an exceptionally strong pulse causes the vessels to expand rhythmically.

This network of blood vessels, called the "fundus," can be seen more directly with the aid of a flashlight. Cover the end of the flashlight with a piece of aluminum foil and punch a 1/8" hole in it to provide a small beam of light. Go into a dark room and shine this beam into one eye at an angle, holding the flashlight directly under the eye just above the chin and aiming the beam toward the top of your head; you will probably have to experiment with the angle in order to get the proper result. Look straight ahead and move the flashlight around slightly. What you will see is a pattern of lines on a glowing reddish background, rather like the veining in a leaf; this is the fundus.

C. A Familiar Sight Not Normally Seen

Another portion of your anatomy, also rarely "seen," is much more obvious than the fundus. If you think about it as you read, you will discover that you can see not only this workbook but also a view of each side of your nose. Unlike the fundus, the invisibility of your nose is not based on recurrent inhibition, but on sensory adaptation or "attention." You are so used to these views of your nose accompanying every scene that you no longer notice them. (If you now have trouble *not* noticing them, don't worry about it; as you turn your attention to other activities, your nose will resume its customary place in the scheme of things.)

D. A Familiar Lack of Sight Not Normally Noticed

Just as you do not normally see your nose, so do you not normally miss what you do not see in the blind spot of each eye. The illustration on page 110 of your text shows you how to locate your blind spots. (For the right eye, you can reverse the description given in the text. Close your left eye and stare at the spot; the cross will disappear.) It's even more instructive to take the example further and show how objects, even people, disappear as well. Try a simple object first. After you have made the dot disappear, as instructed on page 110, hold that position and slide your pencil across the book so that the eraser moves over the dot and thus into the blind spot. The eraser should also disappear. Notice that you do not *perceive* a hole or blank spot; you just do not see the eraser.

With a little practice, you can achieve the same effect in the real world. Remember that the blind spot is a few degrees to the outside of the fovea, that is, your point of gaze; this is a little more than the width of your outstretched hand. With your right eye closed, a small object about a hand's width to the left of your direct gaze is not seen. Thus if you point your gaze about that far to the right of someone's face as you look at them (with your right eye closed, remember), you should be able to decapitate them, so to speak. A person across a table is about the proper distance; at that range you can get clothes, a ring of hair, and nothing in the middle. This exercise is not only useful as a perceptual demonstration; it's a great time killer if you are trapped at a boring lecture.

E. Seeing Color

Surprisingly, people often do not know that they are colorblind. We are not normally aware of how we learn to label colors or of how color constancy works to keep our perception of colors stable. A familiar object appears to be the same color regardless of the light conditions under which we view it. But it is possible to overcome the effects of constancy. Pick something you know the color of very well—your bike or car, some item of clothing, and so on. Then look at it in various light conditions—from brilliant sun to as dark as you can still see at all. If you try to look at the object as if you and it were completely new to the world, you may be able to overcome the constancy effect and see how different its color appears under differing conditions. (Note that you will be able to observe these differences much more easily for a friend's object and vice versa, since the constancy will not be as strong for an unfamiliar object.)

You can also experiment with color constancy by wearing tinted glasses. One aspect of looking at the world through rose-colored glasses is that after a while you adapt, and it tends to look like the same old world. Try some of the brilliant lenses available in department stores—green, orange, violet, or even rose—the ones apparently designed more to be looked *at* than to look through. You will find that at first everything seems brighter than usual, and colors appear peculiar. But if you wear the glasses for a while, the world will seem more normal—as if you had been born with this particular kind of vision. You will still be able to name most colors appropriately, although a careful test will show some problems—just as it does with those who are colorblind from birth. One final experience awaits you, however. When you take the glasses off, the world will seem unusually drab for a time; your innate tendency to compensate for changes in visual stimulation will overcompensate when the lenses are first removed. Mercifully, your visual adaptation system will soon have things normal again.

F. The Importance of Vision

Finally, give a moment's thought to the extent to which sight dominates our lives. If you have never had a blind friend, imagine now that you do and think about trying to explain something to him or her. Whether your explanation concerns people, cars, clothes, schoolwork, how to get somewhere, or whatever, you will be surprised to discover the extent to which you rely on vision and think in visual terms.

You may even wish to try the exercise, developed by sensory-awareness groups, of being "blind for a day" and being led about by someone as you concentrate on your other senses. (Remember if you attempt this exercise that you are still thinking in visual terms—something the congenitally blind cannot do.)

As a last way of noting the extent to which sight, when not blocked off, overrides the other senses, think about where the sound comes from in a movie or TV. Obviously, it actually comes from the speaker(s), which are often discriminably separated from the picture. But equally obvious, the sound *seems* to be located in the visually apparent source, for example, the moving mouth on the screen. Similarly, a ventriloquist does not "throw" his or her voice. The ventriloquist simply provides cues, such as a different voice and movement of the dummy. *You* "throw" the voice to the dummy.

When some other sense conflicts with vision, it is almost always vision that prevails. The same phenomenon causes airplane pilots many problems because they tend to attempt to align the aircraft visually, even in the face of evidence and training to the contrary.

5
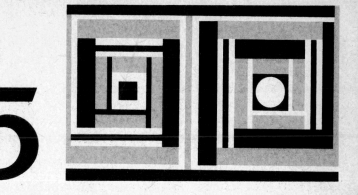

Perception

LEARNING OBJECTIVES

5-1.   Be able to show, with examples, how each of the five object constancies contributes to our perception of stable wholes. Be familiar with evidence for the role of learning in size and location constancy.

5-2.   Be able to discuss figure-ground organization, including that seen in reversible figures, and to show how this is basic to stimulus patterning.

5-3.   Be familiar with the visual illusions and understand their relationship to our perceptual structuring into three dimensions.

5-4.   Understand the concept of perceptual hypothesis testing, including the analysis-by-synthesis theory.

5-5.   Be able to describe two types of apparent motion and give examples of each. Be familiar with the factors that influence the perception of real motion.

5-6.   Know the major cue in binocular depth perception and be able to demonstrate it. Be able to list the major monocular cues to depth perception and show how an artist would use each.

5-7.   Understand the difference between simple, complex, and hypercomplex cells in the visual cortex. Be able to show, in general, how they function in a hierarchical manner in coding information.

5-8.   Be able to discuss the nativist and empiricist views of perception, presenting relevant evidence from several areas of research.

5-9.   Be familiar with the factors that determine which stimuli will gain our attention. Know how the orienting reflex is involved and the factors that affect it.

5-10. Be able to define three types of ESP plus PK. Be familiar with how some of these are investigated in the laboratory, as well as the reasons why many psychologists are skeptical of the results.

PROGRAMMED UNIT

patterns

1. In our perception of the world around us, we respond not to isolated stimuli but to *patterns of stimuli* that are organized into a *meaningful whole.* When looking at a painting of a landscape, you perceive not isolated daubs of paint but _____ of stimuli that are organized in some meaningful way.

patterns

meaningful

2. In listening to a piece of music, you hear _____ of tones rather than isolated tones. The word "pattern" implies that the tones are organized in some m_____ way.

stimuli

3. As you sit at your desk reading this unit, there are many stimuli impinging on your sense organs, but what you actually perceive depends on your *past experience* with patterns of _____ .

experience

4. When we say that perception depends on past _____ , we imply that at least some aspects of perception must be learned.

stimuli

shape

5. When you look at a silver dollar held at eye level, the pattern of _____ impinging on your eyes is quite different from the pattern produced by the same coin lying on a table. In both instances, however, you perceive the shape of the coin as round. In other words, the _____ of the coin is perceived as *constant* regardless of the viewing angle.

constant

6. Similarly, we tend to perceive an object as having a *constant* brightness regardless of the degree of illumination on it. A tennis ball is perceived as just as white whether it is lying in the bright sunlight or in the shade of a tree. That is, the tennis ball is perceived as having a _____ brightness.

color

7. The color of a familiar object does not appear to change with changes in illumination. The owner of a blue car sees it as blue whether looking at it in bright sunlight, in dim illumination, or under a yellow street light. Its _____ is perceived as constant.

object

8. The tendency to perceive objects as the same regardless of changes in the conditions of perception is called *object constancy.* We recognize a tin can as being cylindrical regardless of its position. This is an example of _____ constancy.

object

constancy

9. The fact that we perceive an object as being of a certain brightness or color even when the illumination is changed is another illustration of _____ _____ .

object constancy

10. A closed door is rectangular in shape, but as it swings toward you its shape goes through a series of distortions. When the door is partially open, it is actually a trapezoid, in terms of the pattern of stimulation on the retina. When it is completely open, we see only a vertical line the thickness of the door. Although we can easily distinguish these changes, what we perceive is an unchanging door swinging on its hinges. The fact that you perceive the door as a rectangle regardless of its position is an illustration of _____ _____ .

11. Psychologists distinguish among several kinds of object constancy. For example, the tendency to perceive objects as the same *shape,* regardless of the viewing angle, is

shape   known as _____ constancy.

12. When we see a man close to us, we may recognize that he is about 6 feet tall. If we perceive this same man at a distance of 100 yards, the image on the retina is much smaller than it was when he was right next to us. Still we perceive him as being

size   approximately the same *size,* 6 feet fall. This is an example of _____ constancy.

13. We perceive a tin can as being cylindrical, regardless of its position because of

shape   _____ constancy.

14. We perceive a fence post at the end of the block as being as tall as the one next to

size constancy   us because of _____ _____ .

15. The fact that a piece of black velvet looks just as dark whether it is viewed in the

constancy   sun or in the shade is an example of brightness _____ .

16. The fact that an orange is perceived as orange even when the conditions of illumina-

color   tion change is an example of _____ constancy.

17. Another kind of object _____ is *location* constancy. Even though

constancy   the stimuli impinging on our senses change rapidly as we move about, we perceive objects as maintaining a fixed location.

18. The tendency to perceive objects as being in a fixed location, regardless of continual

location constancy   changes in stimulation, is known as _____ _____ .

19. When we speak of object constancy, then, we are speaking about the tendency to

constant   perceive objects as _____ regardless of alterations in illumination,
(or the same)   viewing angle, distance, or other conditions of perception.

20. The general name given to the tendency to perceive objects as the same regardless of

object constancy   changes in the conditions of perception is _____ _____ .

location, color   21. We have examined five kinds of object constancy: _____ , _____ ,

shape, size, brightness   _____ , _____ , and _____ constancy.
(any order)

22. The perceptual constancies suggest that our perceptions are organized in some way. If you look around, you will notice that certain objects seem bolder and better defined than others. Writing on a blackboard stands out against the background of the blackboard. We call what stands out the *figure* and the background the *ground.* The perceptual organization of figure and ground—in the example above, white

figure   against black—constitutes the _____ -*ground* relationship.

23. When we look at a picture of a woman standing on a beach with the ocean behind

figure, ground   her, the woman is the _____ and the ocean is the _____ .

24. An object standing out against a uniform background is an example of a

figure-ground _____-_____ relationship.

25. Another example of organization within perception is the tendency to *group* stimuli into some sort of pattern or structure. This is known as *perceptual grouping.* In the top figure below, you tend to perceive three pairs of straight lines with an extra line

right on the _____. In the bottom figure, the addition of extensions to the same

left lines makes you perceive three broken squares and an extra line on the _____.

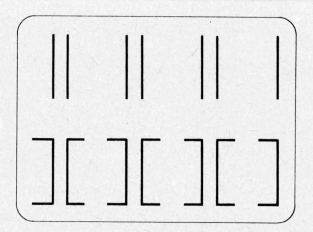

26. The tendency to group stimuli according to a pattern of some sort is called per-

grouping ceptual _____.

figure-ground **27.** Two examples of organization within perception are _____-_____

perceptual grouping relationships and _____ _____.

28. Many problems in perception are still not well understood. One of these is *visual illusions.* You are probably familiar with geometrical illusions like those below. For

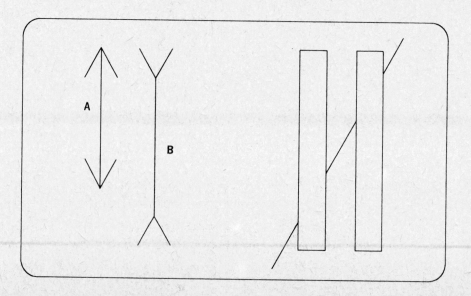

the figure on the left, line segment B looks longer than line segment A, although

illusion

both are actually the same length; this is an example of a visual _____.

For the figure on the right, the line that projects through the two rectangles is actu-

visual

ally straight, though it appears staggered. This is another example of a _____

illusion

_____ .

29. Related to visual illusions are *reversible figures* such as the *Necker cube* shown below. Because the tinted surface can appear as either the front or the rear surface

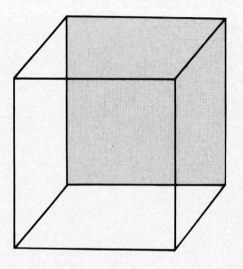

reversible

of a transparent cube, the figure is called _____ .

cube

30. Reversible figures like the Necker _____ indicate that our perceptions are not a static mirroring of visual stimuli; perception is an *active* process of *hypothesis testing.*

figures

31. In looking at reversible _____ our perception jumps back and forth between the two perspectives. Since the pattern of the cube gives us no clue as to which of two alternative hypotheses is correct, our perceptual system tests first one,

hypothesis

then the other, hy_____ and never settles on an answer.

32. The problem arises because the Necker cube is a three-dimensional object represented on a two-dimensional surface. If we were to see it in three-dimensional form,

hypothesis

there would be many cues to tell us which _____ to choose.

active

33. The notion of hypothesis testing emphasizes the (*active/passive*) nature of perception.

34. The perceptual system does not passively sense inputs, but searches for the percept that is most consistent with the sensory data. In most situations there is only one reasonable interpretation of the sensory data, and the search for the correct percept

testing

proceeds so quickly that we are unaware of the hypothesis-_____ nature of perception.

35. The hypotheses tested depend not only on the features of the object but also on

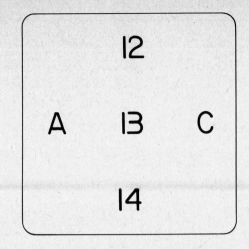

the *context* within which the object is viewed, as the figure above illustrates. The center of the figure can be seen either as the letter B or as the number 13, depending on the con_____ in which it appears.

context

hypotheses

36. We use both object features and context in testing perceptual hy_____ .

37. Events are organized in *time* as well as in space. When you perceive movement, you sense action in space taking place over _____ .

time

38. What cues enable us to perceive *motion?* The facts are not certain, but one theory proposed by *Gibson* is that we see an object in m_____ because as it moves, it successively *covers and uncovers portions of the immobile background.*

motion

39. According to Gibson, movement is perceived when the moving object successively _____ and _____ portions of the background.

covers, uncovers

40. In addition, objects in motion change their orientation in space; we see new portions which other portions disappear. Thus, even if we focus on the moving object and ignore the immobile _____ , we still perceive motion.

background

41. According to G_____ theory, it does not matter whether we track the moving object or look also at the background; we still perceive an object in _____ .

Gibson's

motion

42. Gibson's theory of motion perception emphasizes the (*changing/unchanging*) portions of the moving object or of the background.

changing

43. It is also possible to perceive motion when there is no real movement. This is called *apparent motion.* If you stare at a fixed spot of light in a dark room, after a few seconds the light will appear to move about in an erratic manner. This phenomenon, called the *autokinetic effect,* is an example of apparent _____ .

motion

44. One example of apparent motion, the movement of a fixed spot of light in a dark room, is the _____ effect.

autokinetic

motion

45. Another example of apparent _____ , familiar to you as the basis of "motion pictures," is called *stroboscopic motion.* If a series of pictures (each picture slightly different from the preceding one) is presented rapidly enough, the pictures blend into smooth motion.

46. The illusion of motion created when separated stimuli, not in motion, are presented

stroboscopic

in rapid succession is called _____ motion.

motion

47. Stroboscopic _____ and the autokinetic effect are both examples of

apparent

_____ motion.

three

48. The perception of depth is another problem in the study of perception. The surface of the retina has only two dimensions, yet we perceive in _____ dimensions.

three

49. The process by which we perceive in _____ dimensions is similar to the effect produced by the old-fashioned stereoscope. The stereoscope is a device by means of which two flat pictures, one presented to each eye, combine to yield an experience of depth. The pictures appear to be identical but are actually photographed from slightly different *angles.*

50. Since our eyes are separated in our head, each views the world from a slightly dif-

angle

ferent _____ . The combination of these two scenes provides the

depth

experience of _____ .

51. The perception of depth that results from the overlapping visual fields of the two eyes is called *stereoscopic vision.* Stereoscopic vision depends on the fact that each

different

of our eyes sees a slightly _____ picture.

stereoscopic vision

52. Having two eyes helps us to perceive depth and distance by means of _____ _____ . But a person with only one eye can still use many cues to determine the distance or depth of an object. Cues that

one (or a single)

require the use of only _____ eye are called *monocular distance cues.*

monocular

53. If one object cuts off the view of another, we assume that the first object is nearer. Since we can make this observation with only one eye, it is a _____ distance cue.

54. Another monocular cue is the fact that parallel lines appear to converge in the distance. When you look down a railroad track, the rails appear to come together at

monocular

the horizon. This is a _____ cue to distance.

55. The fact that objects appear to decrease in size with distance is another cue that a

distance

person with only one eye could use to estimate dis_____ .

56. Thus we see that there are many cues that can be utilized to judge the depth or distance of an object. Some of these require the use of only one eye. These are

monocular

called _____ distance cues. Others require the use of both eyes; these are *binocular* cues.

57. When we judge the distance of an object, we generally depend upon both
_____ and _____ cues.

monocular, binocular
(either order)

binocular

58. Stereoscopic vision is a _____ cue, while the fact that objects
appear to decrease in size with increasing distance is a _____ cue.

monocular

59. As adults, we know that we are capable of certain kinds of visual perception. But
disagreements remain over whether our abilities to perceive the spatial aspects of
our environment are learned or whether we are born with them. Those who support
the role of *learning* are called *empiricists*. Those who maintain that we are born
with the ability to perceive the way we do are called *nativists*. If one argues that the
perceptual constancies must be learned, he or she is supporting the viewpoint of the

empiricists

_____ .

empiricists

60. The _____ feel that we have to learn to perceive the world in
the way that we do. The _____ , on the other hand, argue that this
ability is innate.

nativists

61. Most psychologists today agree that practice and experience play a vital role in
determining what we perceive. In other words, they emphasize the importance of

learning, empiricists

_____ in perception. This is the position of the _____ .
The question that remains is whether we are born with some ability to perceive the
world or whether it is all learned.

62. When by the removal of cataracts vision is given to people who have been blind all
their lives, they cannot distinguish a square from a triangle or tell which of two
sticks is longer without feeling them. This evidence supports the role of

learning

_____ in perception.

63. On the other hand, as you will see in the text, there is evidence for some innate
basis for what we perceive. Thus, the _____ viewpoint is not com-
pletely wrong.

nativist

64. Perception is *selective*. We pay *attention* to only a few of the many stimuli that sur-
round us. As you read you are probably unaware of the pressure of your clothing or
the sounds coming from outside the room. Your unawareness of these stimuli points

selective

up the s_____ nature of perception.

65. But any *change* in your surroundings—an unfamiliar noise or change in illumination—
quickly attracts your _____ , and you perform certain body move-
ments to *facilitate reception* of the stimulus.

attention

66. For example, if the stimulus is visual, you turn your head in the proper direction
and move your eyes so that the image falls on the fovea. These movements

facilitate

_____ reception of the stimulus.

67. A faint sound may cause you to turn one ear in that direction while keeping the
rest of your body still so as to facilitate _____ of the stimulus.

reception

68. These body movements in response to changes in the environment are accompanied by a pattern of physiological reactions called the *orienting reflex.* The orienting

reflex

_____ occurs in response to even slight changes in the environment. It includes such physiological changes as constriction of the peripheral blood vessels and changes in muscle tone, heart rate, and respiration.

orienting

reflex

69. These physiological accompaniments of attention, called the _____

_____, facilitate the reception of stimuli and prepare the organism to respond quickly in case action is needed.

70. A loud tone arouses the orienting reflex in a laboratory subject. The subject then reports seeing a light that was too faint to be detected before the tone sounded.

facilitates

This demonstrates the fact that the orienting reflex _____ the reception of stimuli.

71. If the same stimulus is repeated a number of times, the orienting reflex gradually diminishes. A *change* in the stimulus or the introduction of a new stimulus will reactivate the orienting reflex in its original strength. Thus the orienting reflex is

changes

responsive to ch_____ in the environment. Such a reflex has important survival value for the organism.

72. When we discuss perception, we are usually speaking of *sensory perception,* that is,

senses

perception that takes place through the _____. It has been suggested that there may be perceptions that do not require any sense-organ stimulation. These phenomena have been called *extrasensory perception* (ESP).

73. Research on extrasensory perception has been carried on for a number of years. Although some psychologists believe that the evidence for the existence of certain

extrasensory

forms of _____ perception is indisputable, most remain unconvinced.

74. There are several different phenomena classified as ESP. *Telepathy* means the transference of thought from one person to another. In more familiar terms,

telepathy

_____ is the word for "mind reading."

75. A person who claims to be able to transmit thoughts across a distance to another

telepathy

person is maintaining that _____ exists. Of course, one who claims to be able to receive such thoughts also supports the existence of this phenomenon.

76. One of the most common types of research in ESP is based on experiments in card guessing. The experimenter may ask the subject to guess the symbol on a card that is in a sealed envelope. No one knows what card it is. The ability of the subject to perceive the card is called *clairvoyance.* The perception of objects or events that are

clairvoyance

not influencing the senses is known as cl_____. At times,

telepathy

one may not be sure whether _____ or clairvoyance is at work. If someone else knows, for instance, what the card is, then the subject might

clairvoyance

be perceiving the card directly (_____) or might be reading

telepathy

the thoughts of the person who knows (_____).

77. Another kind of ESP is *precognition,* or the perception of a future event. For a

precognition

person who bets on horse races, _____ would seem to be the most valuable kind of ESP.

78. The phenomena of ESP are discussed under a number of classifications:

telepathy

a. Thought transference from one person to another, or _____ .

precognition

b. The perception of a future event, or _____ .

c. The perception of an object or event that is not influencing the senses, or

clairvoyance

_____ .

79. A related phenomenon has to do with the influence of a mental operation over a material body or an energy system—for example, the idea that wishing for a given number affects the number that will come up in a throw of dice. This is called *psychokinesis.* If you can move a vase on your desk by merely willing it to move,

psychokinesis

you are demonstrating the operation of _____ .

80. A person who feels that he or she is a better roulette player than others is (unless

psychokinesis

cheating) operating with some belief in _____ .

TERMS AND CONCEPTS

brightness constancy _____

_____

_____

color constancy _____

_____

_____

shape constancy _____

_____

_____

size constancy _____

_____

_____

location constancy _____

_____

_____

figure-ground perception _____

_____

_____

perceptual hypothesis testing _____

_____

_____

analysis-by-synthesis _____

_____

_____

apparent motion _____

_____

_____

autokinetic effect _____

_____

_____

stroboscopic motion _____

_____

_____

phi phenomenon _____

_____

_____

stereoscopic vision _____

_____

_____

binocular disparity _____

_____

_____

monocular cues _____

_____

_____

feature detectors _____

_____

_____

simple cells _____

_____

_____

complex cells _____

_____

feature list* _____

_____

_____

sorting tree* _____

_____

_____

nativist theory of perception _____

_____

_____

empiricist theory of perception _____

_____

_____

visual cliff _____

_____

_____

attention _____

_____

_____

orienting reflex _____

_____

_____

extrasensory perception (ESP) _____

_____

_____

_____

telepathy _____

_____

_____

clairvoyance _____

_____

_____

precognition _____

_____

_____

psychokinesis (PK) _____

_____

_____

_____

psi* _____

_____

_____

*Indicates terms used in Critical Discussions

_____ 1. When we judge the color of an object we do so on the basis of
   a. wavelength of the light being reflected
   b. information about the color of surrounding objects
   c. information about the nature of the illuminating light
   d. all of the above

_____ 2. Persons blind from birth because of cataracts *cannot,* soon after the cataracts are removed,
   a. distinguish a triangle from a square
   b. distinguish figure from ground
   c. fixate a figure
   d. follow moving objects with their eyes

_____ 3. Studies with the "visual cliff" show that
   a. depth perception is present at birth for most species
   b. very young animals sometimes step off on the deep side, while older ones do not
   c. animals freeze in a state of immobility when placed on the deep side
   d. stereoscopic depth cues are necessary to perceive the danger of the deep side

_____ 4. If one could influence the numbers turning up on dice by thinking about them, this would be an example of
   a. clairvoyance
   b. psychokinesis
   c. telepathy
   d. precognition

_____ 5. The ability to focus on stimuli in which we are interested while resisting distracting stimuli is called
   a. concentrated attending
   b. stimulus focusing
   c. structured perceiving
   d. selective attention

_____ 6. When we look at a distant object, we usually judge its size by
   a. object size
   b. retinal size
   c. a compromise between object size and retinal size
   d. perspective size

_____ 7. Monocular cues that an artist may use to give depth to a picture include
   a. placing distant objects higher in the picture
   b. making the "grain," or texture gradient, finer as distance decreases
   c. making nearer objects smaller
   d. all of the above

_____ 8. The apparent movement that occurs when you stare at a single spot of light in a dark room is called
   a. induced movement
   b. the autokinetic effect
   c. stroboscopic motion
   d. the phi phenomenon

_____ 9. The view that we are born with the ability to perceive the way we do is held by
   a. sensory psychologists
   b. nativists
   c. empiricists
   d. most contemporary psychologists

_____ 10. The phenomenon of induced movement is involved in
   a. the apparent movement of the moon when viewed through moving clouds
   b. the apparent movement of a single spot of light in a dark room
   c. the apparent movement of a spot of light when several lights are turned on and off in sequence
   d. a motion picture

_____ 11. A person with vision in only one eye *cannot* see
   a. spatial relationships
   b. three-dimensional configurations
   c. well in dim light conditions
   d. with stereoscopic vision

_____ 12. Most psychologists remain skeptical about ESP because
   a. improved methods fail to yield better results than crude methods
   b. no statistically significant results have been obtained
   c. they reject the legitimacy of the basic inquiries
   d. all of the above

_____ 13. The perceptual constancies (for example, size, shape, and location constancy) suggest that perception
   a. is oriented toward constant sensory features
   b. is oriented toward things rather than sensory features

c. is based on one constancy per sensory feature

d. provides constant-feature inputs that must be further integrated

_____ 14. Subjects attending to two different spoken messages, one in each ear,

a. can listen to either one at will

b. can repeat aloud one of the messages

c. will know if their name is mentioned, even while attending to the message in the other ear

d. all of the above

_____ 15. In research investigating the effects of experience on visual development, kittens were raised with visual exposure only to bright dots. Subsequent testing showed that the kittens'

a. retinas had deteriorated

b. visual cortex contained neurons unusually responsive to spots of light

c. ability to discriminate forms was very poor

d. vision was essentially normal

_____ 16. While the full explanations for geometrical illusions remain uncertain, it seems that

a. some illusions are based on relative size in contrast with surroundings

b. some illusions are based on a tendency to see flat figures as if they were representations of three dimensions

c. some illusions depend for their full effect on our learning to use linear perspective cues

d. all of the above

_____ 17. Laboratory studies of the orienting reflex show that

a. after the orienting reflex has habituated, any change in the stimulus will reactivate it

b. arousal of the reflex by a loud tone increases auditory sensitivity at the expense of the other senses

c. a new stimulus is much more effective in reestablishing a habituated orienting reflex than a change in the old one

d. all of the above

_____ 18. The Necker cube is a classic

a. apparatus for testing children's vision

b. size constancy illusion

c. reversible figure

d. test of shape constancy

_____ 19. Simple and complex cells in the visual system function in such a way that

a. a complex cell responds to a shape, such as a square

b. a complex cell responds to a line at a particular angle and particular location in the visual field

c. a complex cell responds to a line with a particular orientation anywhere in the visual field

d. a complex cell responds to a line at any angle in the visual field

_____ 20. Proponents of Gestalt psychology might be expected to approach questions of perception with one of their favorite phrases:

a. "the whole is only the sum of its parts"

b. "the parts of an object together create the whole"

c. "the whole is different from the sum of its parts"

d. "the whole is an integration of all its parts"

KEY TO SELF-QUIZ

1. d p.130	6. c p.131	11. d p.139	16. d p.135	
2. a p.145	7. a p.140	12. a p.153	17. a p.150	
3. c p.147	8. b p.138	13. b p.130	18. c p.136	
4. b p.150	9. b p.144	14. d p.148	19. c p.143	
5. d p.147	10. a p.139	15. b p.146	20. c p.129	

CLASS EXERCISE

EXTRASENSORY PERCEPTION

Introduction

Extrasensory perception is a controversial topic in psychology. Many psychologists doubt that it is possible to transfer thoughts from one person to another without any physical intermediary. Others claim that thought transference—a form of ESP known as telepathy—has been adequately demonstrated in the laboratory. This exercise is similar to some laboratory experiments that have been conducted to demonstrate the existence of telepathy. The procedure has been simplified, however, to avoid the necessity of elaborate statistical analysis.

Equipment Needed

Any familiar coin and a screen to shield the "sender" from view of the class.

Procedure

The instructor will select from the class someone who feels that he or she might be a good "sender of thoughts." The sender will sit behind a screen and toss the coin for ten separate trials, each time concentrating on the side of the coin that faces up (heads or tails) and trying to transfer this image to the class, which will act as subjects. One student will observe the sender and record the results of each toss. It is best if the sender shakes the coin in a glass or cup and then inverts the container to deposit the coin on a flat surface.

The instructor will start each trial by saying the word "now"; the sender will toss the coin and concentrate on the upturned image; the instructor will say "receive," and the students will try to concentrate on the image being sent; when the instructor says "record," students will write by the proper trial number the word "heads" or "tails," depending on the image they feel they have received.

Treatment of Data

On the basis of chance we would expect five heads and five tails from ten coin tosses. And if subjects' guesses were based on chance alone, rather than ESP, we would expect them to be correct on five out of ten guesses—or 50 percent of the time. With only ten trials we would expect considerable chance variation from the 50/50 results. Many more trials would be required before chance effects would become insignificant. But our experiment should give us a rough approximation.

The instructor will read the results of the ten trials so that you can score your guesses. He or she will then determine by a show of hands the number of students obtaining one correct guess, two correct guesses, and so on. How many students had results that were below chance level? How many above chance level? How many exactly at chance level? What do you think the results demonstrate concerning the possibility of ESP?

The instructor will now select the three students with the lowest number of correct guesses and the three with the highest number and repeat the experiment with the same sender and these students.

Questions for Discussion

1. Are the students who were good receivers in the first part of the experiment still scoring above chance for the second ten trials? Are the students who were initially poor receivers still poor?

2. How do these results affect your interpretation of the findings from the first experiment?

3. What additional controls would you want to see enforced to make this a better ESP experiment?

INDIVIDUAL EXERCISES

THE PHI PHENOMENON

This drawing illustrates the phi phenomenon. Hold your hand in either position and alternately close your right and left eyes. While actually seen in a stationary position, your index finger appears to move. Thus you get a perception of motion without a moving stimulus.

Why does this occur? Can you think of an industry that depends on this same phenomenon?

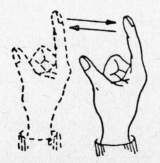 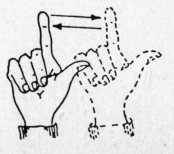

PERCEPTUAL REORGANIZATION

Look at the figures shown below and try to figure out what the next one in the sequence would be like and why.

If you decide you do not know, look again at the figures, using this clue: Look only at the right half of each figure. Now you should experience the shock of perceptual reorganization as the figures suddenly make sense. (If you have not, see the answer at the bottom of this page.)

Now that this perceptual hypothesis has been confirmed

and "locked in," notice something else. It is probably not possible for you to now see them as the mysterious, complex figures they were before. They are now irreversibly obvious to you, so much so that if you show them to friends who have not seen them before, you will find it hard to understand why they are not immediately and glaringly obvious. It is this organizing of visual images into perceptions that is both useful to us and inhibitory—useful in quickly sorting the world for us, inhibitory in keeping us from seeing things "with a fresh eye," as in art or problem solving.

THE AFTEREFFECTS OF MOTION

Cut out the spiral disk on page 81 and paste it on a piece of cardboard. Attach it with a thumbtack to the end of a pencil. Spin the disk slowly and stare steadily at it as it moves. Stop the disk and notice what happens. Does it seem to be turning in the opposite direction? If you were turning the disk so that the spiral was expanding, it will seem to contract when stopped, and vice versa. When the spiral is turning steadily, our visual system tends to suppress the perceived motion, apparently by generating some sort of opposing process. When the actual movement stops, the opposing process continues for a while, and you see it as apparent motion in the opposite direction.

Now look at the spiral again as it spins slowly, then turn to look at a blank wall or a picture. The opposing process will make even the wall or picture appear to move in the opposite direction to the direction of the spiral's movement. The process apparently is not limited to spirals but applies to anything in the visual field.[1]

You may have noticed a similar effect in nature. If you look steadily at a waterfall or a flowing river for a while and then transfer your gaze to the rocks beside the falls or the river bank, whatever you are looking at appears to move in the opposite direction from the flow of water.

[1] Courtesy of Dr. Cornsweet.

They are the numerals 1 through 5, with mirror images.

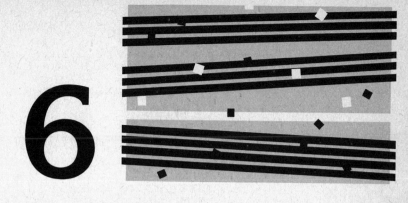

6
Consciousness and Control

LEARNING OBJECTIVES

6-1. Be able to differentiate between nonconscious, preconscious, unconscious, and subconscious processes. Understand how consciousness itself may be considered active or passive.

6-2. Understand the complexities of defining consciousness as an agent of control, including the concept of dissociated consciousness.

6-3. Be familiar with the phenomena of divided consciousness as illustrated by research on divided attention and multiple personalities.

6-4. Be able to discuss in some detail sleep schedules, stages of sleep depth, and voluntary and involuntary controls of sleep.

6-5. Be familiar with Freud's theory of dreams and what research says about it. Know the answers to the basic questions about dreams discussed in the text.

6-6. Be able to define meditation and to describe similarities and differences between the form called TM and the technique developed by Benson.

6-7. Know what is meant by a psychoactive drug and be able to give examples of each of the three subcategories. Be familiar with some typical patterns of use of these drugs.

6-8. Be able to describe the procedure and typical effects of a hypnosis session. Be familiar with the phenomena of posthypnotic amnesia and other posthypnotic suggestions; understand the questions of conscious control that these phenomena raise.

6-9. Be familiar with the phenomena of hypnotic age regression, automatic writing, and other dissociated tasks. Understand what is meant by the "hidden observer" and how it is studied.

6-10. Know the difference between unusual but scientifically demonstrable phenomena and other claimed phenomena that either cannot be demonstrated or have been demonstrated to be fraudulent. Be able to discuss the role of psychology in the study of both types of phenomena.

1. We think of consciousness as an alert and active state, but a little reflection makes it clear that there are various *degrees of conscious awareness.* While reading this page you may be only dimly aware of the sounds outside the room until something (a sudden noise, your name mentioned in a conversation) attracts your attention. This

conscious   illustrates the fact that there are degrees of _____ awareness.

2. You may perform a habitual act, such as driving a car, while engrossed in thought. On reaching your destination you realize that you recall nothing about the actions you performed while driving or the street corners you passed. Again, we see that

degrees   there are _____ of conscious awareness.

3. Some activities within the body never become conscious; these are called *nonconscious processes.* You are not aware of changes in hormone secretions or the concentration of salt in your blood. These bodily activities are what we mean by

nonconscious   non _____ processes.

4. Sometimes there are conscious effects that are associated with these bodily changes— for example, you may be aware of the rapid heart rate that accompanies the secretion of the hormone adrenalin. But the processes themselves are

nonconscious   _____ .

conscious

5. In contrast to nonconscious processes, which never become _____ , are *preconscious processes.* These are memories that are *available* to consciousness but are not conscious at a given moment.

6. You may not be aware now of the trip you took last weekend, but the memory is

available   av _____ to awareness if you wish to recall it. Memories that are available to awareness but are not presently conscious are called

preconscious   _____ .

preconscious

7. Available memories are (*nonconscious/preconscious*) processes. But some memories or experiences are not available to consciousness, and these are called *unconscious.*

8. *Unconscious processes* were proposed by Freud to explain certain behaviors—such as slips of speech, forgotten memories, or emotions we do not understand. For example, a man says to his sister, "I'm sad you came," when what he intended to say was, "I'm glad you came." Freud would speculate that the man had negative feelings

unconscious   toward his sister of which he was unaware. These feelings are un _____ .

9. According to psychoanalytic theory, unconscious processes are very much like con-

awareness   scious mental activities except that they go on without our aware _____ .
Freud believed that for emotional reasons, some consciously experienced events are driven out of consciousness and lost to memory; they are *repressed* to the unconscious.

10. A young boy has strong feelings of hostility toward his newborn sister, who has usurped his place as the center of parental affection; but whenever he expresses

such feelings, he is punished. According to Freud, the angry feelings may then be

repressed   re_____ to the unconscious.

11. In later life the boy may show, in various indirect ways, that he resents his sister. If he is not aware of any feelings of resentment, such feelings may be said to be

unconscious (or repressed)   _____.

12. Experiences that affect what we do but are so hidden that we become aware of

unconscious   them only through *indirect methods* are called _____ processes.

13. Sometimes the terms *unconscious* and *subconscious* are used synonymously, but we can make some distinctions between them. Subconscious experiences operate very much as conscious ones do except that they are so far toward the outer margins of consciousness that we are unaware of them at the moment. But they are not deeply

unconscious   buried, or repressed, as are _____ experiences.

14. For example, you may not be conscious of hearing a clock strike the hour until, after a few strokes, you become alert. Then you can count the strokes that you did

subconsciously   not know you heard; they influenced you sub_____.

15. While driving to work and engaging in conversation with your passenger, you fail to notice several police cars pulled up in front of the bank. Later, when hearing news of a bank robbery on the radio, you recall the scene. The events registered

subconsciously   _____, even though you were not aware of them at the time.

repressed   16. Unlike unconscious experiences, which are assumed to be re_____
indirect   and are available to consciousness only through (*direct/indirect*) methods, subconscious experiences can be brought to awareness.

17. We have discussed various degrees of conscious awareness. (These are distinguished

nonconscious   from activities within the body, _____ processes, which
preconscious   never become conscious.) They include available memories, or _____
unconscious   processes, experiences that are repressed, or _____, and
subconscious   _____ experiences of which we may be unaware at the time but which can be brought to awareness when attention is drawn to them later.

18. To complicate matters still further, even our everyday consciousness includes two quite different modes: *passive,* receptive states (as when we relax and listen to music) and *active,* productive mental states (as when we make plans or initiate activities). As you concentrate on this paragraph, your consciousness would be

active   described as _____; while meditating or watching the sunset, you are
passive   probably in a _____ state.

19. It is easy to distinguish on paper between the two modes of consciousness,

active, passive   _____ and _____. In reality, however, the boundaries be-
(either order)   tween the two are blurred—as are the boundaries between the different degrees of

consciousness discussed earlier. This becomes apparent when we consider the relation between consciousness and *control*.

20. We think of control as one function of consciousness. But not all controls are conscious. The various controls that regulate such bodily processes as temperature and heart rate operate automatically without our awareness; they correspond to what

    nonconscious   we referred to earlier as _____ processes. While such inter-

    voluntary   nal controls are *involuntary,* most behavior is (*voluntary/involuntary*).

21. We think of voluntary behavior as being under conscious control because it depends on a deliberate decision to engage in a particular activity. You decide to go for a

    voluntary   bicycle ride and get your bike from the garage. Your behavior is v_____

    conscious   and under _____ control.

22. But as voluntary actions become habitual, they require less conscious control. Learn-

    control   ing to ride a bicycle involves intense concentration and voluntary _____
    of movements. But once you learn to ride, your actions became automatic and you no longer have to concentrate on what you are doing.

23. Bicycle riding is still voluntary (you decide when to start and stop riding), but the

    control   activity itself no longer requires much conscious _____.

    less   24. As voluntary activities become habitual, they require (*less/more*) conscious control.

25. After you have learned a piano piece well, you may be able to play it automatically with little attention to your fingers or the piano keys. You may even be able to carry on a conversation while playing. An activity that once required intense con-

    conscious   scious control now requires little _____ control.

26. If you hit a wrong note, however, your attention is immediately drawn to the keyboard, and your conversation may be disrupted. Your consciousness is *divided*

    divided   between two activities. Consciousness is often d_____ when we shift
    attention from one activity to another. The text gives several examples of divided consciousness and shows how multiple personalities may be viewed as extreme cases

    consciousness   of divided _____.

27. Conscious activities may take place under conditions that are different from those of normal waking; these conditions can be described as *altered states of consciousness.* A person who is drunk or in a hypnotic trance behaves differently from that same person under normal waking conditions. Hence alcoholic intoxication and

    altered   hypnosis are considered _____ states of consciousness.

    consciousness   28. Sleep is also an altered state of _____. If sleep were an

    state   entirely unconscious state, it would not be considered an altered _____ of
    consciousness. But since we can recall dreams we experienced while asleep, we cannot have been entirely unconscious.

29. Scientists have discovered that there are *five stages* of sleep—*four stages of depth* and a fifth stage known as *rapid-eye-movement* (*REM*) *sleep,* during which dreams

five

commonly occur. One method of studying the _____ (*number*) stages of sleep is by using the *electroencephalogram* (abbreviated *EEG*), which measures the electrical activity of the brain.

30. When we measure the electrical activity of the brain with the electroencephalogram

EEG, depth

(abbreviated _____) we find that the four stages of d_____ of sleep are characterized by different *brain waves.*

waves

31. We can tell how deeply a person is sleeping by the kind of brain _____

electroencephalogram

recorded by the electro_____ .

four

32. There are _____ (*number*) stages of depth of sleep. Stages 1 through 4 represent a scale of increasing depth of sleep, with stage 1 the lightest sleep and stage 4 the deepest.

easier

33. You would expect it to be (*easier/more difficult*) to arouse a person from stage 1 sleep than from stage 4.

34. During a fifth stage of sleep, rapid movements of the eyes occur. This stage is known

REM

as rapid-eye-movement, or _____, sleep. It is this stage of sleep that is associated

dreams (or dreaming)

with d_____ .

35. Since rapid eye movements are not observed during the other four stages of sleep, they are known collectively as non-REM, or *NREM,* sleep. Dreams usually take place

REM

during (*REM/NREM*) sleep.

36. During REM sleep the EEG pattern is similar to that of stage 1 sleep. (You recall

brain

that the EEG is a method of measuring the electrical activity of the _____.) The EEG pattern during REM sleep indicates that it should be easy to arouse the

1

person, since it is similar to stage _____ , which is light sleep. But actually it is as difficult to arouse a person from REM sleep as it is from stage 4 NREM sleep.

37. When a person is in REM sleep there is a *decrease in muscle tone* of the body mus-

difficult

cles. This may be one reason why it is (*easy/difficult*) to awaken someone from REM sleep.

38. The stage of sleep during which dreams occur can be distinguished from the other

eye movements

four stages by two measures: rapid _____ _____ and decrease in

muscle

_____ tone. The stages of sleep vary throughout the night, but REM sleep tends to be more prominent during the second half of the night.

39. Does everyone dream? If we accept REM sleep as evidence, then it is true that *every-one* dreams, though some people recall very few dreams. Thus we can say that

everyone

(*everyone/not everyone*) dreams.

40. Another interesting question is, "Can the sleeper react to stimuli from the environment without awakening?" During REM sleep, if stimuli such as spoken names are presented while the person is dreaming, the subject is not likely to awaken but instead will *incorporate* the external stimuli into his or her dreams in some manner. Thus, if John is in REM sleep and he hears the name "Mary" (the name of his girl-

incorporate

friend) spoken to him, he is likely to _____ her name into his dream in some manner.

41. The answer to the question "Can the sleeper react to the environment without awakening?" is (yes/no).

yes

42. Both *sleeptalking* and *sleepwalking* occur primarily during NREM sleep and probably not in relation to dreaming, which occurs during _____ sleep.

REM

43. Occurring primarily in NREM sleep are two phenomena, sleep _____

sleepwalking

and sleep _____.

sleeptalking (either order)

44. The most influential theory of dreams within the last half-century has been that of Freud. He believed that *unconscious* impulses were responsible for the dream, and that the aim of the dream was the *gratification* of some *drive.* Jane, who has been married two years, dreams that she is single. According to Freud, Jane has an

unconscious

_____ wish that she were single.

45. According to Freud, dreams express _____ impulses and provide the_____ of some drive.

unconscious

gratification

46. According to Freud's analysis, the *remembered* aspects of a dream constitute the *manifest content* of the dream. However, the *real meaning* of the same dream, or the *latent content,* is not directly expressed but is instead dramatized in *disguised form;* even the dreamer cannot readily discern its hidden meaning. If Bob recalls that he dreamed last night that he was flying over the campus grounds, this would

manifest

be the dream's _____ content, since it is the remembered content of the dream.

47. The real meaning of Bob's dream may be incomprehensible to him; it is the

latent

_____ content of the dream.

48. Freud believed that dreams serve to *protect sleep.* In dreams, unfulfilled impulses

disguised

appear in dis_____ form; thus the dreams prevent the sleeper from being awakened by the disturbing impulses. In this sense, dreams serve to

protect

_____ sleep.

49. Some experimental findings, however, cast doubt on Freud's notion that dreams

sleep

serve to protect _____. The prevalence of REM states in newborn infants and in lower animals makes it unlikely that the purpose of REM sleep is to discharge

drives (or wishes, or impulses)

unfulfilled _____.

50. Unlike sleep, which is a change of state that occurs naturally, *meditation* is an effort

consciousness

to produce an altered state of _____ by *following prescribed exercises.*

51. Zen Buddhism, yoga, and Transcendental Meditation all prescribe certain

exercises

_____, or techniques, that must be followed to achieve a state of consciousness characterized by relaxation, peace of mind, and a sense of well-being.

meditation

52. While these approaches to _____ all involve mystical, or spiritual, associations, laboratory studies have shown that a similar state of consciousness can be attained by following a simple procedure of relaxation.

are not

53. Mystical, or spiritual, associations (*are/are not*) necessary to achieve the benefits of meditation.

54. Profound changes in conscious awareness can also be produced by the use of drugs. Drugs that affect behavior and conscious experience are called *psychoactive drugs.* Alcohol reduces anxiety, produces relaxation, and releases some of our social inhibi-

psychoactive

tions; it is one kind of psycho_____ drug.

55. Tranquilizers, alcohol, barbiturates, and narcotics such as heroin form one group of

psychoactive

_____ drugs that are called *depressants*. They vary in their effects, but all slow down the activity of the *central nervous system.*

56. Alcohol in small quantities may make a person more talkative and sociable, because it inhibits some of the restraints on social behavior. But several drinks produce slowed reaction times and drowsiness. Therefore, alcohol is classed as a

depressant

_____ .

psychoactive

nervous system

57. Another group of psycho_____ drugs are called *stimulants* because they speed up the activity of the central _____ _____ .

58. Amphetamines and cocaine increase alertness and wakefulness. They are classed as

stimulants

_____ .

depressants

stimulants (either order)

59. Two classes of psychoactive drugs are _____ and _____ .

behavior

experience (or awareness)

60. Psychoactive drugs are drugs that affect a person's _____ and conscious _____ .

61. A third class of psychoactive drugs are called *hallucinogens* or *psychedelic drugs* because they produce profound alterations in one's perceptions and conscious experience. LSD may produce serious distortions of consciousness, including hallu-

psychedelic

cinations; it is therefore classed as a hallucinogen or _____ drug.

62. Marijuana, while much milder in its effect than LSD, tends to distort one's time

hallucinogen

sense. Consequently, it is also classed as a _____ gen.

63. To recapitulate: drugs that affect behavior and conscious experience are called

psychoactive, depressants

_____ drugs. They fall into three classes: _____ ,

stimulants, hallucinogens
(or psychedelic drugs)
(any order)

_____ , and _____ . (The text discusses a number of patterns of drug use and the risks each entails.)

consciousness

64. We have discussed three altered states of _____ . These

sleep

include the natural state of _____ , as well as self-induced states attained

meditation, drugs
(either order)

through the use of _____ and _____. A fourth state of altered consciousness is *hypnosis.*

65. To induce hypnosis, the hypnotist uses a number of methods to lead the person to *relinquish some control of behavior* and to *accept some reality distortion.* Hypnosis was once believed to be similar to sleep, but EEG measures taken during hypnosis

stages

are like those of waking rather than any of the five _____ of sleep.

is not

66. While hypnosis (*is/is not*) similar to sleep, it differs from the normal waking state in several ways. An individual in a *hypnotic state* relinquishes some control of

behavior

_____ to the hypnotist; he or she does not like to make plans and would rather wait for the hypnotist to suggest what to do.

67. A *decreased interest in planning* or initiating activity is thus one characteristic of

hypnotic

the _____ state.

68. Another characteristic of the hypnotic state, in addition to a decreased interest in

planning

p_____, is a *reduction in reality testing.* A hypnotized individual will readily accept reality distortion or hallucinated experiences (for example, petting an imaginary rabbit that the person has been told is sitting on his or her lap). The same person in the normal waking state would usually reject such a distortion of

reality

_____ .

69. The hypnotic state thus differs from the normal waking state in (1) a decrease in

planning, reality

_____ and (2) a reduction in _____ testing.

testing

70. Closely related to the reduction in reality _____ under hypnosis is an increase in *suggestibility.* The hypnotized person will readily accept suggestions. If the hypnotist says, "You are very warm," the subject may begin to perspire. If the hypnotist says, "You are angry," the subject may show signs of irritability.

suggestibility

71. Another characteristic of the hypnotic state is increased sug_____ .

planning

72. Three characteristics of the hypnotic state are a decrease in _____ , a

testing, suggestibility

reduction in reality _____ , and increased _____ .

73. Several of the phenomena that can be demonstrated with deeply hypnotized individ-

suggestibility

uals are related to increased _____ . For example, the hypnotist may suggest that the subject will forget all that transpired during the hypnotic session. This is called *posthypnotic amnesia.*

amnesia

74. In posthypnotic am_____ the memories are not "lost"; when the hypnotist gives a prearranged signal, the subject recalls what took place during the hypnotic state.

75. The temporary loss of memory for events during hypnosis is called posthypnotic

amnesia

_____ . Amnesia is one form of *posthypnotic suggestion.* The hypnotist may make other suggestions while the subject is in the hypnotic state—for example, suggesting that after coming out of hypnosis the subject will open the window when the hypnotist pulls out a handkerchief but will not remember being so instructed.

76. If the subject opens the window at the prearranged signal but does not recall that the

posthypnotic

act was suggested by the experimenter, this is an example of post_____ suggestion.

amnesia, posthypnotic

77. Posthypnotic _____ is one form of _____

suggestion

_____ .

78. Another hypnotic phenomenon that occurs with highly responsive subjects involves performing two tasks at the same time while being aware of only one of them;

subconsciously

that is, one of the tasks is being carried on sub_____ . The text discusses this phenomenon as it relates to divided consciousness and dissociations.

TERMS AND CONCEPTS

consciousness _____

_____

_____

_____

nonconscious processes _____

_____

_____

_____

preconscious processes _____

_____

_____

_____

unconscious processes _____

_____

_____

_____

subconscious processes _____

_____

_____

_____

subliminal perception _____

_____

_____

_____

dissociation _____

_____

_____

_____

passive consciousness _____

_____

_____

_____

active consciousness _____

_____

_____

_____

divided consciousness _____

_____

_____

_____

multiple personalities _____

_____

_____

_____

altered states of consciousness _____

_____

_____

_____

sleep schedules _____

_____

_____

_____

circadian rhythm _____

_____

_____

_____

REM sleep _____

_____

_____

_____

narcolepsy _____

_____

_____

_____

apnea _____

_____

_____

_____

manifest content _____

_____

_____

_____

latent content _____

_____

_____

_____

REM deprivation* _____

_____

_____

_____

meditation _____

_____

_____

_____

Transcendental Meditation (TM) _____

_____

_____

_____

mantra _____

_____

_____

_____

psychoactive drugs _____

_____

_____

_____

depressants _____

_____

_____

_____

stimulants _____

_____

_____

_____

hallucinogens _____

_____

_____

_____

state-dependent learning _____

_____

_____

_____

psychedelic drugs _____

_____

_____

_____

hypnosis _____

_____

_____

_____

posthypnotic amnesia _____

_____

_____

_____

posthypnotic suggestion _____

_____

_____

_____

age regression _____

_____

_____

_____

automatic writing _____

_____

_____

_____

"hidden observer" _____

_____

_____

_____

*Indicates terms used in Critical Discussions

_____ 1. The four stages of NREM sleep are defined according to
  a. subjective ratings of depth of sleep
  b. the amount of dreaming per stage
  c. the duration of each stage
  d. EEG patterns

_____ 2. The general term for drugs that produce subjective changes in consciousness is
  a. psychoactive
  b. psychotomimetic
  c. psychedelic
  d. tranquilizing

_____ 3. A mantra is a key element in
  a. Zen Buddhism
  b. Benson's relaxation technique
  c. Transcendental Meditation
  d. yoga

_____ 4. The case of Jonah shows that in multiple personalities
  a. fusing the personalities into one is the best cure, if possible
  b. the separate personalities are always aware of each other
  c. the separate personalities score quite differently on both emotion and intelligence measures
  d. each personality may or may not be aware of the other

_____ 5. In studying who can be hypnotized, it has been found that
  a. anyone can be hypnotized if enough attempts are made
  b. childhood experiences can be important in determining whether a person can be hypnotized
  c. studies of twins show no evidence of a hereditary factor in susceptibility
  d. measures of susceptibility are useful when given, but the results cease to be meaningful as the subjects grow older

_____ 6. What are often simply classified as _available memories_ may be more specifically termed
_____ processes.
  a. nonconscious
  b. subconscious
  c. unconscious
  d. preconscious

_____ 7. Which of the following is _not_ a characteristic of the hypnotic state?
  a. The subject loses the sense of his or her own identity.
  b. Attention is redistributed.
  c. The subject ceases to make plans.
  d. Reality testing is reduced.

_____ 8. The relaxation technique developed by Benson does _not_ make use of
  a. a comfortable sitting position
  b. a sound specially chosen for each individual
  c. a focus on breathing
  d. daily practice

_____ 9. Alcohol is classified as a
  a. depressant
  b. stimulant
  c. hallucinogen
  d. narcotic

_____ 10. Adverse LSD reactions (that is, "bad trips")
  a. occur only in those who have such reactions outside the drugged state
  b. occur only in the first few uses of the drug
  c. can occur in any user
  d. tend to be brief and transient

_____ 11. The "hidden observer" of a hypnotized subject typically reports
  a. less pain than the nonhypnotic reports
  b. the same pain as the nonhypnotic reports
  c. more pain than the nonhypnotic reports
  d. no pain at all

_____ 12. Subjects who attempted to monitor two videotaped games presented simultaneously on the same screen
  a. were inaccurate on either game because of interference from the other one
  b. were able to simultaneously monitor both games accurately
  c. were able to monitor one game accurately if they ignored the other
  d. either b or c, depending on whether they used serial or parallel processing techniques

_____ 13. Studies of sleepwalking and sleeptalking have shown that
  a. sleeptalking is primarily associated with NREM sleep, although 20–25 percent is associated with REM

b. sleepwalking is primarily associated with REM sleep, although 20-25 percent is associated with NREM

c. sleepwalkers believe they are dreaming, since their reports of dreams match what they were doing while sleepwalking

d. sleepwalking only occurs during REM sleep

_____ 14. In testing whether sleepers can react to the environment without awakening, it has been found that subjects

a. can learn simple auditory material using sleep-learning techniques during REM sleep

b. sometimes incorporate auditory signals given during REM sleep into their dreams

c. can discriminate auditory signals better during REM sleep than during stages 1 and 2

d. all of the above

_____ 15. Some hypnosis studies have used a "hidden observer," that is, a(n)

a. experimenter concealed from the subject by a one-way mirror

b. member of the subject's own family who could observe responses at home

c. second personality of a multiple personality patient

d. concealed part of the subject's consciousness

_____ 16. Which of the following has been experimentally verified as possible?

a. "psychic surgery"

b. walking barefoot on hot coals

c. fixing watches through mental processes

d. reincarnation

_____ 17. Studies of the effects on performance of "jet lag" and loss of sleep have shown that

a. students who flew to Germany and back recov-covered in two or three days

b. students flying to Germany and back adjusted to the new German schedule in less time than it took to readjust back to the home schedule

c. the effects of jet lag are due to interference with the normal circadian rhythm

d. the effects of jet lag are due primarily to the loss of sleep

_____ 18. Studies of consciousness as an agent of control show that our experience of consciousness as unitary and continuous

a. accurately reflects the stability of consciousness

b. occurs because conscious controls are involuntary

c. occurs because voluntary controls are unconscious

d. is something of an illusion sustained by memory continuity

_____ 19. The modern induction of hypnosis often involves

a. convincing subjects that they are going to sleep

b. authoritarian commands by the hypnotist

c. asking a subject to concentrate on a visual target

d. hypnotizing an uncooperative subject

_____ 20. While occasional low doses of _____ can be beneficial, sustained and increased doses may cause persecutory delusions.

a. heroin

b. amphetamines

c. LSD

d. marijuana

KEY TO SELF-QUIZ

INDIVIDUAL EXERCISES

THE CHEVREUL PENDULUM

Introduction

While psychologists differ in their conception of a "subconscious" or "unconscious" portion of the mind, most would agree that some of our thoughts, motives, and emo-tional responses are more available for self-inspection than others. A variety of techniques have been developed to aid us in better understanding such "unconscious" mental activity. These range from Freud's free association to Zen and other forms of meditation. The Chevreul Pendulum[1]

[1] Named after the Frenchman, Michael Chevreul, who investigated the phenomenon in 1883, relating it to the use of a divining rod to discover water or precious metals beneath the earth.

technique falls into this spectrum. However, it is not an accepted research technique, as are most of the other procedures in this *Study Guide.* (The Chevreul Pendulum has been widely used in the manner to be described below, but rarely as part of a carefully controlled scientific study.) It is presented as a possible way for getting more in touch with ourselves or perhaps contacting our "hidden observer."

Equipment Needed

A pendulum, made up of a small weight on six to ten inches of string or fine chain. A locket on a chain will do. Or make a pendulum from a fishing weight, an eraser, etc., tied to a length of string.

Procedure

1. The Chevreul Pendulum is a device for what hypnotists term "ideomotor answering." The "answering" refers to the subject's answering questions, while "ideomotor" means doing so by a special kind of motor performance, one that reflects a thought yet is different from normal, deliberate body movements. Those hypnotists who use the "unconscious" as an explanatory system say this device allows the unconscious to answer. Others, less convinced of an unconscious "mind" lurking in our heads somewhere, still agree that such answering may yield responses different from simple verbal replies.

2. The pendulum works by allowing very fine muscular movements to provide answers to questions, movements so fine as to seem to happen by themselves. To help this happen, sit down, hold the string of the pendulum between your index finger and your thumb, and rest your elbow on a table. Pick a comfortable angle of the arm and let the pendulum hang to within an inch or two of the table. You will find that you can cause the pendulum to oscillate along a line, forward and back or left and right, and to rotate in either direction, by very small, almost imperceptible, movements.

3. In order to answer questions, you should have pendulum movements for "yes," "no," "maybe," "I don't know," and perhaps "I don't want to answer." A typical setup could be right-left for "yes," forward-back for "no," an indeterminate movement for "maybe," a circle one way for "I don't know," and the other way for "I don't want to answer." But don't just use these movements; let the pendulum tell you. Rest your elbow comfortably with the pendulum motionless and tell yourself, out loud or silently, that the pendulum will soon move appropriately for "yes." The movement

may be uncertain at first, but don't force it. Just keep thinking "yes" and expecting some movement. If all goes well the pendulum will slowly being to move. Use the same procedure for the other answers.

4. If you can get the answering to work, then ask yourself questions—ones, for example, about which you are confused. You may get a "maybe" or "I don't know" answer, but you may be surprised to find a definite answer forthcoming.

5. You might also let someone else try the pendulum while you ask the questions.

6. Note that there is no suggestion of magic, spirits, or other psychic causation in this procedure. The answers come from you. But normal verbal consciousness is not the totality of all our thoughts and desires. The pendulum may simply allow you to listen to parts of yourself usually overridden or overlooked.

Questions for Discussion

1. Do you think that the pendulum might react differently when you use your left hand than when you use your right? (Try it.)

2. If you observe differences between the right and left hands, might they be related to the differences between the two hemispheres of your brain, as discussed in Chapter 2 of the text? If so, why?

OBSERVING REM SLEEP

Defining the REM sleep cycle and relating this phase of sleeping to dreams has probably been the most significant finding in the study of sleep and dreams. There are two ways you can study the process of REM sleep: by observing its outer signs in animals or other people and by observing your own dreams.

It is part of our folklore that when Rover whimpers and twitches while sleeping, he is dreaming of chasing cats. Based on the similarity of the sleep cycles across a variety of species and on interviews with human subjects, we now presume that something of the sort really is going on, not only in sleeping dogs, but in a variety of other species. Researchers studying cats' sleep have noted, for example, that it is difficult for even an expert to tell the difference in the EEGs of a sleeping cat and a sleeping human.

The signs of REM and the cycles into and out of it can be observed in a sleeping pet or zoo animal. Consider, for example, a pet cat sleeping on your lap. As the cat goes deeper asleep, it still occasionally shifts position. But after a while, it will be quite still. Often, however, heavy breathing or twitching of the limbs will occur as signals from the aroused brain overcome the limb paralysis of REM. At these times the eye movements themselves will be quite noticeable beneath the closed eyelids; the eyelids may even open a bit, allowing the eye movements to be seen directly. After some minutes, the REM period will end; eye movements will cease and the cat will yawn, stretch, change position, and settle down for another cycle. Similar behavior can be seen in other pets and often in wild animals at the zoo, especially the various great cats, who sleep a great deal during the day. If you observe a sleeping human, the same pattern will also be seen.

While you cannot observe your own sleep cycles without the aid of videotape or film, you can make some observations of your dreams. One way is via a dream diary. Put writing materials beside your bed, so that they can be easily reached, and leave on a very dim light. As you go to sleep, remind yourself that you are interested in your dreams and really want to write them down. At first you may only write down a few fragments recalled in the morning, after the last sleep cycle. But if you keep at it, you may find that you are able to take advantage of that brief semi-waking at the end of a REM period (when the cat stretches and yawns) to write down your dream. Some people find, on awakening in the morning, that they have written at length about dreams that are now remembered only poorly, if at all. Even the act of writing may be forgotten, the result of an amnesia barrier that normally helps us keep dream events from intruding into daytime memories.

If you do get useful reports with this procedure, you may wish to analyze them for content—not with the intent of "interpreting" them, but simply for scientific curiosity. Much of what we believe about dreams is probably a result of the amnesia barrier. For example, we tend to remember unusual and vivid dreams, but most dreams reported in the laboratory are about everyday events. Although we may not remember color or detail from our dreams, laboratory results suggest both are common. How do your dreams compare?

As you keep your diary and focus attention on your dreams, you may find yourself experiencing one of the most striking of dream phenomena, the so-called "lucid dream." In a lucid dream, the setting and your actions seem so vivid and undreamlike that you question whether you are dreaming. You may "see" your surroundings (sometimes the room in which you are sleeping) so clearly that you feel certain you are awake. Only on actually awakening are you convinced that you were indeed dreaming.

You may also be able to specify a topic for a night's dreaming by setting it as a "program" as you go to sleep; some people claim to be able to do so regularly.

Observing your own REM sleep and that of others should provide you with a better understanding of the processes in-volved as well as some insight into the excitement of sleep research that motivates people to give up their own sleep to study that of others.

EXPERIMENTAL MEDITATION

There are a number of ways of attaining a sense of detachment or meditation. The text describes Benson's technique, derived from Transcendental Meditation (p. 171), and two other techniques are noted below: the first is a form of what has been termed "concentrative meditation," similar to Zen, while the second is a form of "opening-up meditation," more akin to yoga. Try each of these three techniques to see which helps you best to free your mind from extraneous thoughts while expanding your awareness. For each procedure you should choose a time when you are not sleepy; sit relaxed in a comfortable chair or on the floor supported by pillows.

For the concentrative procedure put an object such as a vase or a bowl on a table about eight feet in front of you, keeping the background as simple as possible. Now concentrate all your attention on the object, excluding all other thoughts or feelings or body sensations. Do not try to analyze the object or associate ideas with it; simply concentrate on it as it is. After a few minutes you will find that it will be difficult to keep your eyes in proper focus. Do not try to retain a sharp focus; let your eyes unfocus but continue to concentrate on the object for at least five minutes.

How did you feel? Were you able to avoid being distracted by events going on around you? Did you have a feeling of detachment, of being able to step aside and watch your feelings and ideas flow by without getting involved in them? Were there any perceptual distortions of the object being viewed? Did you have a feeling of more intense perception of the object? Was the state a pleasurable one?

Now try the opening-up technique and see if you get the same results. Again sit in a comfortable position, but do not be so relaxed that you will go to sleep. Breathe naturally and focus your attention on your breathing: the movements of your chest and stomach, not the sensations in your nose and throat. Try to avoid being distracted by extraneous thoughts or stimuli. Keep your attention on your breathing, turning aside all other thoughts.

What are your feelings? Are they similar to, or different from, those elicited by the first technique? How do the sensations in both cases differ from those you experience while drowsy or in a half-asleep state?

Now try Benson's technique (p. 172 of the text). How do the effects compare to those of the other procedures? (Note that this technique has similarities to both of the others: it focuses on breathing, as does the general opening-up technique, and the repeated use of the word "one" is somewhat similar to the concentration on the vase of the general concentrative technique.)

7

Conditioning and Learning

1. *Learning* is a *relatively permanent change* in *behavior* that occurs as the result of

learning *prior experience*. Not all changes in behavior can be called l_____ ; thus
the definition must be qualified.

permanent 2. Learning is a relatively _____ change in behavior. This specifica-
tion excludes changes in behavior resulting from such temporary conditions as
fatigue or adaptation.

experience 3. Learning occurs as a result of prior _____. By this statement we
exclude from the definition of learning behavioral changes due to maturation, disease, or physical injury.

change 4. Therefore we say that learning is a relatively permanent _____ in

behavior, prior _____ that occurs as the result of _____

experience _____ .

5. One of the most basic forms of learning is called *associative learning;* it involves

association making a new connection, or as_____ , between events in
the environment.

learning 6. Associative _____ means to make a new association between events
in the environment. Psychologists distinguish between two forms of associative
learning: *classical conditioning* and *operant conditioning.*

conditioning 7. In classical _____ the organism learns that two *stimuli* tend
to go together. For example, a baby learns that the sight of a nursing bottle (one

stimulus stimulus) is associated with the taste of milk (another _____).

8. A child learns that the sound of a tinkling bell is associated with the appearance of

classical the ice cream truck. This is another example of _____ conditioning.

stimuli 9. In classical conditioning the organism learns that two _____ tend to go
together.

conditioning 10. In operant _____ the organism learns that some *response* it
makes leads to a particular *consequence.* For example, a baby learns that raising a
bottle to his or her mouth (the response) brings milk (the consequence).

11. A toddler learns that putting a hand in the flame of a candle (the response)

consequence brings pain (the _____). This is an example of operant

conditioning _____ .

classical 12. Learning an association between two stimuli is called _____ conditioning. Learning an association between a response and its consequences is called

operant, associative _____ conditioning. Both are forms of _____
learning.

13. The method of classical conditioning, in which a new association is made between

stimuli   two _____ , is illustrated by the diagram below.

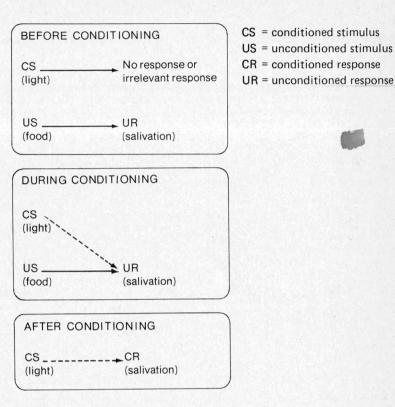

BEFORE CONDITIONING

CS ————————→ No response or
(light)   irrelevant response

US ————————→ UR
(food)   (salivation)

CS = conditioned stimulus
US = unconditioned stimulus
CR = conditioned response
UR = unconditioned response

DURING CONDITIONING

CS ⟍
(light)   ⟍
             ⟍
US ————————→ UR
(food)   (salivation)

AFTER CONDITIONING

CS - - - - - - - - →CR
(light)   (salivation)

To understand the diagram, let's discuss the laboratory arrangement used by Pavlov to study classical conditioning. A dog is placed in a harness and a device attached to its cheek to measure salivary flow; meat powder can be delivered to a pan in front of the dog by remote control. A light is turned on, and a few seconds later meat powder is delivered to the pan. The dog eats, and the recording device measures copious salivation. After this procedure has been repeated a number of times, the experimenter turns on the light without delivering meat powder. The dog

food (or meat powder)   salivates nevertheless. The animal has learned to associate the light with _____ .

14. The dog will salivate the first time that meat powder is placed on its tongue, even if the animal has never been exposed to meat powder before. Because salivation to meat powder does not depend on learning, or conditioning, it is called an *unconditioned response* (UR). We call a response that does not depend on learning an

unconditioned   _____ response.

15. A puff of air aimed at the eye will cause an infant to blink, even though the infant has never experienced an air puff before. Since such eye-blinking does not depend

unconditioned   on learning, it can be called an _____ response.

16. Any response to a stimulus that is unlearned can be called an unconditioned

response   _____ .

17. The stimulus that gives rise to the unconditioned response is called an *uncondi-*

tioned stimulus (US). In Pavlov's arrangement, the meat powder that elicits saliva-

unconditioned

tion is called an _____ stimulus.

stimulus, response

18. An unconditioned _____ elicits an unconditioned _____ without any prior learning.

19. In Pavlov's arrangement the stimulus that did not originally elicit salivation, but

light

came to do so after repeated pairings with meat powder, was a l_____ .The stimulus that becomes associated with the unconditioned response through the process of classical conditioning is called the _conditioned stimulus_ (CS).

conditioned

20. The light is called a(n) _____ stimulus because it acquires

response

its power to elicit salivation (the unconditioned _____) through learning.

21. A conditioned stimulus is a stimulus that would not by itself elicit the desired response but gains the power to do so only by being associated with an

unconditioned

un_____ stimulus.

22. If putting a bottle into the mouth of an infant produces sucking, this illustrates an unconditioned stimulus (bottle in mouth) that elicits an unconditioned response (sucking). If, later on, the child begins to suck at the _sight_ of the bottle, then this

conditioned

stimulus (sight of bottle) would be called a(n) _____ stimulus.

23. A stimulus that elicits a response the first time the stimulus is offered is called a(n)

unconditioned

_____ stimulus and the response a(n)

unconditioned

_____ response.

24. If we have to associate a stimulus with an unconditioned stimulus in order to evoke

conditioned

a response, the learned stimulus is called a(n) _____ stimulus.

25. If the reponse to an unconditioned stimulus is called an unconditioned response,

conditioned

then the response to a conditioned stimulus will be called a(n) _____ response (CR).

conditioned

26. The learned response to a conditioned stimulus is called a _____ response.

response

27. The conditioned response resembles the unconditioned r_____ but is not always identical; it may differ in some respects.

28. The association between the unconditioned stimulus and the unconditioned re-

unlearned

sponse is (_learned/unlearned_); the association between the conditioned stimulus and

learned

the conditioned response is (_learned/unlearned_).

29. When a new association is formed between a conditioned stimulus and a response, through repeated pairings of the CS with a US that normally elicits the response, the

classical conditioning

process is called _____ _____ .

30. The more times we present the conditioned stimulus with the unconditioned stimulus, the stronger will be the response to the _____ stimulus.

conditioned

31. In other words, the more often the conditioned stimulus is associated with the unconditioned stimulus, the better the animal will learn the association. The pairing of the conditioned stimulus with the u_____ stimulus is called *reinforcement*, because the pairing makes the conditioned response stronger.

unconditioned

32. If we pair a light (*the CS/US*) with meat powder (*the CS/US*) twenty times, the salivation to the light will be stronger than if we only pair them ten times. The association between the two stimuli is stronger in the former case because the association has been re_____ more often.

CS, US

reinforced

33. The paired presentation of the CS and the US, which strengthens the conditioned response, is called _____.

reinforcement

34. However, if we condition a dog to salivate to a light (the CS) and then continually turn on the light without giving any meat powder (the _____), eventually the dog will stop salivating to the light.

US (or unconditioned stimulus)

35. In other words, if we pair the conditioned and unconditioned stimuli until the dog responds with salivation to the conditioned stimulus and then continually present only the conditioned stimulus, so that there is no re_____, gradually the dog will stop salivating to the stimulus.

reinforcement

36. Repetition of the conditioned stimulus without reinforcement is called *extinction*. The association between the light and the meat powder is weakened by presenting one without the other. In *extinction* we repeatedly present the _____ stimulus without the unconditioned stimulus.

conditioned

37. When we present the conditioned stimulus without the unconditioned stimulus, the conditioned response is weakened because it is not being re_____.

reinforced

38. Suppose we condition a dog to respond with salivation to a touch on the back near the hindquarters. To do this, we touch the dog on the back and, a second later, put meat powder on its tongue. Let us call the touch near the hindquarters (which is the _____ stimulus) stimulus 1 (S_1).

conditioned

39. Once this conditioning has been established, if we touch the dog on another spot on its back (S_2), we find that the dog will make the response of salivation to this stimulus as well, although it has never been reinforced for this stimulus. Therefore S_2 has substituted for _____.

S_1

40. Responding to S_2 with the response that was conditioned to S_1, even though S_2 has not been established as a conditioned stimulus, is called *generalization*. The more similar S_2 is to S_1, the stronger will be the tendency to generalize. In _____ the organism makes the *same* response to

generalization

a new stimulus that it learned to make to an old stimulus; it does so because the new stimulus is similar in some way to the old stimulus.

41. Generalization consists of the following sequence: (1) a stimulus is conditioned to a response; (2) the organism is presented with a new stimulus that is similar to, but not identical with, the conditioned stimulus; (3) the organism responds to the new

same   stimulus as though it were the _____ as the old one.

42. When an organism makes the same response to a new stimulus (S_2) that it has learned to make to a different stimulus (S_1), we note the operation of the principle

generalization   of _____.

43. Let us suppose that, in the experiment described above, every time we touch the dog near the hindquarters (S_1) we put meat powder on its tongue and we never put meat powder on its tongue after touching the dog on the other spot (S_2). Eventually the dog will no longer respond to S_2, although it will continue to

respond   _____ to S_1. The animal has learned to tell the two stimuli apart (to react to them differently).

44. In the situation just described, the dog has learned to *discriminate* between the two

same (or conditioned)   stimuli and thus does not make the _____ response to both of them.

45. When the organism learns *not* to make the same response to both of the stimuli— that is, when it distinguishes between them—we call the process *discrimination*. When there are two stimuli, one of which is *always* reinforced and the other *never*

discriminate   reinforced, the organism will in time _____ between them
(or distinguish)   and respond to the former and not to the latter.

46. If we condition a dog to salivate to a tone of 1,000 Hz, reinforcing the tone with food, and then present a 500 Hz (lower) tone, the dog will probably salivate in response to both tones. However, if we never reinforce the 500 Hz tone with food but always reinforce the 1,000 Hz tone, the dog will eventually stop salivating in response to the 500 Hz tone but will continue to salivate to the 1,000 Hz tone. This

discrimination   is an example of the process of _____.

learning   47. Classical conditionion is one form of associative l_____; another is operant conditioning.

48. In operant conditioning the organism learns an association between a response and

consequences   its con_____.

49. Operant conditioning differs from classical conditioning in several ways. In classical conditioning the conditioned response resembles the normal response to the unconditioned stimulus; for example, salivation is a dog's normal response to

food (or meat powder)   _____. Behavior that occurs automatically in direct response to a stimulus is called *respondent behavior*.

50. Salivation to food or an eye-blink to an air puff are essentially involuntary responses

respondent   to a particular stimulus. They would thus be considered r_____ behavior.

51. *Operant behavior,* in contrast, is voluntary and spontaneous; it is not an automatic
response to a specific _____ .

stimulus

52. A baby bats at a rattle and kicks the covers; a dog sniffs at a ball and scratches at
the rug. Since these responses are voluntary and spontaneous, they are considered
_____ behavior. Operant responses usually *"operate"* on the environment.

operant

53. If we put a hungry rat in a maze that contains food, it will make certain responses
to get to the place where the food is; if we cover the food, the rat will learn to turn
over the cover. These are _____ responses.

operant

54. A certain stimulus may make an operant response more likely to occur, but does
not automatically elicit it. For example, the doorbell rings and you go to open the
door. The ringing bell is a stimulus that tells you someone is at the door, but it does
not force you to answer the door. Going to the door is a (*voluntary/involuntary*)
response, and hence is considered operant behavior.

voluntary

55. The ringing bell is a discriminative stimulus that provides the occasion for an operant response, but it does not elicit the response is the same way that a US elicits a
_____ .

UR (or unconditioned
response)

56. Operant conditioning differs from classical conditioning in another way. In Pavlov's
laboratory arrangement the animal was passive; it did not have to do anything in
order to receive the unconditioned stimulus (the reinforcement). In teaching the
dog to salivate to the light, the experimenter turned on the light and then delivered
the meat powder (the _____ stimulus) regardless
of what the animal did.

unconditioned

57. In op_____ conditioning, however, the animal must make some kind
of response in order to get the reinforcement.

operant

58. In classical conditioning the animal can be passive and still be reinforced; in
_____ conditioning the animal must be active in order to be reinforced.

operant

59. In operant conditioning we increase the probability of a response by following the
response with _____ .

reinforcement

60. For example, we want Mary to develop the habit of working hard in school. To do
this we give her extra spending money for each high grade she receives. If the
extra money strengthens the response of working hard in school, it constitutes a
_____ of the response of working hard in school.

reinforcement

61. Jimmy continually comes home late for dinner. His mother wants to strengthen the
response of mealtime promptness, so she gives Jimmy a special dessert whenever he
is on time. The dessert constitutes a _____ of the
response of promptness.

reinforcement

62. We have been assuming that every time an organism did something we would rein-

force it. Thus every time a rat ran to the end of the maze, we would give it food. Suppose, however, we gave the rat reinforcement only every other time it performed the act that led to reinforcement. This procedure is called *partial reinforcement*. When we reinforce an organism only part of the time, we are using

partial reinforcement

_____ _____ .

63. Since a child's mother is not always present to reinforce a desired response,

partial

_____ reinforcement is the state of affairs that is most prevalent in children's lives.

64. One of the characteristics of partial reinforcement is that it makes the behavior more resistant to extinction than the behavior that is subject to 100 percent rein-

partially

forcement. Thus when a child is _____ly reinforced for a given behavior, this behavior tends to persist against many nonreinforcements.

65. When Jimmy cleans his room his mother notices his efforts only 40 percent of the time. She rewards him each time that she notices. With this reinforcement schedule,

longer than

Jimmy's behavior of cleaning the room will last (*longer than/not as long as*) it would if 100 percent reinforcement were used.

66. As in classical conditioning, an operant response can be extinguished. If we suddenly stop giving Mary extra spending money for making good grades, we run the risk that Mary will eventually stop working hard (if money was her only reason for working). We would be producing *extinction* of the response of working hard by

reinforcement

withdrawing _____ .

67. If a rat has learned to press a bar to receive food and the delivery of food no longer follows a bar press, we say that the operant response of bar-pressing is undergoing

extinction

_____ .

68. Classical conditioning and operant conditioning are two important but clearly different forms of learning. In classical conditioning, learning depends on the experimenter's pairing of the unconditioned stimulus with the conditioned stimulus; in

passive

this sense the learning is (*active/passive*), since the organism cannot determine when the pairing will occur. In operant conditioning, the organism acts on the environment in order to obtain reinforcement. The strength of the organism's response in-

reinforcement

creases whenever the response is followed by _____ .

69. So far we have discussed classical and operant conditioning—two simple forms of

associative

learning that are called _____ learning. More complex forms of learning (such as playing chess, finding your way about a new city, or learning a language) are difficult to explain in terms of conditioned associations.

70. Learning in these situations undoubtedly involves more than simple associations

responses

between stimuli and r_____; it requires perceiving and understanding the relationships among events occurring in the environment. Perceiving and understanding relationships among events are called *cognitive processes*.

71. In learning to play chess, for example, you must perceive the relationships among the chess pieces and understand how these relate to your knowledge of the rules of the game and the moves your opponent is making. Learning the game is not simply

a matter of stimulus-response associations but of perception and understanding,

cognitive   which are _____ processes.

72. Simple forms of learning may be governed by the law of classical and operant conditioning. But associative learning alone cannot account for some of the complex forms of learning (such as language learning and problem solving) that we will encounter in later chapters. These involve our ability to perceive and

understand   _____ relationships among objects and events in our environment.

73. To explain learning one needs to take into account both associative and

cognitive   _____ processes.

TERMS AND CONCEPTS

learning _____

_____

_____

_____

classical conditioning _____

_____

_____

conditioned response (CR) _____

_____

_____

unconditioned response (UR) _____

_____

_____

unconditioned stimulus (US) _____

_____

_____

conditioned stimulus (CS) _____

_____

_____

acquisition _____

_____

_____

simultaneous conditioning _____

_____

_____

delayed conditioning _____

_____

_____

_____

trace conditioning _____

_____

_____

extinction _____

_____

_____

generalization _____

_____

_____

discrimination _____

_____

_____

operant conditioning _____

_____

_____

respondent behavior _____

_____

_____

cumulative curve _____

_____

_____

partial reinforcement _____

_____

_____

reinforcement schedule* _____

_____

_____

_____

conditioned reinforcer _____

_____

_____

_____

shaping _____

_____

_____

_____

reinforcement _____

_____

_____

_____

positive reinforcer _____

_____

_____

_____

negative reinforcer _____

_____

_____

_____

punishment_____

_____

_____

_____

cognitive processes _____

_____

_____

_____

insight _____

_____

_____

_____

cognitive map _____

_____

_____

_____

latent learning _____

_____

_____

_____

schema* _____

_____

_____

_____

CAL _____

_____

_____

_____

linear program _____

_____

_____

_____

branching program _____

_____

_____

_____

*Indicates terms used in Critical Discussions

_____ 1. Generalization and the complementary process of _____ operate to produce specific appropriate behavior, such as a child saying "bow-wow" only in response to dogs.
  a. conditioning
  b. reinforcement
  c. discrimination
  d. extinction

_____ 2. When a phone rings, we usually answer it. In Skinner's terms, the ringing is a _____, which tells you to answer but does not force you to.
  a. conditioned stimulus
  b. operant stimulus
  c. respondent stimulus
  d. discriminative stimulus

_____ 3. In Pavlov's experiments with dogs, the CR was _____ and the UR was _____.
  a. meat powder, salivation
  b. salivation, salivation
  c. a light, meat powder
  d. salivation, a light

_____ 4. "A relatively permanent change in behavior that occurs as the result of prior experience" is a formal definition of
  a. classical conditioning
  b. operant conditioning
  c. learning
  d. conditioning

_____ 5. Which of the following is *not* one of the learning principles used in programmed instruction?
  a. progress at the student's own rate
  b. information feedback
  c. active participation
  d. delayed reinforcement

_____ 6. In demonstrating operant conditioning of human behavior, a student's statements of opinion were reinforced by
  a. statements such as "You're right"
  b. food
  c. money
  d. the opportunity for social interaction

_____ 7. In his analysis of latent learning experiments, Tolman distinguished between
  a. learning and expectation
  b. knowledge and learning
  c. learning and performance
  d. response probability and behavior

_____ 8. A person who has been trained to respond with salivation to the word "good" because it has been paired with food is found to salivate also to the sentence "Leningrad is a wonderful city"; this illustrates
  a. classical conditioning
  b. generalization
  c. semantic conditioning
  d. all of the above

_____ 9. Which of the following is *not* true of insight?
  a. Insight is independent of the arrangement of the problem situation.
  b. Once the solution occurs, it can be repeated promptly.
  c. The solution achieved with insight can be applied to new situations.
  d. Insight depends on the arrangement of the problem situation.

_____ 10. If a student receiving CAL gives a wrong answer, the computer
  a. branches to appropriate remedial work
  b. records the error
  c. evaluates the type of error
  d. all of the above

_____ 11. The _____ viewpoint argues that the dogs in Pavlov's experiments were not forming associations but were learning to anticipate food.
  a. insight
  b. cognitive
  c. encoding
  d. mixture theory

_____ 12. The technique of shaping behavior is important because it provides a means of training _____ responses.
  a. respondent
  b. reflexive
  c. novel
  d. conditioned

_____ 13. Which of the following is *not* a true statement regarding reinforcement by brain stimulation?
  a. Human patients reported that it made them feel relief from anxiety.

b. It follows the same rules as learning with food reinforcement.

c. While brief stimulation in some areas is reinforcing, prolonged stimulation is aversive.

d. Hungry rats will endure more shock for it than they will for food.

_____ 14. Conditioned reinforcement has important practical implications because it

a. can strengthen responses other than the one used in its establishment

b. can function with drives other than the one operating when it was originally established

c. greatly increases the range of possible conditioning

d. all of the above

_____ 15. In comparing the value of associative and cognitive theories of learning, the text points out that

a. it is possible to view them as complementary

b. the S-R approach has proved most satisfactory for complex human learning

c. the cognitive approach in itself provides a complete explanation

d. all of the above

_____ 16. Extinction of a classically conditioned response is likely to occur when

a. there is only partial or intermittent reinforcement

b. the conditioned response generalizes to other stimuli

c. the unconditioned stimulus is presented repeatedly without the conditioned stimulus

d. the conditioned stimulus is presented repeatedly without the unconditioned stimulus

_____ 17. Rats exposed to a light while being injected with insulin eventually produce an insulin shock reaction to the injection of saline solution in the presence of the light. In this experiment the CS is _____, while the UR is _____.

a. light, insulin shock

b. insulin shock, light

c. saline solution, light

d. insulin, insulin shock

_____ 18. One crucial difference between the two major types of conditioning is that in classical conditioning reinforcement _____ the response, while in operant conditioing reinforcement _____ the response.

a. maintains, produces

b. elicits, follows

c. precedes, produces

d. produces, elicits

_____ 19. If we wish to produce the optimum conditions for learning, we provide

a. the largest amount of reinforcement available, presented immediately after the behavior

b. a moderate amount of reinforcement, presented immediately after the behavior

c. the largest amount of reinforcement available, presented with a one- to five-second delay after the behavior

d. the smallest amount of reinforcement that is functional, presented with a two-second delay after the behavior

_____ 20. An advantage of a branching program is that

a. the learner progresses along a single track from one frame to the next

b. each learner may take a different path through the curriculum

c. the learner moves along at a preprogrammed rate

d. errors are not pointed out, so that the effects of punishment are avoided

KEY TO SELF-QUIZ

1. c p.197	6. a p.202	11. b p.208	16. d p.194
2. d p.198	7. c p.210	12. c p.202	17. a p.195
3. b p.193	8. d p.196	13. b p.207	18. b p.204
4. c p.191	9. a p.210	14. d p.200	19. a p.204
5. d p.217	10. d p.214	15. a p.211	20. b p.197

INDIVIDUAL EXERCISE

MODIFYING ANIMAL BEHAVIOR

The procedure of shaping behavior described in Chapter 7 can be used effectively, even by those who are not professional animal trainers. All it takes is ready access to an animal subject, whether a pet or wild, and a bit of patience.

Pets are the most accessible subjects, of course, and many can be quickly trained. One student, for example, taught her dog to close the front door whenever someone accidentally left it ajar. On verbal command, the dog would stand on its hind paws and push the door shut with its front paws until the door latched. Then it would come for its reward, loving attention backed up sometimes with food treats. As suggested in the text (p. 202), you must begin with an existing behavior and selectively reinforce that which comes closest to what you want, gradually sharpening or tightening your criteria for reinforcement as the behavior changes. This dog's polished performance was reasonably easy to shape, beginning with the dog's tendency to prance about when spoken to, but the final result was very impressive for visitors.

To shape the behavior of wild animals, you must be able to get close enough to provide contingent reinforcement. Your first task, then, is to "tame" the animal so that it will approach you without fear. Do this by providing food simultaneously with your presence and then gradually moving the animal closer. Initially, you may have to put out the food before the animal approaches; a peanut thrown toward a wild squirrel or raccoon usually just scares it away. But after the animal has eaten in sight of you for a number of times, you can probably begin to throw the food, tossing each piece a bit closer to you. Always move slowly and speak softly, if at all, until the animal becomes less frightened of you. Always change cues gradually, as wild animals are very sensitive to them; quick movement or sudden noise may badly startle the animal and set back your progress.

If the distance is decreased too rapidly, the animal may exhibit what the text describes as an approach-avoidance conflict (p. 418): a squirrel, for example, will move toward you but stop short, perhaps only an inch short of its goal, apparently transfixed with the conflict and trembling all over. If this happens, you are trying to push it too far too fast.

Note that what you are doing is not only shaping, in an operant conditioning sense, but also desensitizing the animal's fear of you; this form of behavioral therapy (described on p. 494 of the text) is based on classical conditioning.

Once wild animals have learned to approach you with confidence, it is possible to shape their behavior further.

Birds, squirrels, and raccoons, for example, have been taught to take food from an outstretched hand, a pocket, a shoulder, or the top of a person's head. They have also learned to appear in response to a particular sound (a discriminative stimulus). All of this, of course, takes considerable patience, so you might prefer to start your experiments with a tame pet.

When working with wild animals be very careful; they can bite and scratch and may carry rabies. An animal that is too easy to approach may be sick. Getting wild animals reasonably close might be a better goal than attempting to handle them.

INDIVIDUAL OR CLASS EXERCISE

THE PROCESS OF LEARNING

Introduction

Learning so pervades human activity that any curiosity about the nature of people and their behavior sooner or later leads to inquiry about how habits are formed, how skills are acquired, how preferences and tastes develop, how knowledge is obtained and put to use. But what exactly is "learning"? Although there are many varied definitions of this process, it might be defined as the modification of behavior through experience. This exercise will enable you to study the process of learning that goes on in modifying previously acquired behavior.

Equipment Needed

Red pencil, or pen with red ink. A stopwatch or watch with a second hand.

Procedure

Turn to page 114, which you are to use for this experiment. If this is to be a class exercise, your instructor will time you; if not, have a friend tell you to start and then, twenty seconds later, to stop. During the twenty-second trial write the letters of the alphabet backward in a vertical column from top to bottom. *Do not sacrifice accuracy for speed.* If you complete the alphabet, start over again. At the end of Trial 1, cover your answers with another sheet of paper. Then use the same procedure for a total of fifteen trials.

Treatment of Data

1. At the end of the fifteenth trial, count the number of correct letters on each trial and record these numbers in the space provided at the bottom of page 114.

2. Copy the number of correct letters for each trial under "Score" in the following table.

Trial	Score	Trial	Score	Trial	Score
1		6		11	
2		7		12	
3		8		13	
4		9		14	
5		10		15	

3. If this is to be a class exercise, record on a slip of paper the number of correct letters you had for each trial, so that the average number of correct letters per trial for the class as a whole can be ascertained. When your instructor reads these group averages for each trial aloud, enter them in the space in the following table.

Trial	Group average	Trial	Group average	Trial	Group average
1		6		11	
2		7		12	
3		8		13	
4		9		14	
5		10		15	

4. Now plot your learning curve and, if available, the learning curve of the class as a whole on the graph on page 115. Use a pencil for your curve and a red pencil or red pen for the class curve.

Questions for Discussion

1. Does you progress from trial to trial indicate gradual learning?

2. Are there differences between the shape of your learning curve and that of the class? How do you account for the difference?

3. Were there uncontrolled variables in this particular learning experiment?

4. How would you test for the permanence of learning to write the alphabet backward?

1	2	3	4	5	6	7	8	9	10	11	12	13	14	15

NUMBER
CORRECT

Trial number	1	2	3	4	5	6	7	8	9	10	11	12	13	14	15
	—	—	—	—	—	—	—	—	—	—	—	—	—	—	—

LEARNING CURVE

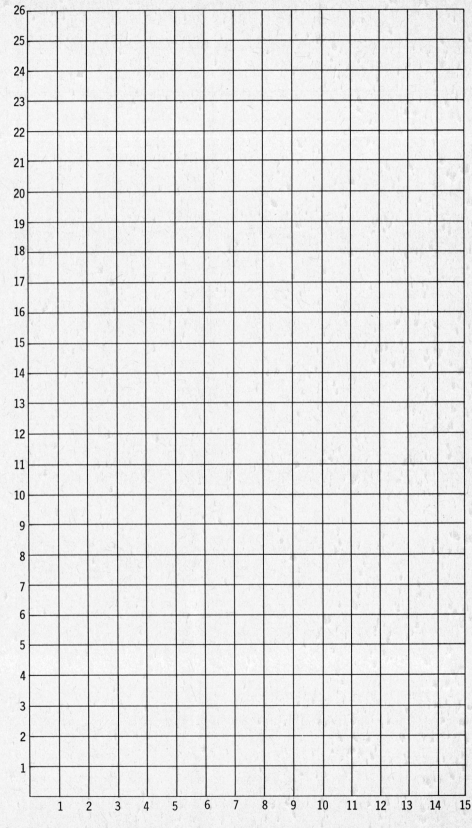

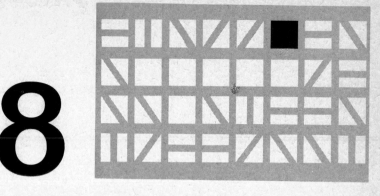

8

Remembering and Forgetting

LEARNING OBJECTIVES

8-1. Understand the distinctions between the three stages and two types of memory described in the text.

8-2. Know the difference between acoustic and visual encoding in short-term memory.

8-3. Be able to discuss the limits of short-term storage represented by the magic number seven and to explain how this is related to displacement and to chunking. Be familiar with the research on short-term retrieval.

8-4. Know the difference between imagery and semantic encoding in long-term memory and know how each may be used to encode meaning.

8-5. Be able to discuss forgetting in terms of storage versus retrieval failure. Be familiar with the research on retrieval cues, the organizing of storage, and the use of context in recall; be able to show how each aids recovery of long-term memories.

8-6. Be able to define, and to differentiate between, retroactive and proactive interference. Be familiar with possible emotional factors in forgetting.

8-7. Know some of the ways to improve memory, through both encoding and retrieval techniques. Be able to explain the particular mnemonic systems called the method of loci and the key-word method.

8-8. Be familiar with the evidence for two kinds of memory. Be able to differentiate between retrograde and anterograde amnesia and show how each relates to the two kinds of memory.

8-9. Be able to describe the Atkinson-Shiffrin theory of dual memory and show how the free-recall evidence supports it. Be familiar with some of the problems encountered by the theory and with the alternative approach called depth-of-processing.

8-10. Know what is meant by constructive memory and be able to show how inferences, stereotypes, and schemata each contribute to constructive memory processes.

PROGRAMMED UNIT

encoding

1. Memory involves three stages: *encoding, storage,* and *retrieval.* The first stage, en_____, refers to the *transformation of physical information* into a kind of *code* that can be deposited in memory.

code

2. Encoding means to transform physical information into a _____ that can be deposited in memory.

3. You look up a telephone number and remember it while dialing. If you remember the number by forming a mental picture of the digits, you are using a *visual* code; if you remember the sound of the names of the digits, you are using an *acoustic*

code

_____.

encoding
information
memory, visual

4. The first stage of memory, _____, involves transforming physical _____ into a code that can be deposited in _____. A code may be acoustic or _____.

three

store

5. The second of the _____ (*number*) stages of memory, storage, refers to the retention of encoded information. In order to retain a telephone number long enough to dial it, you must somehow s_____ it in memory.

encoding, storage

6. The first two stages of memory are _____ and _____. The third stage, retrieval, is the process by which information is recovered from memory when needed.

retrieve

7. In order to dial the telephone number you must ret_____ it from memory storage.

8. Thus, even the simple act of remembering a telephone number requires three stages:

encoding, storage, retrieval

_____, _____, and _____.

three

9. These _____ (*number*) stages of memory may operate differently in situations that require us to remember material for a few seconds or minutes—*short-term memory*—than in situations that require us to store material for longer intervals—*long-term memory.*

10. Thus, in addition to three stages of memory, there are also *two types* of memory. Remembering a telephone number long enough to dial it is one type, called

short-term

_____-_____ memory.

11. Remembering your own telephone number for months or years is another type,

long-term

called _____-_____ memory.

encoding, storage
retrieval

12. The three stages of memory—_____, _____, and _____—may operate differently in the two situations.

13. For example, items that are to be remembered only a few seconds—an example of

short-term

_____-_____ memory—are often encoded according to the sound

acoustic
of the names of the digits. This is called a(n) _____ code. Or they may be encoded in the form of a mental picture of the digits, that is, as a(n)

visual
_____ code.

long-term
14. Information that is stored for longer intervals—an example of _____-_____ memory—is usually encoded in terms of its *meaning.*

15. If you now try to retrieve the first sentence of this programmed unit, which lists the three stages of memory, you probably do not recall the exact words—either how they looked or how they sounded. You are more likely to remember the

meaning
_____ of the sentence.

short-term,
long-term (either order)
16. Information may be encoded differently, depending on whether it is stored in _____-_____ or _____-_____ memory.

17. Short-term memory has a very *limited* storage capacity. It can store only about *seven* items, plus or minus two (7 ± 2). That is, some people can store only five

short-term
items in _____-_____ memory and some can store as many as

seven
nine. But, on the average the storage capacity of short-term memory is _____ items.

18. If I read a list of 20 names and ask you immediately how many you can remember,

seven, two
you are apt to recall _____ names, plus or minus _____.

limited
19. Short-term memory has a very _____ storage capacity. The storage capacity for long-term memory, in contrast, is virtually *unlimited.*

20. Some people are memory experts, while others have very poor memories. We must conclude that they differ in their (*short/long*)-term memory capacity.

long

encoding, storage
(either order)
21. So far, we have seen that the two types of memory differ in both their _____ and _____ stages.

7 ± 2
22. We have said that short-term memory storage is limited to ___±___ items. But what is an item? Surely, you can remember a sentence you have just heard even though it is longer than seven words.

23. An item is the *largest meaningful unit,* or *chunk,* you can find in the material presented. The string YTDRAES contains seven single-letter items. But if we rearrange

chunk
the letters to form the word STRAYED, we have only one item, or ch_____.

24. The sequence YELL A LOUD GAVE THE BOY has five word units. But we can rearrange the words into meaningful phrases, THE BOY GAVE A LOUD YELL, to

chunks
reduce it to three _____.

25. Language provides a natural chunking device, since it groups letters and words into

meaningful
larger m_____ units.

short-term
26. Even though its storage capacity is limited, we can store more in _____-

_____ memory if we regroup sequences of letters or words into mean-

chunks

ingful units, or _____ .

encoding

27. We have been discussing the first two stages of memory, _____ and

storage (either order)

_____ . The third stage, which involves retrieving information from

retrieval

memory storage, is called _____ .

28. We can retrieve information from short-term memory fairly quickly because its

limited

storage capacity is (*limited/unlimited*); we don't have far to search. Retrieving information from long-term memory is often more difficult because its storage capac-

unlimited

ity is _____ .

29. One factor that determines the ease with which information can be retrieved from
long-term memory is the manner in which it is transformed for deposit in memory,

encoded

or en_____ .

30. We noted earlier that information in long-term memory is usually encoded in terms

meaning

of its m_____ . One way to encode and store meaning is to use a mental picture, or *imagery code*.

31. Suppose you want to remember the meaning of the word ''submarine.'' If you
formed a mental picture, or image, of a submarine, you would be using an

imagery

im_____ code. If, instead, you said to yourself, ''A submarine is an
underwater vehicle made of metal,'' you would be using a *semantic code*.

pictures (or images)

32. An imagery code stores information in the form of mental _____ .

semantic

A se_____ code stores information in the form of verbal meaning.

33. Suppose you have to memorize a list of 20 pairs of unrelated words (for example,
''horse-table,'' ''rabbit-bucket'') so that when given the first word you can respond
with the second. If you remember the pair ''horse-table'' by forming a mental

imagery

picture of a horse kicking a table, you are using a(n) _____ code. If
you remember the pair by thinking of a sentence to connect the two words—''the

semantic

horse jumped over the table''—you are using a(n) _____ code.

imagery

34. Meanings can be encoded and stored in the form of either _____ or

semantic (either order)

_____ codes. While meaning is the dominant way of storing infor-

long-term

mation in _____-_____ memory, we sometimes code other aspects as
well. For example, we may memorize a poem word for word. In this case we have

words

stored not only the meaning of the poem but the individual _____ as well.

35. Coding by meaning, however, results in the best memory. You are more apt to re-

meaning

member a point made in the textbook if you concentrate on its m_____
rather than the exact words. And the more you think about and elaborate on the
meaning, the better your memory.

encoding

36. Let's review. The three stages of memory, in order, are _____ ,

storage, retrieval	_____, and _____. The two types of memory
short-term, long-term (either order)	are called _____-_____ and _____-_____. Information may be transformed for deposit in short-term memory by means of either
acoustic, visual (either order)	a(n) _____ or _____ code. Short-term memory stor-
7 ± 2, chunks	age is limited to _____±_____ items, or _____. Long-term memory
unlimited	is un_____ in storage capacity; information is usually encoded in
meaning, imagery	terms of its _____, which may be in the form of _____
semantic (either order)	or _____ codes.

37. Forgetting often results from difficulty in retrieving information from long-term memory; the information may be stored—that is, it hasn't been lost from memory—

retrieving   but we have problems _____ it.

retrieval   38. In other words, forgetting often reflects (*storage/retrieval*) failure rather than loss of information from memory.

39. During an exam you struggle unsuccessfully to remember the specific term that answers a question. Five seconds after leaving the room the correct word comes to

retrieval   you, much to your chagrin. This is an example of _____ failure.

40. You may have experienced a similar situation when a person's name seems on the tip of your tongue, but you just cannot remember it. You are pretty certain the name begins with "G," and you start through the alphabet, adding various second letters to the "G" sound. Finally, when you get to "Gr" you suddenly recall the name—"Graham." This tip-of-the-tongue experience indicates that memories often

are not   (*are/are not*) lost; they simply require the right kind of *retrieval cue.*

cue   41. A retrieval _____ is anything that can help us retrieve a memory. In the example

retrieval   above, the sound "Gr" is the _____ cue for remembering the name Graham. If I told you that the name you were searching for is the same name

retrieval cue   as a type of cracker, that would be another kind of _____ _____.

42. People usually do better on recognition tests (for example, "Place a check mark by the words that identify parts of a neuron") than they do on recall tests (for example, "Name the parts of a neuron"), because recognition tests provide better

retrieval   _____ cues.

43. While some memories may be lost from storage, retrieval failures are the major

long-term   cause of forgetting information in _____-_____ memory. Thus, if we want to improve our memory, it will help to know what factors increase the speed and accuracy of retrieval.

44. One important factor is *organization*; the more we organize the material we want to remember, the easier it is to retrieve. Thus, if you want to remember the names of a

organize   large number of people you met at a party, it would help to or_____ the names according to professions—that is, to think of the doctors as one group, the lawyers as another, and so on.

45. After you have read the chapter "Remembering and Forgetting" in the text, the best way to remember the material is to go through the chapter again, noting the headings and subheadings. Then put the book aside and make your own outline.

organization

This is another example of using _____ to encode material.

organization

46. One aid to retrieval is _____; another is *similarity of context.* It is easier to retrieve a particular bit of information if the context in

context

which you are trying to recall it is similar to the _____ in which the information was encoded.

47. You will probably do better on your psychology exam if it is given in the same room in which you attended lectures, because the context in which you are trying

similar

to retrieve information is _____ to the context in which it was encoded.

48. If you want to recall the name of your high school chemistry teacher, you might try to mentally reconstruct the chemistry classroom—visualize the room, the teacher

context

at the blackboard, and so on. This is another example of using _____ to aid memory.

49. Memory is better when the context during retrieval is similar to that during

encoding

_____ .

organization

50. Two factors that increase the ease of retrieval are _____

similarity, context

and _____ of _____ . A factor that *decreases* retrieval is *interference.*

51. When we learn different things that are similar to one another, trying to retrieve one of them will bring to mind the other similar items. That is, the similar items

interfere

will inter_____ with the one you are trying to recall.

52. Suppose your friend moves across town temporarily and acquires a new telephone number in the process. You finally learn the new number. Your friend returns to the former address, and now you have difficulty remembering the old telephone number that you once knew so well. When you attempt to retrieve the old number,

interferes

the new one comes to mind and _____ with the old one. This is an example of *retroactive interference:* the learning of new materials interferes with the retrieval of old ones.

53. Sometimes new learning interferes with old. Such interference is called

retroactive

_____ .

54. The following procedure can be used to study retroactive interference. An experimental group learns a list of words (list A), then learns a second list (list B), and after an interval of time tries to recall the words in list A. A control group learns list A, rests, and then tries to recall list A. If the control group does much better in recalling list A than the experimental group, we attribute the difference to

retroactive interference

_____ _____ .

55.

Experimental group	Learn A	Learn B	Recall A
Control group	Learn A	Rest	Recall A

retroactive

The above is an arrangement for testing _____ interference. (Note that this is a simplified version of the procedure discussed in the text.)

56. A different kind of interference, called *proactive interference,* occurs when *prior* learning interferes with an attempt to recall *new* information. When you move to a new city you may have difficulty at first remembering your new zip code. When asked for it, the old one comes to mind. When previously learned information inter-

proactive

feres with an attempt to retrieve new information, it is called _____ interference.

57. The following procedure can be used to study proactive interference.

Experimental group	Learn A	Learn B	Recall B
Control group	Rest	Learn B	Recall B

proactive interference

If the control group does better than the experimental group in recalling list B, we attribute the difference to _____ _____.

prior, new
new
prior

58. Proactive interference occurs when (*prior/new*) learning interferes with (*prior/new*) learning. Retroactive interference occurs when (*prior/new*) material interferes with the retrieval of (*prior/new*) information.

retroactive, proactive
(either order)

59. Numerous experiments using the above procedures have shown that a great deal of forgetting is caused by both _____ and _____ interference.

organization, context

60. We have discussed several factors that influence forgetting. Two that aid retrieval are _____ of material and similarity of _____ between the encoding and retrieval conditions. Two that may hinder retrieval are

retroactive interference

_____ _____ and

proactive interference
(either order)

_____ _____. Another set of variables that can influence memory involves *emotions*.

emotion

61. We tend to remember exciting events (pleasant or unpleasant) more readily than we remember neutral ones; in this case em_____ improves memory. On the other hand, if we become extremely anxious during an exam, we may forget much

hinder

of what we had studied. In this case our emotions (*help/hinder*) retrieval.

62. Sometimes an emotional experience may be so traumatic that we block it from conscious awareness, or *repress* it. When a person cannot consciously recall certain events that are associated with extreme anxiety, the memories are said to be

repressed

re_____.

63. The fact that the person may become aware of these anxiety-producing memories during psychotherapy or while under hypnosis indicates that such memories (*are/*

are not, repressed

are not) lost from long-term memory. They are simply _____.

emotional

64. Thus, we see that _____ factors can influence memory in a variety of ways.

65. Memory usually involves more than simply recalling names or numbers or dates. We remember complex materials such as sentences, stories, and scenes. Memory for these more complex materials involves a *constructive process.* For example, we often take sentences as incomplete descriptions of events, and we use our general

construct   knowledge of the world to con_____ a more complete description.

66. When we say that our total memory goes beyond the information given, we mean

constructive   that memory is a _____ process.

67. One way we construct memories is by *drawing inferences* from the information given. For example, if I tell you that "Mark was injured while riding to work," you may later recall that Mark was involved in an automobile accident. Since the word

inference   "automobile" was not mentioned, your memory includes an in_____. Mark could have been riding on a bicycle or subway train.

inferences

68. One way we construct memories is by drawing _____. Another is by using *social stereotypes.* For example, if you learn that the man you just met is a basketball player, you may later remember him as tall. He is actually

stereotype   only average height, but you used a social _____ to reconstruct your memory of him.

inferences

social stereotypes

69. Two ways we construct memories are by drawing _____ and using _____ _____ . A third method, closely related to the notion of stereotypes, is to use a *schema* (plural *schemata*). A schema is a packet of general knowledge about some situation that occurs frequently.

70. A packet of general knowledge about some situation that occurs frequently is called

schema   a _____ . For example, you undoubtedly have a schema for how to drive a car—sit behind the wheel, insert the ignition key, turn the key while pressing the gas pedal, and so on. People often try to fit their experience to a schema and end up with a memory that is partly constructed from it.

71. The text describes more fully the notion of schemata and the way we use them,

inferences, social   along with in_____ and _____ stereotypes, to construct memories. In our memories we preserve information about what has happened in the past, but we also add some new material of our own devising. This is

constructive   what we mean when we say that memory is a _____ process.

TERMS AND CONCEPTS

encoding _____

_____

_____

_____

storage _____

_____

_____

_____

retrieval _____

_____

_____

_____

short-term memory _____

_____

_____

_____

long-term memory _____

_____

_____

_____

acoustic code _____

_____

_____

_____

visual code _____

_____

_____

_____

eidetic imagery* _____

_____

_____

_____

magic number seven _____

_____

_____

_____

displacement _____

_____

_____

_____

probe _____

_____

_____

_____

rehearsal _____

_____

_____

_____

chunks _____

_____

_____

_____

limited-capacity process* _____

_____

_____

_____

imagery code _____

_____

_____

_____

semantic code _____

_____

_____

_____

retrieval cue _____

_____

_____

_____

*Indicates terms used in Critical Discussions

RNA* _____

_____

_____

_____

state-dependent learning _____

_____

_____

retroactive interference _____

_____

_____

proactive interference _____

_____

_____

repression _____

_____

_____

mnemonic system _____

_____

_____

method of loci _____

_____

_____

key-word method _____

_____

_____

_____

retrograde amnesia _____

_____

_____

_____

anterograde amnesia _____

_____

_____

dual-memory theory _____

_____

_____

free recall _____

_____

_____

depth-of-processing approach _____

_____

_____

constructive memory _____

_____

_____

stereotype _____

_____

_____

schema _____

_____

_____

_____

_____ 1. Individuals suffering from anterograde amnesia
a. probably cannot remember their name
b. have deficiencies in short-term memory
c. will be unable to remember their new address if they move
d. are unlikely to be able to remember previously learned skills

_____ 2. The mnemonic system of taking an imaginary walk and locating images of objects to be remembered along the route is called the
a. mental-walk system
b. method of imagery
c. image-organization technique
d. method of loci

_____ 3. A dual-memory theory says that long-term recall may fail because
a. information was never transferred from short-term memory to long-term memory
b. not enough cues may be available at the time of attempted recall to locate information in short-term memory
c. the capacity of long-term memory is limited
d. all of the above

_____ 4. The kind of forgetting in which memories become inaccessible because of the way in which they relate to our childhood emotional experiences is
a. retroactive interference
b. proactive interference
c. repression
d. context interference

_____ 5. Psychologists divide memory into three stages:
a. organization, storage, and retrieval
b. encoding, processing, and organization
c. storage, retrieval, and processing
d. encoding, storage, and retrieval

_____ 6. In the mnemonic system that used imagery in teaching Spanish words, the key word for "caballo" was
a. caballo
b. horse
c. cob-eye-yo
d. eye

_____ 7. Because better retrieval cues are provided, we usually do better on tests of
a. state-dependent learning
b. recognition
c. state-independent learning
d. recall

_____ 8. Studies of the encoding techniques used in short-term memory show that
a. the favored code is an acoustic one
b. errors in remembered letters tend to be those that look like the target letter
c. the favored code is a visual one
d. both visual and acoustic codes are used, with the acoustic fading quickly and the visual retained longer

_____ 9. Which of the following is *not* an example of constructive memory?
a. relying on schemata
b. using mnemonic systems
c. drawing inferences
d. using social stereotypes

_____ 10. A subject is shown a list, then, after a few seconds, asked if a probe item was on the list. The plot of decision time versus number of items on the list is a straight line, indicating that
a. more retrieval cues are needed for longer lists
b. short-term memory is hierarchically organized
c. retrieval from short-term memory involves a search through all items
d. all of the above

_____ 11. In free-recall experiments, when subjects are asked to do 30 seconds of mental arithmetic between seeing the list of words and trying to recall them, their recall of _____ items is decreased.
a. the first
b. the last
c. the middle
d. all

_____ 12. The magic number seven refers to
a. the best number of items to combine into a chunk for long-term storage
b. the maximum number of items that can be encoded into long-term memory without a mnemonic system
c. the number of items that can be encoded by a visual code
d. the limited number of chunks that short-term memory can hold

13. Previously learned material interferes with our attempt to remember new information in
    a. proactive interference
    b. repression
    c. retroactive interference
    d. displacement

14. The depth-of-processing approach
    a. helps to explain why memory is constructive
    b. helps to explain the effects of repression
    c. is an alternative to a dual-memory theory
    d. all of the above

15. The kind of information that a dictionary gives, for example, about "helicopters," is the form of meaning used to encode via a _____ code.
    a. visual
    b. semantic
    c. acoustic
    d. imagery

16. People suffering from retrograde amnesia typically cannot remember
    a. who and where they are
    b. events just prior to a head injury
    c. particularly traumatic events of childhood
    d. what has happened to them following brain surgery

17. When we say that a memory is lost because of displacement, we refer to
    a. exceeding the capacity of short-term memory
    b. the effect of retroactive interference
    c. blocking from consciousness an emotionally disturbing memory
    d. the effect of proactive interference

18. Subjects asked how fast cars were going when they smashed into each other later reported broken glass that they had not, in fact, seen. This illustrates the functioning of _____ in constructing memories.
    a. inferences
    b. schemata
    c. visual encoding
    d. social stereotypes

19. _____ is a powerful cue for retrieval of memories from long-term storage.
    a. Repeating the context in which the original learning occurred
    b. Organizing material as it is stored
    c. Retaking any drug that was present at the time material was originally learned
    d. all of the above

20. The best long-term memory for verbal materials seems to result from the use of _____ in the original encoding process.
    a. semantic codes
    b. acoustic codes
    c. meaning codes, whether semantic or imagery
    d. imagery codes

KEY TO SELF-QUIZ

1. c p. 242	6. d p. 239	11. b p. 244	16. b p. 241	
2. d p. 238	7. b p. 232	12. d p. 224	17. a p. 225	
3. a p. 243	8. a p. 223	13. a p. 235	18. a p. 246	
4. c p. 237	9. b p. 245	14. c p. 244	19. d p. 234	
5. d p. 221	10. c p. 227	15. b p. 229	20. c p. 230	

INDIVIDUAL OR CLASS EXERCISES

DIGIT SPAN

Introduction

As discussed in the text (pp. 224–26), short-term memory seems to be limited to 7 ± 2 items. Psychologists arrived at this figure via a test of memory span; they also noted that the number of single items could be increased by combining, or "chunking," them. The following experiment deals with one type of memory-span test, called digit span. It allows you to demonstrate both the magic number seven and the effects of chunking.

Procedure

Read the following sets of numbers to your listeners in a regularly paced monotone, approximately one per second. (If this is to be a class exercise, the instructor will read them for the class; if not, you may do so with any size group, or have a friend read them to you.) For each set of numbers, the listeners should wait until the reader has read all numbers and only then try to write down the entire set in the order presented. After all sets have been presented (from length 4 to 10), all numbers should be reread so the listeners can check the correctness of what they have written.

DIGIT-SPAN TEST NUMBERS

Length of set	Numbers
4	4–2–8–6
5	6–8–0–9–1
6	2–1–4–7–2–9
7	1–5–7–1–8–6–1
8	9–0–3–6–8–3–0–2
9	7–0–2–1–9–8–1–3–6
10	5–7–1–9–4–1–6–7–5–2

As the sets reach and exceed seven digits the task becomes noticeably harder, then virtually impossible. Those attempting it can *feel* their short-term memory losing the first numbers as the last ones are read; audible gasps and laughter usually mark the class reaction to the longer sets.

If this is a class exercise, the instructor may wish to tabulate the results so as to demonstrate both the generality of the phenomenon and the individual differences. The instructor can note how many students had four correct, five correct, and so on. The resulting numbers will drop from virtually 100 percent to near zero as the set length increases from five through nine, though rare individuals can retain ten or more.

Next try the second set of numbers below. Read each chunk rapidly, then allow a pause similar to the one used between single digits. If desired, the results may be tabulated as before. Whether formally tabulated or not, it will be recognized by all that the chunking allows substantially more digits to be remembered. It is not accidental that telephone numbers are chunked; otherwise, seven-digit numbers would be near the limits of short-term memory, while telephone numbers plus area codes would be virtually impossible!

DIGIT-SPAN TEST NUMBERS IN CHUNKED FORM

Length of set		
digits	*chunks*	**Number**
6	2	507–413
7	3	439–106–8
8	3	692–630–52
9	3	726–859–613
10	4	318–402–179–6
11	4	015–972–605–52
12	4	591–807–924–613

IMAGERY VERSUS REHEARSAL IN MEMORIZING

Introduction

The purpose of this exercise is to determine the effectiveness of two different techniques for memorizing a list of word pairs (called paired associates). One technique is simply to repeat the two words several times; this is the sort of procedure one might use in memorizing the vocabulary of a foreign language. The other technique involves associating the two words by means of some kind of mental image.

Equipment Needed

Stopwatch or watch with a second hand.

Procedure

The experimenter, whether you or the instructor, should find a willing subject and read him or her the following instructions.

The purpose of this experiment is to investigate two different techniques for memorizing word pairs. I will read a list of 20 paired nouns, one at a time. Your task is to learn the pairs so that later, when I give you the first word of a pair, you will be able to tell me the word that goes with it. There are two memory techniques I want you to use. For some pairs you are to repeat the two words aloud four times. For other pairs you are to remain silent while forming a mental image or picture in which the words are associated or interacting in some way—the more vivid or unusual the image the better. For example, if I give you the word pair "dog-bicycle," you might picture a dog dressed in a clown suit riding on a bicycle. Just before I give you each word pair, I will tell you which method of memorizing to use by saying either "repeat" or "image." For the pairs you are to rehearse aloud four times, try to avoid forming any mental images.

After you have been given all 20 pairs, I will say "count," and you are to count backward from 99 until I tell you to stop. I will then test your memory by saying the first word in each pair, and you are to tell me the word that goes with it.

Do you have any questions?

Answer any questions by repeating the appropriate part of the instructions. Start with the first paired associate in the study list below, give the appropriate instruction, and then say the pair aloud. Continue in the same way until the list is completed. Time the presentation, allowing approximately ten seconds for the study of each pair. You should practice the procedure at least once before trying it out on your subject.

After all 20 paired associates have been presented, ask your subject to count backward from 99 for approximately 30 seconds. This task will prevent him or her from rehearsing the last few paired associates. Now test your subject's memory by reading aloud the words in the first column of the test list (S_1) below and recording his or her responses in the second column (S_2). After you have completed the list, check your subject's responses for errors and tabulate the number of correct responses for repetition pairs and the number correct for imagery pairs. Record these numbers in the appropriate space. If this is to be a class exercise, bring your results to class so that your instructor can tabulate the results for the entire class.

Questions for Discussion

1. Which learning technique was most effective for your subject?

2. If done as a class exercise, how did your subject's results compare with those from the entire class?

3. If done as a class exercise, were there individual differences in the total number of words recalled? In the effectiveness of the two memory techniques?

4. Why does the test list present the paired associates in a different order from the study list?

5. Why does the study list present the repetition and imagery pairs in a random order rather than some fixed order, such as alternating repetition and imagery pairs?

6. How might the results of this study be applied to memorization tasks you encounter?

7. A properly controlled study would include one group of subjects who learn the list as given and a second group for whom the repetition and imagery paired associates are switched; that is, word pairs the first group memorized by repetition would be learned by the second group through imagery, and vice versa. What variables that might have influenced the present exercise would be controlled by this procedure?

PAIRED-ASSOCIATE STUDY LIST

Instruction	Paired associates
repeat	1. rabbit—house
repeat	2. boy—rope
image	3. shoe—mountain
repeat	4. table—skull
image	5. doctor—flag
image	6. book—fish
repeat	7. slave—party
image	8. lamp—bird
image	9. heart—water
repeat	10. ladder—baby
repeat	11. teacher—pudding
image	12. mule—dress

PAIRED-ASSOCIATE TEST LIST

S_1	S_2
1. clock	_____
2. table	_____
3. snake*	_____
4. shoe*	_____
5. flower	_____
6. lamp*	_____
7. boy	_____
8. horse*	_____
9. book*	_____
10. rabbit	_____
11. harp*	_____
12. slave	_____

Instruction	Paired associates	S₁	S₂
repeat	13. kettle—fox	13. mule*	_____
image	14. snake—fire	14. heart*	_____
image	15. tree—queen	15. bear	_____
repeat	16. flower—money	16. ladder	_____
image	17. harp—elephant	17. doctor*	_____
repeat	18. bear—candle	18. kettle	_____
repeat	19. clock—moon	19. teacher	_____
image	20. horse—potato	20. tree*	_____

*Imagery pair

Total correct (repetition) _____

Total correct (imagery) _____

9

Language and Thought

LEARNING OBJECTIVES

9-1. Be able to define a concept, including the aspects of common properties and typicality. Be able to describe how our knowledge of the world might be represented as a hierarchy of concepts.

9-2. Be familiar with the acquisition of concepts by children and adults. Be able to explain what a child's overextensions and an adult's biased use of hypothesis testing tell us about such acquisition.

9-3. Understand how sentences may be broken down into propositions that reflect thoughts, and be able to explain the difference between a given sentence and the proposition(s) it expresses. Be familiar with the ways of further subdividing sentences into noun versus verb phrases and subjects versus predicates.

9-4. Be able to define, and to differentiate between, phonemes and morphemes. Be able to describe the levels of language.

9-5. Be familiar with children's progression from primitive to complex sentences and how telegraphic speech and grammatical morphemes fit into this progression.

9-6. Be able to describe the three models proposed to explain how children learn to speak in sentences. Be able to suggest what role each of these is likely to play in such learning.

9-7. Be familiar with the evidence bearing on the question of whether human language learning is innate.

9-8. Be able to explain what is meant by visual thinking, how it may be studied experimentally, and how it may be involved in creative thought.

9-9. Know what is meant by stages of problem solving. Be able to discuss how and why such stages may be simulated by computers.

9-10. Be familiar with the General Problem Solver. Know what its two basic processes are and be able to describe how they interact to solve problems.

1. Thinking requires an ability to *represent objects* and *events* that are *not physically present*. When you think, for example, "I'm going out for a cup of coffee," you are

present   referring to an object that is not physically _____ ; somehow you must represent this object to yourself.

represent   2. Thinking requires an ability to _____ objects and events that are not present.

events   3. One way we represent objects and _____ is by means of *concepts*. A concept is a class of objects or events with *common properties*.

properties   4. To have a concept of *bird,* for example, means to know the _____ common to all or most birds.

common   5. A concept is a class of objects or events with _____ properties.

6. Since the word "fruit" refers to a class of objects that are edible and usually sweet,

concept   we can say that fruit is a _____ .

7. Concepts enable us to *infer properties* that are not directly observed. For example, if someone hands you a strange object and tells you it is a fruit, you assume that it

infer   is edible. The concept *fruit* allows you to _____ properties not observed.

8. If you are told that the woman you just met is a doctor, you immediately know certain things about her (for example, that she has a medical degree). The concept

infer   enables you to _____ properties that are common to all doctors.

9. Some properties are *common* to *all instances* of the concept. For example, all birds

common   lay eggs, so this property is _____ to all instances of the concept *birds*.

10. Some properties are *characteristic* of only the more *typical* members of the concept. Most, but not all, birds can fly. The ability to fly is characteristic only of the more

typical   _____ instances of the concept.

11. A property that is true of most, but not all, birds is said to be

characteristic   ch_____ of the concept *bird*.

12. Typical members of a concept have *more* characteristic properties of their concept

typical   than do less typical ones. We think of a robin as more ty_____ of the concept *bird* than penguins because robins can fly.

more   13. Typical members have (*more/fewer*) characteristics of the concept than do less typical members.

typical   14. When we think of a concept, we are apt to think of a ty_____ instance of it, and this may lead us to think in terms of *stereotypes*.

15. We may think of senators as typically middle-aged men and thus be surprised when

we meet a female senator. If our concepts are too narrow we may think in terms

stereotypes of s_____.

16. In learning to speak, children learn the proper words to apply to concepts. In learn-

concept ing which word goes with which _____, they form *hypotheses* about

the crucial properties of a word's meaning.

17. The parents say "doggie" whenever they refer to the family dog. The child, noting

hypothesis that the dog has four legs and moves, may form the hy_____

that these two characteristics define "doggie."

18. The child may then apply the word "doggie" to cats and horses, which also have

four legs and move. This is an example of *overextension*. The child's initial

hypothesis _____ is based on only a few properties of the concept, and

he or she overextends the meaning of the word.

overextension 19. A two-year-old calls all men "daddy." This is an over_____

of the word.

20. Another child calls all animals with soft fur "bunny." This is another example

overextension of _____.

21. Overextensions occur because the child's initial hypothesis is based on only a few

properties p_____ of the concept. As children learn more about differ-

ent animals, they begin to differentiate the relevant properties of each (for example,

bunnies have long ears and hop).

22. Adults, too, use *hypothesis testing* in forming new concepts. We hypothesize that

properties certain _____ are characteristic of a concept and then look

for evidence to confirm or disprove our hypothesis.

hypothesis 23. In our _____ testing, however, we tend to be biased toward

evidence that confirms our hypothesis while ignoring evidence that might disprove

it.

24. If your concept of *lawyer* includes the property "politically conservative," you may

tend to note those law students you know who are Young Republicans but fail to

note those who are members of Americans for Democratic Action. You are biased

confirms toward evidence that (*confirms/disproves*) your hypothesis.

25. Concepts may be combined to form thoughts that can be expressed in sentences.

Such thoughts often take the form of *propositions*. "John likes music" is an exam-

proposition ple of a pro_____.

26. Each proposition contains a *subject* and a *predicate*. In the above example, the

John predicate, *likes music,* asserts something about the subject, _____.

27. "The girl laughed at the joke" is another proposition. *The girl* constitutes the

subject _____; and the assertion about her (*laughed at the joke*) is the

predicate _____.

subject, predicate (either order)	28. A proposition consists of a _____ and a _____.
	29. A simple sentence like "The baby smiled" contains only one proposition. The sentence "The baby smiled and mother laughed" contains two
propositions, baby	_____. There are two subjects, _____ and
mother (either order)	_____, and two predicates.
	30. All sentences, no matter how complex, can be broken down into
propositions	_____ containing subjects and predicates.
	31. The sentence "The baby laughed when the cat spilled the milk, but mother got
three	mad" contains _____ (*number*) propositions.
	32. A sentence and the proposition it expresses are not identical, because the same proposition can be expressed by different sentences. "The man shut the door" and "The door was shut by the man" are two different sentences, but they express the
proposition	same thought, or _____. The text describes how we extract propositions from sentences by breaking the sentence into phrases.
	33. All languages are based on a certain number of *elementary sounds,* or *phonemes.* The English language is composed of about forty phonemes, or
elementary	_____ sounds, which correspond roughly to the different ways we pronounce the vowels and consonants of our alphabet. The number of phonemes varies from one language to the next.
Phonemes	34. _____ are the elementary sounds of a language, and they may vary in number from one language to the next.
	35. Each language has *rules* that specify how the elementary sounds, or
phonemes	_____, may be combined or sequenced to form a word. For example, in English we have words that start with "stri" or "spl" but none beginning with "zb" or "vg," as is common in some Slavic languages.
	36. Not all phonemes can be used in all combinations. Each language has
rules	_____ that specify how phonemes may be sequenced.
	37. The smallest *meaningful* units in the structure of a language are called *morphemes.*
phoneme	Do not confuse the word "morpheme" with _____, which refers to elementary sounds of a language.
meaningful	38. Morphemes are the smallest _____ units in the structure of a language. Morphemes may be root words, prefixes, or suffixes, and may consist of from two to six phonemes.
	39. The words "banana," "god," and "sweet" are single morphemes. That is, they are
meaningful	among the smallest _____ units in the English language.
	40. Some words consist of two or more morphemes. The word "sweetness" consists
morphemes	of two _____, "sweet" and "ness," since both parts have

meanings of their own (the suffix "ness" implies "being" or "having the quality of").

two

41. The word "sincere" consists of a single morpheme. However, if we add the prefix "in" which means "without" to form "insincere," we have _____ (*number*) morpheme(s).

morphemes

42. The smallest meaningful units in the structure of a language are called _____. One word, however, may combine several morphemes and have several units of sound, or phonemes.

phonemes

morphemes

43. Words can be analyzed in terms of elementary sounds, or _____, and meaningful units, or _____.

proposition

44. When we produce a sentence we start with a thought, or p_____. We translate this thought into words, which consist of one or more meaningful

morphemes

phonemes

units called _____. Finally, we translate the words into speech sounds, or _____.

phonemes

morphemes

proposition

45. To understand a sentence, however, we proceed in the opposite direction. What we hear are ph_____. We use these to construct the meaningful units of the sentence—phrases, words, and _____—to arrive at the thought, or _____, intended by the speaker.

phonemes

concepts

46. In learning to talk, children must learn to combine the elementary speech sounds, or _____, into words. And they use hypothesis testing to discover the proper words to apply to various con_____.

concepts

47. By the time they are about a year old, children begin to utter single words (such as "doggie," "dada," and "foot") that refer to simple _____. At around a year and a half they begin to combine single words into two-word utterances ("there doggie," "see baby," "go car") that have a *telegraphic* quality.

48. These two-word utterances contain words that carry the most important meaning, while leaving out articles ("the," "a"), auxiliary verbs ("is," "are"), and prepositions ("on," "in"). Because they convey meaning with a minimum of words, such

telegraphic

utterances have been called tele_____.

12

18

49. Children utter single words at about _____ months of age and progress to two-word utterances at around _____ months. They rapidly proceed to more complex sentences by expanding the *verb phrase*. "Daddy hat" becomes "Daddy wear hat" and, finally, "Daddy is wearing a hat."

verb

50. In forming more complex sentences children first expand the _____ phrase and then *use conjunctions* (like "and" and "so") to form compound sentences.

telegraphic

verb phrase

51. Children progress from tele_____ two-word utterances to more complex sentences by expanding the _____ _____ and

conjunctions

using _____ . At the same time, they learn to use certain morphemes that are essential for making sentences *grammatical.*

morphemes

52. We noted earlier that suffixes and prefixes are (*phonemes/morphemes*). The suffix "ing" is a morpheme because it carries meaning when added to a verb to form the progressive ("kick"—"kicking").

grammatical

53. Other morphemes that are essential for making a sentence gr_____ include "ed" to form the past tense of regular verbs ("kick"—"kicked") and "s" added to nouns to form the plural ("boy"—"boys") or to verbs in the present tense for the third person singular ("The boy kicks").

verb phrase, conjunctions

grammatical

54. Children progress from simple two-word utterances to more complex sentences by expanding the _____ _____, using _____ to form compound sentences, and learning the morphemes that make a sentence _____. And this sequence of language development is remarkably the *same for all children.*

same

55. Children learn to use the suffix "ing" before "ed" and to use the plural "s" before the third person "s." This illustrates the fact that the sequence of language development is the _____ for all children.

language

56. The fact that the sequence of _____ development is the same for all children has led some experts to believe that some of our language-learning abilities are *innate;* we are genetically programmed to learn a language.

testing

57. How do children learn all of the complexities involved in speaking a language? The most important process appears to be one we mentioned earlier in discussing how concepts are acquired, namely, hypothesis _____.

hypothesis

58. Children seem to learn by forming a hy_____ about some aspect of language, testing it out, and keeping it as a rule if it works.

hypotheses

principle

59. Studies indicate that there are a small number of *operating principles* that children everywhere use as a guide to forming _____ about language. For example, one operating _____ is to pay attention to the *ends of words.*

operating

principle

60. Paying attention to the ends of words is one _____ _____ that children use as a guide to forming hypotheses about language; another is to look for prefixes and suffixes that indicate a *change in meaning.*

meaning

61. The past tense of regular verbs is formed by adding the morpheme "ed" (for example, "look"—"looked"). By observing that "ed" at the end of verbs changes the m_____ of the verb, children arrive at the hypothesis that "ed" at the end of verbs signals the past tense.

62. We make this assumption by noting what happens to some verbs that have an irregular past tense and do not follow the "ed" rule (for example, "run"—"ran" and "go"—"went"). These are common verbs that children learn early, and initially they

use the correct past tense; they say "went" and "ran." After learning the "ed" past tense of some regular verbs, children often begin saying "goed" and "runned," which they have never heard or said before. This change suggests that they are

hypothesis   testing a new _____ in their use of language. Eventually, children learn that some verbs are irregular, and they stop overgeneralizing their use of "ed."

63. Some language learning may occur through imitation of adult speech or through conditioning—being rewarded for grammatically correct sentences and reprimanded for mistakes. But more important is the process of learning general rules about

hypothesis testing   language through _____ _____.

64. In generating hypotheses, children appear to be guided by a small number of

operating   _____ principles.

TERMS AND CONCEPTS

concept _____

_____

_____

_____

semantic concept _____

_____

_____

_____

hierarchy of concepts _____

_____

_____

_____

linguistic relativity hypothesis* _____

_____

_____

_____

overextension _____

_____

_____

_____

propositions _____

_____

_____

_____

predicate _____

_____

_____

_____

subject _____

_____

_____

syntactic analysis* _____

_____

_____

*Indicates terms used in Critical Discussions

phoneme _____

_____

_____

_____

morpheme _____

_____

_____

_____

telegraphic speech _____

_____

_____

_____

grammatical morphemes _____

_____

_____

_____

operating principles _____

_____

_____

_____

motherese _____

_____

_____

_____

productivity* _____

_____

_____

_____

computer simulation _____

_____

_____

General Problem Solver (GPS) _____

_____

_____

_____

SELF-QUIZ

_____ 1. All languages are made up of _____ such as _____.
   a. phonemes, "strange"
   b. phonemes, /s/
   c. morphemes, "strangeness"
   d. phonemes, "ness"

_____ 2. Young children often "overextend" in learning a language—for example, by
   a. treating "large" as if it meant "gigantic"
   b. presuming something that is "gone" is gone forever
   c. calling a cat a "doggie"
   d. using words they hear without knowing what they mean

_____ 3. The spontaneous speech of a two-year-old has been termed _____ because of such sentences as "Jimmy bike" and "car go."
   a. truncated speech
   b. telegraphic speech
   c. abbreviated speech
   d. primitive speech

_____ 4. Subjects asked questions about a mental image, for example, of a car,
   a. are typically unable to answer in any detail
   b. can answer questions about any aspect of the image equally quickly, as if they could see all of it at once
   c. seem to scan the image in the same way as they might a real object
   d. find that the details of their image keep changing as they attempt to answer questions about it

_____ 5. To a psychologist, a "concept" refers to
   a. a set of objects that share common properties
   b. an abstract idea, such as _justice_
   c. a state of humans, such as _being old_
   d. all of the above

_____ 6. Children's sentences such as "Annie goed home" and "Harry taked the book" provide evidence supporting the _____ view of language development.
   a. hypothesis testing
   b. innate pattern
   c. conditioning
   d. imitation

_____ 7. To produce a sentence we go through three levels of language in the following order:
   a. thoughts, propositions, sentences
   b. propositions, phonemes, morphemes
   c. sentences, phonemes, propositions
   d. propositions, phrases, phonemes

_____ 8. Researchers working with language use by chimpanzees have _not_ been able to teach them to
   a. speak words
   b. combine or generalize signs in ASL
   c. type out messages
   d. any of the above

_____ 9. In analyzing the components of speech we note that a simple thought is often expressed as a _____ with two major components, the _____ and the _____.
   a. predicate, subject, proposition
   b. proposition, predicate, subject
   c. proposition, predicate, verb phrase
   d. predicate, noun phrase, verb phrase

_____ 10. Which of the following true statements is _not_ evidence in favor of an innate tendency for children to learn language?
   a. Perceptual and motor skills follow an orderly development similar to that of language.
   b. Children do not generate hypotheses about language at random
   c. Children do not have to learn each step in language through observation and imitation.
   d. Children acquire new grammatical constructions in a predictable order.

_____ 11. Computer simulation programs are designed for the purpose of
   a. demonstrating that human problem solving works via the same steps that a computer takes
   b. demonstrating that a computer can solve problems faster than humans can
   c. trying to understand how humans solve problems
   d. trying to find a better way to program computers

_____ 12. During the first year of life, children learn
   a. the roles that different things play in their world
   b. how to communicate with gestures
   c. specific facts about their world
   d. all of the above

13. When we break up the sentence "My friend Lorri is a doctor," we note that
    a. "My friend Lorri" is a noun phrase
    b. "friend" is the subject
    c. "My friend Lorri" is the predicate
    d. "is a doctor" is a noun phrase

14. Our speed in judging whether a particular example is a member of a concept depends on the typicality of the concept. Which of the following is likely to take the longest decision time?
    a. a dog as an animal
    b. a chair as furniture
    c. an ostrich as a bird
    d. a house as a building

15. The General Problem Solver makes use of two basic processes that cycle; it _____ and _____.
    a. analyzes the problem, tries a solution
    b. breaks the problem into steps, tries each of its subroutines on each step
    c. specifies how a human would handle the problem, tries to duplicate that
    d. sets up a subgoal, reduces the discrepancy between current status and a subgoal

16. To use language fully, children must acquire concepts and learn the words that define them. When we study children's learning of color concepts, we find that
    a. children learn the names first, then the concept
    b. children learn the concept first, then the name
    c. children learn concept and name simultaneously
    d. any of the above, depending on the particular child

17. The language form called "motherese" refers to
    a. special words used only between mother and child

b. the tendency of children to learn the accents spoken by their mothers
c. simplified and slowed sentences used by adults to children
d. the tendency of children to directly mimic or imitate adult speech

18. Certain word endings used to marked verb tense and plurals (for example, "ing," "ed," "s") are called
    a. grammatical morphemes
    b. semantic phonemes
    c. grammatical phonemes
    d. telegraphic morphemes

19. To test the hypothesis "If a card has a consonant on one side, it has an odd number on the other," which of the following cards should you turn over: E, K, 2, 5?
    a. E and 5
    b. E and K
    c. 2 and 5
    d. K and 2

20. Given an upside-down letter "R" and asked if it is normal or backward, subjects
    a. were often incorrect
    b. mentally rotated the image to find out
    c. used a verbal code to help decide
    d. all of the above

KEY TO SELF-QUIZ

1. b p. 260	6. a p. 265	11. c p. 274	16. b p. 253
2. c p. 255	7. d p. 261	12. d p. 262	17. c p. 266
3. b p. 262	8. a p. 267	13. a p. 258	18. a p. 264
4. c p. 272	9. b p. 257	14. c p. 252	19. d p. 256
5. d p. 251	10. a p. 266	15. d p. 275	20. b p. 273

INDIVIDUAL EXERCISES

CONFLICT IN CODING

Introduction

We normally encode events in a manner appropriate to them. Our memory of material we have read is verbal, while our recollection of a sunset may be pictorial. This exercise, based on the Stroop Test, intentionally sets two forms of coding into conflict. It demonstrates not only how disconcerting such conflict can be, but also how difficult it is to override firmly established verbal responses.

Equipment Needed

Display cards in color, to be created from white paper and colored marker pens as described on the next page.

1. Make up three display sheets as follows. If you want to do the test for a group, make them as large as necessary for clear viewing by the group. (The experiment makes an interesting party game.) For individual usage, sheets of standard size typewriter paper are large enough. You should use plain white opaque paper or cardboard that will take ink well and bright felt-tip markers that will produce distinctly different colors.

2. On the first sheet, the experimental one, print the names of colors in large, thick block letters: YELLOW, GREEN, etc. But print them in *different* colors from the color names. The first word thus could be YEL-LOW but printed in thick block *green* letters. Make at least four or five lines, with about five words per line, a total of perhaps 25 words; each word will be repeated several times in the display, but the same word should not be used twice in succession. Use only basic color names and easily discriminable colors: perhaps red, yellow, blue, green, orange, and brown. Vary the color used to print a particular color name; that is, don't print YELLOW in green ink every time it appears.

3. Make up two control sheets, one with patches of color that are not words, the other with the color names printed all in black. Make the color patches similar in size and color density to the words on the first sheet, and make the black-ink names similar in size to the colored ones on the first sheet. (It is not necessary to have the colors and words in the same order as on the experimental sheet.)

4. Present the sheets to your subject (yourself, if no one else is handy) in any order. The tasks for the control sheets are to name the colors on one and to read the color names on the other. Use a stopwatch to time each performance as precisely as possible. Subjects will of course find these tasks so easy as to be trivial. The experimental task, however, using the third sheet, is to correctly name the *ink* colors used as fast as possible; that is, to name the color that a word is printed in and not the word itself. (If the word YEL-LOW is printed in green ink, the subject should say "green" when he or she comes to it.) A subject who makes a mistake must correct it before continuing. This is not nearly as easy as it sounds; a reasonably quick, errorless run through 25 names is a surprisingly difficult task.

5. Compare the time needed for the experimental task to that of the control tasks; it will undoubtedly be substantially longer.

1. Why is this task so difficult? Would it be more or less difficult for a five-year-old child? For a nonnative speaker of English?

2. Can you figure out any way to become more proficient at the task? What do you want to do? (Hint: try turning the page upside down. Can you think of ways of achieving similar results without turning the page upside down?)

CONFLICT IN PROBLEM SOLVING

Introduction

As noted in the text, some problems are easier to solve visually (p. 271), while others require a logical and sequential approach (p. 274). Although there are problems that can be solved by either approach, some problems may respond to only one; use of the other approach may inhibit or prevent a solution. This exercise is designed to let you experience some of the conflict in strategies that often accompanies problem solving.

Procedure

Try to solve the following problem before reading further. As you do, pay attention to the strategies you use.

Which line does the "Z" go on and why?

```
A    EF HI KLMN      T VWXY
 BCD   G  J      OPQRS U
```

Most people seek to solve such a problem by logic, usually by an analysis similar to that of the series problems described on page 274 of the text. It looks like a sequence, and the use of letters probably tends to bias you toward the logical thought processes of the left hemisphere (as described in Chapter 2 of the text). But this is actually more of a right-hemisphere task, one calling for visual thought and analysis. Try it again from this perspective before going on.

If you have not solved it yet, consider what information is available to you. By saying that the solution is not sequential, we have eliminated any "1–3–2–1 . . ." pattern. It can't be based on initial letters, as in the "OTTFFSS" sequence (p. 274 of the text), since this is the alphabet itself. What property of these letters do you have left? Try the problem again.

If you still do not get it, consider a final clue: the property you are seeking is letter *shape.* The solution should now be obvious. Is it?

The answer is that the "Z" goes on the top line, with all the other letters made of straight lines. Any attention paid to the numbers of letters on each line, to words beginning with the letter, and so on, simply interferes with finding such a solution. Note that the effect here is similar to that of the color-naming task in the preceding exercise: previously learned associations to visual patterns interfere with the task. But here the associations are less specific; rather than a simple interference of word name, complex patterns of logical problem solving intrude.

Questions for Discussion

1. What strategies did you use? Did they include visual as well as logical ones before you were told to do so? Were you able to use visual strategies when directed to do so? Are these as easy to describe or explain as the logical-verbal ones?

2. How might you manipulate conditions so that someone else would find the problem easier or harder to solve? (Hint: consider the effect of giving the series problems on page 274 of the text just before giving this problem. How would that differ from giving the problem on page 271 first? What about the hint in question 2 of "Conflict in Coding" on page 143; might it be applicable here?)

LANGUAGE USE AS PROBLEM SOLVING

While you use language in problem solving, your understanding of language itself often has elements of problem solving. The examples in this section focus on some of these problem-solving elements.

Many of these problems involve reading. Making sense of a written message can be considered akin to decoding or to problem solving. First the basic elements, the letters, must be recognized. Before you write this take off as trivial consider the following sentence.

THE CAT SAT THERE

You probably had no difficulty reading it, but look again. Is the open-topped figure an "H" or an "A"? Obviously it can be either for you, depending on context. A similar example is the figure shown in the middle below; it is seen as a letter in one context and a number in another.

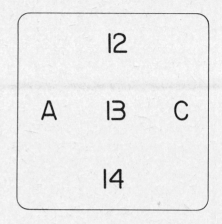

Once you have decoded the letters and/or numbers, you must deal with the meaning of individual words. Here again you find that context often specifies them. English uses words like "fly," for example, as either a verb or a noun, with the context specifying which. Thus the answer to

WHAT HAS SIX WHEELS AND FLIES?

can be either two Cessnas or a large garbage truck.

Sometimes punctuation is used to help you. Try to punctuate the following so that it makes sense.

TIME FLIES YOU CANNOT THEY FLY TOO FAST

Part of the difficulty is that the first words are well known in one context, that is, where "flies" is a verb and "time" a noun. But you can only punctuate this if you reverse the grammatical relationship. If you consider the first two words above to be a question about using a stopwatch on flying insects, the rest of the punctuation follows.

Minor punctuation marks such as commas can be important, even necessary, clues. Consider the meanings of the following sentence, depending on whether or not it has two commas in it.

THE REPUBLICANS SAY THE DEMOCRATS ARE LIARS.
THE REPUBLICANS, SAY THE DEMOCRATS, ARE LIARS.

But even brief and unpunctuated sentences can offer several meanings if such multipurpose words as "time" and "fly" are used. Consider the following:

TIME FLIES LIKE AN ARROW.

Because of the common usage of "time flies," you probably read this sentence to mean that the passage of time is swift. But a Harvard computer simulation program designed to interpret English came up with four interpretations for the same sentence.[1] Can you supply the other three? The answers are given at the bottom of the right column. (Remember that they do not have to make a great deal of sense; they only need to be possible English constructions.)

In some cases where we have difficulty interpreting sentences, the problem is sequence. While most sentences are unambiguous, extracting the intended proposition(s) from more complex, or nested, ones can become difficult. Consider the following. What does it say?

THE LEATHER RACING SADDLES ARE MADE OF IS VERY SMOOTH.

The jolt and retracking you probably experienced in reading this results from the use of a sequence that seems to be of one form but turns out to be another. Consider how it would read if "of is very smooth" were replaced with "by hand." Of course one could help the reader by inserting "that" before "racing," but it is not required by the rules of English.

Other legitimate sentences remain ambiguous even when reread. For example, in the sentence "They are eating apples," "they" may refer to people or to apples. The need for brevity in newspaper headlines often yields similar examples, as in this one from a recent story.

OFF-DUTY POLICEMAN KILLS MAN WITH A CLUB
(Who had the club?)

While problems of ambiguity arise more frequently with written language, they may also occur in interpreting speech, despite the fact that speech is usually less complex and offers more contextual cues. Some of the possible ambiguous interpretations of phonemes and morphemes, for example, have entered folklore as children's games or adult jokes. "I scream for ice cream" delights children who are just discovering such possible ambiguities, but adults are not immune to the charms of such word play. Remember knock-knock jokes?

[1] Raphael, B., *The thinking computer: Mind inside matter* (San Francisco: W. H. Freeman, 1976) p. 186.

KNOCK KNOCK
WHO'S THERE?
SAM AND JANET
SAM AND JANET WHO?
SAM AND JANET EVENING

Some "trick" problems make use of verbal constructions deliberately designed to mislead you through your own normal interpretation process. Consider the following:

I have in my hand two U.S. coins totaling 55 cents and one of them is not a nickel. What are they?

Obviously the coins must be a half dollar and a nickel. How? Well, one of them is *not* a nickel; the *other one* is. If you recognized the deception, it may be because the problem is easier when it is in front of you where it can be reexamined. This trick works best as a verbal problem because once the words have been turned into meaning, the original form is lost. When you try to review the problem, you tend to remember not the exact original statement but instead your interpretation that "Neither one is a nickel."

Part of learning any language is learning the rules for recognizing and interpreting its sounds, words, and sentences. Yet, as we have seen, problems and ambiguities remain. Remember, when you consider how much of your thought process is verbally based, that your thoughts are also subject to such problems. Those who teach creative problem solving often focus on the need to carefully analyze one's verbal processes both in the interpretation of the problem and in search patterns for solutions.

Answers for problem on page 144.

1. Time moves in the same manner that an arrow moves.
2. Measure the speed of flies in the same way that you measure the speed of an arrow.
3. Measure the speed of the flies that resemble an arrow.
4. A particular variety of flies called "time-flies" are fond of an arrow.

10 Basic Drives and Motives

LEARNING OBJECTIVES 10-1. Be familiar with the definition of motivation and the historical development of motivational concepts. Be able to show how instinct and drive theories reflect this history. Be able to define homeostasis.

10-2. Understand some of the problems with drive theories of motivation and how incentive theory was intended to solve those problems.

10-3. Be familiar with the functioning of the LH and VMH in regulating hunger on both a short-term and a long-term basis.

10-4. Understand how taste and smell affect eating behavior. Be familiar with the relevant research on animals, including research on specific hungers.

10-5. Be familiar with the research on human obesity, including the findings on external versus internal cues and restrained versus unrestrained eaters.

10-6. Understand the mechanisms by which an organism can replenish its water deficit and how these are involved in thirst.

10-7. Be able to specify the major male and female sex hormones and to discuss their role in sexual differentiation and sexual behavior.

10-8. Be familiar with research on the role of experience in the sexual behavior of monkeys and implications this work may have for humans. Be able to discuss how attempts to explain homosexuality and transsexuality point up the need to consider both hormonal and cultural factors.

10-9. Be able to discuss the motives implicit in maternal behavior, avoidance of pain, and curiosity. Understand the problems that curiosity and stimulus-seeking behaviors pose for a drive-reduction theory of motivation.

10-10. Understand how the concept of arousal level may overcome some of the problems of drive and homeostasis in formulating an integrated concept of motivation.

1. By a *motive* we mean something that incites the organism to *action.* Hunger can incite an organism to action; therefore hunger can act as a _____ .

motive

2. When an organism is quiescent, we say that it is *not* motivated; when it is incited to action, we say that it is _____ .

motivated

3. Motivated behavior is also characterized by *direction.* When an organism is incited to action by hunger, it does not simply act at random; its action (or behavior) is in the _____ of food.

direction

4. Motivation has to do with two variables: _____ and direction.

action

5. An animal motivated by thirst will go in the _____ of water.

direction

6. Any behavior, then, that is characterized by action and direction is called _____ behavior.

motivated

7. Most of the motives discussed in this chapter are based on bodily needs; these are called *physiological* motives. Hunger is a function of certain bodily needs that result from lack of food. Hunger is thus a _____ motive.

physiological

8. Thirst results from dryness of the throat and mouth plus other specific bodily needs that occur from lack of water. Thirst is thus a _____ motive.

physiological

9. In discussing physiological motives a distinction is made between the terms *need* and *drive.* A *need* is defined as a *bodily deficit.* If we lack food, we have a *need* for food. If we lack water, we have a _____ for water.

need

10. A lack of food creates a bodily _____ ; we call this lack a need.

deficit

11. Any bodily deficit, or state of deprivation (such as lack of oxygen, food, or water), can be defined as a _____ .

need

12. The need for food is physiological, not psychological, but a state of physiological need has *psychological consequences.* The psychological consequences of a need are called a *drive.* The need for food leads to the hunger dr_____ . While need and drive are related, they are not the same. For example, drive does not necessarily get stronger as need gets stronger. People who have fasted for a long time report that their feelings of hunger come and go, although their need for food persists. The need persists but the psychological consequences of the need, the _____ drive, fluctuate.

drive

hunger

13. Drive, then, refers to the _____ consequences of a need.

psychological

14. The body attempts to maintain a state of *homeostasis,* that is, to maintain a *con-*

stant internal environment. Body temperature, for example, is maintained within a few degrees in a healthy individual. When you get hot you perspire, and perspiration evaporating from the body surface has a cooling effect. Perspiring is thus one of the

homeostasis   automatic mechanisms that helps maintain homeo _____ by keeping body temperature within normal range.

constant   **15.** Homeostasis refers to the body's attempt to maintain a _____ internal environment.

16. When the concentration of sugar in the blood drops below a certain level, the liver releases stored sugar (in the form of glycogen) to restore the proper blood-sugar

homeostasis   level. This is another example of _____ .

internal   **17.** Homeostasis refers to the body's attempt to maintain a constant _____ environment. There are many internal states that must be maintained within narrow limits; presumably, there are sensors in the body that detect changes from the optimal level and activate certain mechanisms that correct the imbalance and restore

homeostasis   _____ .

18. When the amount of water in the body cells becomes low, you feel thirsty and are motivated to drink water to restore the balance of fluid in the cells. This is another

homeostasis   example of _____ .

need   **19.** Any bodily deficit, or n_____ , alters the state of homeostasis and initiates a

drive   _____ , the psychological consequences of a need. When homeostasis is restored, the drive is reduced, and motivated activity ceases.

20. But not all motivated activity is initiated by internal drives. *Incentives* in the en-

drive (or need)   vironment can motivate behavior even in the absence of an internal _____ .

21. An hour after lunch, feeling not a bit hungry, you pass a bakery window full of delicious-looking cakes and go in to buy one. Your behavior in this instance is not

incentive   motivated by an internal drive but by an _____ in the environment.

22. An object or condition in the environment that motivates behavior is called an

incentive   _____ . There are *positive incentives* that an individual will *approach* and *negative incentives* that he or she will *avoid.*

positive   **23.** If you are hungry and thirsty, food and water would be_____ incen-

negative   tives. A live electric wire or a clump of poison ivy is a _____ incentive because you are motivated to avoid it.

24. A positive incentive is any object or condition in the environment that the organism

approach   is motivated to _____ . A negative incentive is any object that the

avoid   organism is motivated to _____ .

25. Motivation is best understood as an interaction between certain objects in the en-

incentives   vironment, called _____ , and the physiological state of the organism. Drives alone do not provide a complete explanation of motivated behavior.

26. Hunger as a source of motivated behavior is aroused by bodily needs as well as by external _____. Psychologists have tried to pinpoint some of the internal and external stimuli that *regulate food intake.*

incentives

intake

27. Because regulation of food _____ is crucial to the survival of the organism, nature has provided several homeostatic controls. These control systems are integrated in a region of the brain called the *hypothalamus.*

28. One area of the hypothalamus, the *lateral hypothalamus (LH),* initiates eating; it is a *"feeding center."* Another area of the hypo_____, the *ventromedial hypothalamus (VMH),* inhibits eating; it is a *"satiety center."*

hypothalamus

29. If the lateral hypothalamus is stimulated with a mild electric current, an animal that has just completed a large meal will begin to eat again. This is evidence that the lateral _____ is a _____ center because its stimulation initiates eating.

hypothalamus, feeding

30. If the ventromedial hypothalamus is stimulated electrically, a hungry animal will stop eating in the midst of a meal. This is evidence that the _____ hypothalamus is a satiety center, because its stimulation_____ eating.

ventromedial

inhibits (or stops)

31. The feeding center is the _____ hypothalamus; the satiety center is the _____ hypothalamus.

lateral

ventromedial

32. Knowing this much, you would guess that if a large part of the ventromedial _____ is removed or destroyed, the animal will eat too (*much/little*).

hypothalamus

much

33. And this is exactly what happens. When tissue in the ventromedial hypothalamus is destroyed, the animal overeats until it becomes obese. This is so because the ventromedial hypothalamus is a _____ center, and if it is destroyed the animal doesn't know when to stop eating.

satiety

34. You might guess that in the opposite case, when tissue in the lateral hypothalamus is destroyed, an animal will eat too (*much/little*).

little

35. What actually happens when the lateral hypothalamus is destroyed is that the animal refuses to eat at all and will die unless fed artificially. This provides further evidence that the_____ hypothalamus functions as a feeding center.

lateral

36. These two regions of the hypothalamus thus appear to act in (*the same/opposite*) way(s) to regulate food intake.

opposite

37. Moreover, there appear to be two kinds of control systems in the hypothalamus: a *short-term control system* that responds to the organism's immediate nutritive needs and tells it when to start and stop a meal, and a *long-term control system* that attempts to maintain a stable body weight over a long period of time, regardless of how much the organism eats in any one meal. The fact that most people maintain

the same body weight from year to year (give or take a few pounds) suggests that

long

the body must have some kind of _____-term control system for regulation of food intake.

control

38. The hypothalamus appears to have both short-term and long-term _____ systems for regulating eating.

39. Experiments have pinpointed three physiological variables that are related to our immediate feeling of hunger: *blood-sugar level, stomach fullness,* and *body temperature.* These are variables to which the hypothalamus responds in controlling when

short

we start and stop eating a given meal; they are thus important to the_____-term control system.

40. When our blood-sugar level is low we feel weak and hungry; studies indicate that cer-

blood

tain cells in the hypothalamus are sensitive to the level of sugar in the bl_____.

41. But we usually stop eating before the food we have consumed can raise the blood-

fullness

sugar level significantly. A more immediate result of eating, stomach _____, apparently signals the brain that food is on the way.

42. Certain cells in the hypothalamus appear to respond to a full stomach to inhibit

ventromedial

further eating. As you would expect, these cells are in the (*lateral/ventromedial*) region of the hypothalamus.

43. When the stomach is empty we have periodic contractions of the stomach walls called hunger pangs. This increased activity of the stomach walls signals cells in the

feeding

lateral hypothalamus or (*feeding/satiety*) center to start the organism eating.

blood-

44. Two variables that affect the short-term control of eating are _____-

sugar, fullness

_____ level and stomach _____. A third short-term control variable is temperature: decreased brain temperature initiates eating; increased brain

less

temperature inhibits eating. This is probably one reason why you have (*more/less*) of an appetite in hot weather.

45. Three variables that are important to the short-term hunger control system

blood-sugar, fullness

are _____ - _____ level, stomach _____, and

temperature

_____.

46. The physiological variables that affect the long-term control system so as to keep

weight

our body w_____ about the same from year to year are not fully known. But experimental evidence suggests that the two hypothalamic regulatory centers,

lateral, ventromedial
(either order)

the _____ and the _____ hypothalamus, interact reciprocally to maintain an individual's weight at a set point. These studies have implications for problems of obesity.

47. Let's review. The two important brain areas for the regulation of food intake are

lateral hypothalamus
ventromedial hypothalamus,
satiety

the _____ _____ , a feeding center, and the _____ _____ , a _____

body

center. These two centers act reciprocally to maintain a stable _____ weight.

They also provide for short-term control of food intake by responding differentially

blood-sugar, fullness

to three bodily variables: _____ - _____ level, stomach _____ ,

temperature

and _____. (The text discusses how learning and environmental factors influence hunger and their importance in obesity. The programmed unit has concentrated on the physiological variables because they are less familiar and more difficult to understand.)

48. Human beings can go without food for weeks, but they cannot survive without water

physiological

for more than a few days. *Thirst,* then, is another important _____ motive.

49. The hypothalamus is important to the regulation of water intake, just as it is for

food

_____ intake.

50. If water is placed directly into a thirsty dog's stomach via a tube that bypasses the mouth and throat, it will still drink its usual amount of water if allowed immediate access to its water bowl. However, if there is a delay of several minutes before the dog is given access to water, the amount consumed decreases as the delay increases; and after 20 minutes the dog does not drink at all. In this experiment the important

time

variable is (*time/degree of thirst*).

51. The results suggest that a certain amount of water must be absorbed through the stomach wall into the bloodstream before the mechanism that responds to

water

_____ intake is activated.

52. Although all the details of water regulation are not yet known, current theories postulate two kinds of internal "receptors" that control thirst: *osmoreceptors* are sensitive to the concentration of certain chemicals in the blood and body fluids;

body

volumetric receptors are sensitive to the total volume of blood and _____ fluids.

53. If you go for a while without water, the chemicals in your blood and in the fluids surrounding your cells become (*more/less*) concentrated. This increased concentra-

more

tion causes water to pass out of the cells, through osmosis, leaving them *dehydrated.*

increased

54. One result of water deficit is (*increased/decreased*) concentration of body fluids

dehydrated

which causes the cells to become _____.

55. All body cells become dehydrated when there is a water deficit, but certain nerve

dehydration

cells in the hypothalamus respond specifically to de_____.

hypothalamus

56. These specialized cells in the _____ are assumed to be the osmoreceptors; when they become dehydrated, they stimulate the organism to drink.

57. Osmoreceptors are cells in the hypothalamus that respond to the dehydration that occurs when a water deficit causes the blood and body fluids to become too

concentrated

_____ .

dehydration

58. But cellular de_____ is not the only signal for thirst. During a fast

game of tennis in hot weather your body loses salt through perspiration. The salt

fluids, decreased

concentration of your blood and body _____ is thus (*decreased/increased*), yet you feel thirsty. There must be receptors that are sensitive to the *total volume*

concentration

of blood and body fluids, regardless of their con_____ .

concentration

59. Thus, in addition to osmoreceptors that are sensitive to the _____ of blood and body fluids, there are volumetric receptors that respond to the total

volume

_____ of blood and body fluids. Both of these receptors act together to control thirst. (The text describes in more detail how the volumetric receptors operate.)

60. Another important physiological motive is sex. Sex is not vital to the survival of the

water

organism, as are food and _____ , but it is essential to the survival of the species.

61. Sexual behavior depends on internal factors, primarily *hormones,* and *stimuli in the environment.* If a female rat is injected with a male hormone, it will try to mount other females when placed in a cage with them. This illustrates the influence of

hormones

h_____ on sexual behavior.

62. If the same rat is placed in a cage with male rats, it will revert to the female sexual pattern when confronted with a sexually aggressive male. This illustrates the influ-

environmental (or external)

ence of _____ stimuli on sexual behavior.

63. As we go from lower to higher mammals, experience and learning play an increasingly important role in sexual behavior. If a rat is raised in isolation with no contact with other rats, it will usually show the proper sexual response when first confronted with a receptive mate. Thus, sexual behavior in the rat appears to be largely

innate

(*learned/innate*).

64. A monkey raised in isolation, on the other hand, seems to have no clear idea of the appropriate sexual behavior when confronted with a receptive member of the oppo-

learning (or experience)

site sex. In monkeys, sexual behavior is primarily influenced by _____ .

65. Harry Harlow, a psychologist who has done extensive research on the importance of early experience in monkeys, has suggested that normal heterosexual behavior in primates depends on three factors: (a) the influence of *hormones;* (b) the development of the *appropriate sexual responses* in early play with other monkeys; and (c) an *affectional bond* between members of the opposite sex, which is formed as an outgrowth of early interactions with the mother and other monkeys.

66. Monkeys reared in isolation do not lack the appropriate sex hormones; but because they have never had the chance to play with other young monkeys, they have not

sexual

learned the appropriate _____ responses. And because they have never interacted with either a mother or other monkeys, they have not learned the trust

bond

necessary to form an affectional _____ .

67. Although we cannot automatically extend these findings with monkeys to sexual development in humans, observations indicate that the same three factors may be important to the development of normal heterosexual behavior: hormones, the

sexual responses

affectional

development of appropriate _____ _____ , and an

_____ bond between members of the opposite sex.

68. Among humans an additional influence on sexual behavior is provided by the *culture* in which a person is raised. All cultures place some restrictions on sexual behavior, and what the culture says is right or wrong will have a significant influence

behavior

on the sexual _____ of its members.

69. Some cultures are very *permissive,* encouraging sex play among the children and placing few restrictions on adult sexual relationships. Some cultures are very *restrictive,* frowning on any indication of sexuality in childhood and restricting adult sexual behavior to narrowly prescribed forms. Most societies would fall somewhere

restrictive

between the very permissive and the very _____ .

70. Until recently, how would you have classified American society in terms of its attitudes toward sexual behavior? Fairly (*restrictive/permissive*)? If you said "restrictive," you are closer to the opinions of most authorities in evaluating the attitude of the average American up until the 1960s.

restrictive

71. There are indications, however, that the United States, along with most other Western nations, has become more permissive in its attitudes toward sexual

behavior

_____ . (The text discusses the reasons and evidence for this change.)

hunger

thirst, sex
(any order)

pain

72. The three physiological motives we have discussed so far are _____ ,

_____ , and _____ . Two other physiological motives covered in the text are *maternal behavior* and *avoidance of pain.* The motivations to care for one's young and to avoid _____ are important determiners of behavior.

73. All of these motives have some basis in the physiological condition of the organism. But there is another determiner of action, important to both animals and humans, whose physiological correlates are unknown—the need for *sensory stimulation.* Both animals and people enjoy exploring new places and manipulating objects.

stimulation

They appear to need a certain amount of sensory _____ .

74. When people participate in experiments where the normal amount of stimulation is greatly reduced, their functioning is impaired and they cannot tolerate the situation

sensory

for very long. A certain amount of _____ stimulation is necessary for the well-being of the organism.

TERMS AND CONCEPTS

motivation _____
_____
_____

rationalism _____
_____

instinct theory _____
_____
_____

drive _____
_____
_____

need _____
_____
_____

drive-reduction theory _____
_____
_____

homeostasis _____
_____
_____

positive incentive _____
_____
_____

negative incentive _____
_____

_____
_____

lateral hypothalamus (LH) _____
_____

ventromedial hypothalamus (VMH) _____
_____
_____

glucoreceptors _____
_____
_____

thermoreceptors _____
_____
_____

specific hungers _____
_____
_____

adipocytes* _____
_____
_____

osmoreceptors _____
_____
_____

volumetric receptors _____
_____
_____

*Indicates terms used in Critical Discussions

estrogen _____

_____

_____

_____

progesterone _____

_____

_____

_____

androgens _____

_____

_____

_____

testosterone _____

_____

_____

_____

estrous cycle _____

_____

_____

_____

hermaphrodite _____

_____

_____

_____

homosexual _____

_____

_____

_____

transsexual _____

_____

_____

_____

ethologist* _____

_____

_____

species-specific behavior* _____

_____

_____

imprinting* _____

_____

_____

releaser* _____

_____

_____

sensory deprivation _____

_____

_____

_____

arousal level _____

_____

_____

_____

_____ 1. Psychologists usually narrow the broad concept of motivation to those particular factors that

_____ and _____ behavior.
   a. organize, control
   b. energize, direct
   c. activate, modify
   d. determine, control

_____ 2. The concepts of need and drive are parallel but not identical, even though they are sometimes used interchangeably. One crucial difference, for example, is that
   a. as need gets stronger drive gets weaker
   b. need is a hypothetical construct
   c. as drive gets stronger it arouses greater need
   d. as need gets stronger drive may get stronger or weaker

_____ 3. When rats have been fed on a fat-free diet, they
   a. eat much more than normal rats
   b. show a marked preference for fat
   c. prefer it to a normal diet
   d. eat enough of it to maintain their calorie intake above normal levels

_____ 4. When water is placed directly into a thirsty dog's stomach, the dog
   a. drinks less than it would have otherwise
   b. drinks the same amount as it would have otherwise
   c. does not drink at all
   d. any of the above, depending on how soon afterwards it is allowed to drink

_____ 5. Cultures differ with regard to their sexual taboos;

_____ is prohibited by most cultures while _____ are viewed with varying degrees of tolerance.
   a. homosexuality, masturbation and incest
   b. sexual activity among children, incest and premarital sex
   c. incest, masturbation and homosexuality
   d. masturbation, premarital sex and homosexuality

_____ 6. The results of experiments on exploration, manipulation, and sensory deprivation can be most easily handled by the concept of
   a. drive
   b. incentive

   c. homeostasis
   d. arousal level

_____ 7. Freud can be said to be an instinct theorist because he believed that behavior was determined

by two basic instincts: _____ and

_____.
   a. sex instincts, competitive instincts
   b. social instincts, competitive instincts
   c. life instincts, death instincts
   d. sex instincts, destructive instincts

_____ 8. In examining centers in the hypothalamus that regulate food intake, researchers have found that
   a. the LH inhibits eating
   b. the VMH initiates eating
   c. both long-term and short-term systems are involved
   d. all of the above

_____ 9. Studies of hunger and eating in animals show us that taste and smell are
   a. necessary for an animal to regulate its food intake
   b. not essential to regulation of food intake
   c. less useful in food regulation for rats with VMH lesions
   d. not sensed at all by rats with VMH lesions

_____ 10. Hormones control sexual behavior
   a. by producing a state of readiness to respond
   b. according to both the type and amount of hormone present in the bloodstream
   c. less as we go from lower to higher vertebrates
   d. all of the above

_____ 11. The best current overall statement about motivational theories is that
   a. each theory has a grain of truth but is incomplete in itself
   b. biological needs are less important for humans than social needs
   c. drive-reduction theory comes closest to a complete explanation of behavior
   d. the concepts of homeostasis and incentive together describe most motivated behavior

_____ 12. A homeostatic model of motivation is _least_ appropriate as a description of
   a. hunger
   b. pain avoidance

c. maternal behavior

d. thirst

_____ 13. Hunger and thirst are good examples of drives that fit the homeostatic mechanism approach, because they

a. initiate behavior to restore the balance of substances in the blood

b. are both necessary to sustain life

c. operate through both internal and external cues

d. are common to all species

_____ 14. Humans have more trouble than animals do in maintaining a regular weight throughout their lifetime, primarily because

a. human diets are less natural and thus confuse the control mechanisms

b. with evolution, the LH and VMH centers have become less well developed

c. human eating is more strongly influenced by social and emotional factors

d. by wearing clothes humans distort the temperature mechanism for controlling diet

_____ 15. Injured persons who have lost a lot of blood help us to understand the mechanisms of

_____ by the fact that they

_____ .

a. thirst, are intensely thirsty

b. hunger and thirst, are neither hungry nor thirsty

c. obesity, will overeat if allowed to

d. pain, are less sensitive to it

_____ 16. Incentive theory adds to our understanding of motivation and helps explain some problems of drive-reduction theory by

a. focusing attention on the motivational effects of external stimuli

b. providing an explanation for seeking the thrills of horror movies or roller-coaster rides

c. looking at the interaction between bodily states and environmental stimuli

d. all of the above

_____ 17. Subjects who experienced experimental sensory deprivation

a. became bored, restless, irritable, and upset

b. found it created a soothingly altered state of consciousness akin to meditation

c. were often better able to concentrate on problems in the absence of distractions

d. experienced subjective time distortions, but gave no evidence of this in the pattern of their response to the experimenters

_____ 18. When obese subjects were tricked into thinking that the time was 6:05 instead of 5:35, they

a. were affected by it, while normal subjects were not

b. ate more crackers

c. reported more frequent hunger pangs

d. all of the above

_____ 19. Study of neural mechanisms for the control of sexual behavior have shown us the complexity of such control. For example, it has been found that

a. men with severed spinal cords can have erections and ejaculate

b. male rats stimulated electrically in the hypothalamus will indiscriminately mount any available partner

c. male monkeys can be switched from eating to sexual behavior by switching electrodes in the posterior hypothalamus

d. all of the above

_____ 20. It is true that

a. most transsexuals are homosexuals

b. most transsexuals are males

c. most homosexuals are transsexuals

d. most transsexuals are bisexual

KEY TO SELF-QUIZ

1. b p. 281	6. d p. 311	11. a p. 311	16. d p. 285	
2. d p. 283	7. c p. 282	12. c p. 309	17. a p. 311	
3. b p. 283	8. c p. 288	13. a p. 283	18. b p. 294	
4. d p. 297	9. b p. 289	14. c p. 289	19. a p. 302	
5. c p. 304	10. d p. 301	15. a p. 298	20. b p. 307	

INDIVIDUAL EXERCISE

CUES FOR EATING

Introduction

Human beings share aspects of such basic motives as hunger with other species, but they also eat for a variety of other reasons: the odor or sight of food acting as an incentive, social customs, personal habits, and so forth. As the text notes, overweight individuals seem to eat more in response to external cues and less to internal cues than normal-weight subjects. Whether you consider yourself to be overweight or simply desire to maintain a well-balanced diet, it is instructive to pay some attention to what, when, and why you eat. One way to do this is to keep a journal or diary of food intake.

Procedure

The easiest way to keep such records is to first develop a one-page form that you can use for each day's food intake. The top of the page should include the date and any other data you might wish to analyze later, for example, day of the week, weather (including temperature), amount of sleep the night before, amount of exercise, and so forth. The main part of the form should have column headings for the primary data—time, food eaten, and hunger pangs or other cues relevant to eating. It might also be useful to include a few additional headings, for example, your location, your activity, other people around, and your mood. If you are serious about some form of diet—to lose or gain weight, or for other reasons—it is probably best also to include spaces for calories eaten as well as any other food components you wish to control, for example, fats or carbohydrates.

Try the first version of your form for a day or two to see if it meets your needs. When you have arrived at an appropriate form, duplicate a supply of them; arrange to fill it in every day, without fail. Add up whatever data you wish to analyze (for example, number of meals and total calories) daily and in a weekly summary. Also try to summarize in a few words the cues for each eating episode and categorize them as internal or external.

Initially, you may not find any obvious pattern, but keep at it for a while. Most people quickly discover patterns in their eating behavior that they were not previously aware of. Even if you do not wish to change the eating habits you discover, you will be learning more about yourself.

As you monitor yourself in this way, you are actually taking the first step of a self-modification program; such programs play an important role in behavior therapy (see Chapter 16 of the text). The next steps involve choosing some aspect(s) of your eating behavior that you wish to change and setting up a personal reward system to shape the desired behavior. If you are interested in such a program, an excellent reference is *Human behavior: Analysis and application,* from which the sample record form and self-management contracts on the following pages are taken. Other references on self-modification of behavior are also noted below.

References

1. Mahoney, M. J., and Thoresen, C. E. (1974) *Self-control: Power to the person.* Monterey, Calif.: Brooks/Cole.

2. Reese, E. P., Howard, J., and Reese, T. W. (1978) *Human behavior: Analysis and application.* Dubuque, Iowa: Wm. C. Brown.

3. Thoresen, C. E., and Mahoney, M. J. (1974) *Behavioral self-control.* New York: Holt, Rinehart and Winston.

4. Watson, D. L., and Tharp, R. G. (1977) *Self-directed behavior: Self-modification for personal adjustment* (2nd ed.) Monterey, Calif.: Brooks/Cole.

EXAMPLE OF DAILY RECORD FORM USED IN SELF-MANAGEMENT OF WEIGHT

Day _Th_ Date _10/11_ WEIGHT _138_ GOAL _118_   CALORIES, eaten _3828_

Baseline _X_ Program _____ Maintenance _____   Calories, exercise _100_

Amt. sleep last night _6 h._ Weather _cold_   Total meals _____ 7

Time	Place	Activity	People	Mood	Amount	FOOD	Calories	Sum
7:30	Dorm	Breakfast	People?	bitchy	1 1 1 2	o.j. h.s. egg revolting coffee w. t.s. toast butter	120 78 40 210	} 448
10:30	College Inn	break	Debbie, Neal Dinny, Barb	BORED	1 1	Danish coffee	125 40	165
Noon	Dorm	lunch	Jill, Pearl Eva, Stephanie	OK	1 1 2	milk spaghetti cake ☺	160 couldn't eat 500	} 660
4:30	Snack bar	after lab	Ed, David, Jerrilynn	Ravenous	1 1	cheeseburger Fr. fries (make up for lunch)	470 250	720
6:30	Dorm	dinner	Jerri, Betsy Denise, Chip, Cathy	good	2 1 2 1	meat (lamb?) peas sm. potatoes choc. ice cream	470 115 120 100	} 805
10:30	Snack bar	a well-deserved break	Tim & Marci Andy, Richard Skye & Talley TOM	tired	2 1	beer sm. potato chips	300 230	530
11-12	Room	studying	Rhea for a while; Esther & Madeleine came by	zonked	½	box (maybe 10?) choc. chip cookies	500?	500

448
465
1365
1835
3828

Total meals ___7___ Total Cal. _3828_

EXERCISE

Moderate (200/hr; 33/10 min)		Vigorous (300/hr; 50/10 min)		Strenuous (400/hr; 70/10 min)	
Walking (slow)	_15_	Walking (3 mph)	_10_	Stren. sports	____
Bicycling	____	Horseback riding	____	Dancing (fast)	____
House work	____	Bowling	____	Jogging	____
	____	Swimming	____		____

Total time _15_ Cal. _50_   Time _10_ Cal. _50_   Time ____ Cal. ____

COMMENTS: _This was not a good day_

SELF-MANAGEMENT CONTRACT FOR WEIGHT CONTROL

Name: _____ General Goal: 20 lb. weight loss _____

Duration of Contract (dates) Oct 4 to Oct 11. Program ✓ Maintenance _____

Data
  Keep daily ✓ or _____ records of:

  weight _____ extra exercise (time) _____

  calories _____ _____

  # between meal snacks _____ _____

  Data will be analysed and plotted: every night _____

Program
  Behavior   Consequences
    Keep records at 5 pts each; 10 pt graph   30 pts
    1600 cal. weekdays; 1800 weekends (2 days)   50
    only 2 snacks a day: Total 300 cal. (500 weekend)   10
    Eat at least 2 balanced meals a day   10
    Exercise 15 min/day (during week)   10

  Stimulus control
    No food in room   10
    Eat only with someone, in regular place   10

  Alternative behavior (if applicable) when feel urge to eat, remember Richard can
    wear my jeans and I can't Resist urge —
    think "gorgeous me"
  Covert (behavior, consequences)

                          If points, possible daily total   130

  Bonus?
    50 points each pound lost
    200 "free" calories if stay within limit whole week

Exchange
          Reinforcers   (Aversive Consequences?)
  movies, TV, reading etc - 10 pts/hr   Point cost: 1 pt each 10 cal.
  shower — 10 pts   over limit
  weekend away - 100 pts   Also: if 200 cal. over,
  gas for car -   10 pts   tell Richard I blew it
  clothes - 100 pts per $10.00 worth   if 300 cal. over, all calls
                                                 from pay phone for a
                                                 week

  Signature _____ Date _____

11

Human Motivation and Emotion

LEARNING OBJECTIVES

11-1. Be familiar with Maslow's hierarchy of motives and Freud's psychoanalytic theory of motivation.

11-2. Know the major concepts of the social learning theory of motivation.

11-3. Be able to discuss the idea of aggression as a drive. Be familiar with research on aggressive crime and brain-stimulated aggression in animals.

11-4. Be able to discuss the social learning theory of aggression as a learned response. Be familiar with the research concerning imitation and reinforcement of aggression; be able to show how the findings do or do not support a social learning theory.

11-5. Understand the concept of aggression as cathartic and the implications of such a concept.

11-6. Be familiar with the problems in classifying emotions and know which aspects of emotion are controlled by the sympathetic and parasympathetic systems.

11-7. Be able to explain the James-Lange theory of emotion. Understand Cannon's objections to the James-Lange theory and be able to show how the Cannon-Bard theory differs. Know the current view concerning the difference between these theories.

11-8. Understand the influences on felt emotions of differences in body arousal and in cognitions. Be familiar with Schachter's study of these variables and be able to show how his cognitive-physiological theory of emotion combines them.

11-9. Be able to discuss the contributions of maturation and learning in emotional expression.

11-10. Be able to discuss the optimal level of arousal and the negative consequences of arousal that is not optimal.

1. Human beings engage in a vast variety of complex activities. Physiological motives, as we saw in the preceding chapter, can account for some of these activities. But many of our motives are *psychological*; they are learned in interaction with other people and are little influenced by biological needs. Security, self-esteem, and

motives   acceptance by others are important psychological _____ .

physiological   2. Hunger is a _____ motive, while the need to feel

psychological   competent is a _____ motive.

biological   3. Psychological motives are influenced primarily by learning and the kind of society
(or physiological)
                      in which the individual is raised rather than by _____ needs.

                  4. Not all societies consider it important for a person to acquire wealth or material

psychological   goods. Consequently, we assume that avarice is a _____ ,
                      rather than a physiological, motive.

                  5. Of the numerous motivational theories, the text discusses two: *psychoanalytic*
                      theory and *social learning theory*. Psychoanalytic theory, which originated
                      with Freud, views human actions as determined by internal impulses that are
                      often unconscious. The idea of unconscious motivation is important to

psychoanalytic   _____ theory.

                  6. When a person engages in behavior but is *not* aware of the real reason for the behav-
                      ior, he or she is directed by *unconscious* motivation. If you meet a stranger and dis-

unconscious   like him or her at first sight, there are probably _____
                      motives operating, especially if you are unaware of why you do not like the
                      individual.

                  7. If you are not aware of the real reason for your behavior, we say that the motiva-

unconscious   tion is _____ .

                  8. Freud believed that unconscious motives reveal themselves in several ways. In
                      dreams the dreamer often expresses desires of which he or she is unaware. *Dreams,*

unconscious   then, are one way in which _____ motives may be ex-
                      pressed.

                  9. *Slips of speech* may also reveal unconscious motives. While expressing sympathy,
                      John says to his ailing sister, "I regret that you will soon be well." His speech slip

unconscious   may express _____ hostile feelings toward her.

slips of speech 10. Dreams and _____ _____ _____ are two ways in which hid-

motives   den or unconscious _____ may be expressed.

                 11. Freud believed that the two basic drives or instincts that motivate human behavior

are sex and aggression. Because parents and society place certain taboos on the child's expression of sexual or aggressive impulses, these impulses are often *repressed* from conscious awareness. They remain active only as _____

unconscious

motives.

sex, aggression (either order)

12. According to psychoanalytic theory, the two most important sources of motivation are _____ and _____ .

13. Because of taboos on the expression of sex and aggression, such impulses may be

repressed

banished from awareness, or re_____ .

14. Repressed impulses remain active as unconscious motives and may find expression

dreams, speech

indirectly in _____ or slips of _____ .

15. A father resents the time and attention his wife devotes to their young son. His resentment leads to aggressive feelings toward the child. But since it is not considered acceptable to feel or express aggression towards one's offspring, these feelings re-

unconscious

main largely un_____ .

16. A second theory of motivation, *social learning theory,* proposes that much of human motivation is *learned* through coping with the social environment as the individual grows. Psychoanalytic theory maintains that behavior is motivated by instinctual drives. Social learning theory, in contrast, claims that many motives are

learned

not innate but are _____ .

17. Behavior patterns that are *rewarded* will tend to be repeated, while those that produce unfavorable results will be discarded. This is the basic premise of social

learning

_____ theory.

18. Every time Margaret, who is four, strikes out in anger, her mother hastens to placate her with a cookie or toy. When she enters kindergarten, Margaret is the most aggressive child in the class. Aggressive behavior patterns have been

rewarded (or reinforced)

re_____ .

learned

19. In this case it is clear that Margaret's aggressiveness is (*learned/innate*).

20. Not all behavior is learned directly. Many behavior patterns are learned by watching the behavior of others and observing its consequences for them. This is called *vicarious learning.* Mary observes that every time her older brother takes out the garbage, mother praises him. Mary begins to take out the garbage. Her learning in this case is

vicarious

_____ because she was not rewarded herself but observed someone else being rewarded.

21. Vicarious learning saves a lot of time. We don't have to experiment with different behaviors and determine whether they produce reward or punishment. Instead, we can observe their consequences for other people and *model* our behavior after

social learning

theirs. Vicarious learning is an important principle of (*social learning/psychoanalytic*) theory.

22. The motivation of aggression is of great concern to psychologists. Some distinguish between *hostile aggression* and *instrumental aggression*. Hostile _____ is designed solely to inflict injury. Instrumental aggression is aimed at obtaining rewards other than the victim's suffering.

aggression

23. A young man shot a store clerk during a robbery. This would probably be called _____ aggression.

instrumental

24. However, the distinction between instrumental aggression and _____ aggression is not always clear-cut. Several motives may be involved in any aggressive act.

hostile

25. Quite different explanations of aggression are proposed by psychoanalytic theory and social _____ theory. As we have seen, Freud considered aggression to be one of the two basic _____. The other was _____.

learning

instincts (or drives)

sex

26. Freud believed that aggression was an innate drive. Later psychoanalytic theorists proposed that aggression was a drive produced by frustration. The *frustration-aggression hypothesis* states that when a person is thwarted in efforts to reach a goal, that person will display _____ toward the source of this frustration.

aggression

27. According to the frustration-aggression hypothesis, aggression (*is/is not*) innate. But since all of us encounter frustration in our daily existence, an aggressive drive is fairly universal.

is not

28. In contrast, social learning theory views aggression as a learned response rather than either an innate or a frustration-_____ drive.

produced

29. According to social learning theory, aggression is (*innate/learned*). Frustration produces an unpleasant emotion; how the individual responds to this emotion depends on the kinds of responses he or she has found successful in coping with stress in the past.

learned

30. Whenever Judy is thwarted she runs to mother, who always solves the problem. In the future, Judy will probably respond with (*aggressive/dependent*) behavior when frustrated.

dependent

31. Psychoanalytic theory sees aggression as a (*drive/learned response*), while social learning theory views aggression as a (*drive/learned response*).

drive
learned response

32. Studies have shown that children will imitate aggressive behavior they see modeled by an adult, especially if they are reinforced for doing so. These findings lend support to the (*psychoanalytic/social learning*) theory of aggression.

social learning

33. If aggression is a drive, then releasing pent-up aggressive feelings should be *cathartic*: expressing aggression should decrease the person's need to aggress. You might expect this view to be proposed by (*psychoanalytic/social learning*) theorists.

psychoanalytic

34. If the expression of aggression is c_____, then hitting a person who has angered you should (*increase/decrease*) your feelings of anger.

cathartic
decrease

35. Studies of children indicate, however, that behaving aggressively does not reduce aggressive behavior, and may even increase it. These findings (*do/do not*) support the idea that expressing aggression is cathartic.

36. When college students are given the opportunity to shock a subject in a laboratory experiment, they give progressively stronger shocks as the trials progress. Acting aggressively appears to increase subsequent aggression. This fails to support the view

that expressing aggression is _____ .

37. Some officials of the television industry defend violent television programs on the grounds that expressing aggression vicariously (by observing violence) is beneficial; viewers discharge their aggressive impulses through viewing and thus become less likely to perform aggressive acts. In light of what we have said about catharsis and about the imitation of aggressive acts, such a claim is probably (*true/false*). The text discusses several ways in which exposure to filmed violence may elicit aggressive behavior.

38. Motivation and emotion are closely related. Emotions can activate and direct behavior in the same way as biological or psychological _____ . When we talk about motivation we usually focus on the goal-directed activity; in discussing emotion our attention is drawn to the subjective, affective experiences that accompany the behavior.

39. Most emotions can be classified according to whether they are *pleasant* or *unpleasant*. Joy and love would be considered pleasant emotions, while anger and fear would be classed as _____ .

40. Emotions can also be scaled according to the *intensity* of the experience. Rage and panic would be classified as intensely un_____ affective states, ecstasy and joy as _____ pleasant emotions.

41. Intense emotions are accompanied by widespread *bodily changes*. Most of these changes are controlled by the *sympathetic division* of the *autonomic nervous system,* which prepares the body for emergency action. The increased heart and respiration rate and the elevated blood-sugar level that occur when one is frightened result from activity of the _____ division of the autonomic _____ system.

42. In fear, also, blood is diverted from the stomach and intestines and sent to the brain and skeletal muscles. These changes prepare the body for _____ action. They result from activity of the (*sympathetic/parasympathetic*) division of the _____ nervous system.

43. Because emotions are accompanied by widespread _____ changes, it might be possible to classify emotions according to the bodily responses involved. If a person always became red-faced and breathed rapidly when angry and became

pale and breathed slowly when afraid, these differences in bodily _____ might prove a useful means of distinguishing between anger and _____ .

44. Unfortunately, attempts to differentiate emotions on the basis of _____ changes have not proved very successful. The physiological symptoms of the different emotions vary from one individual to the next, and there is considerable overlap between the symptoms. The face may flush during fear as readily as during anger. Hence redness of the face (*would/would not*) be a useful measure for distinguishing between the two emotions.

would not

45. The problem of distinguishing among emotional states is further complicated because the *situation* in which the bodily _____ of emotion occur will often influence how the person *labels* the emotion.

changes (or responses)

46. For example, if subjects are given a drug that produces profound bodily changes, they may tend to label their emotional state in accordance with the behavior of those around them. If their fellow subjects are acting in a joyous and euphoric manner, they may label their emotional state as euphoria; if their fellow subjects are expressing angry feelings, they may tend to _____ their emotion as anger.

label

47. The label that a person attaches to the bodily changes of emotion depends to some extent upon the s_____ in which these changes occur. Situational factors influence how a person will _____ his or her emotional state.

situation

label

48. One of the earliest theories of emotion was the *James-Lange theory*, which proposed that what we feel as emotional is the *feedback* from the bodily changes. According to the _____-Lange theory, we see a wildcat, start to run, and then experience the emotion we call fear.

James

49. The notion that the feeling of sorrow results from the tears that flow when a person hears tragic news is a statement of the _____-_____ theory of emotion.

James-Lange

50. The James-Lange theory maintains that emotion is defined by _____ responses that are perceived and labeled after they occur. The experience of emotion is fe_____ from the bodily changes.

bodily

feedback

51. An alternative explanation of emotion, the Cannon-Bard theory, proposes that the bodily changes and the experience of emotion occur at the same time. According to the Cannon-Bard theory of _____, "butterflies" in the stomach and the felt emotion of fear occur together; the brain and the sympathetic nervous system are aroused simultaneously by an emotion-producing situation.

emotion

52. Because an emotional experience is not a momentary event but takes place over time, it is difficult to determine whether the physiological responses precede or accompany the emotion. When you are suddenly confronted with possible danger (for example, a loud sound that might be an explosion, a narrowly avoided accident), your pounding heart and feeling of weakness in the knees may precede full awareness of the danger. In this instance the (*James-Lange/Cannon-Bard*) theory of emotion is correct.

James-Lange

53. More often, however, physiological arousal follows the appraisal of a situation as dangerous. You realize that the gray shape behind the door is not a shadow but a man with a gun; the emotional experience of fear precedes or occurs at the same

Cannon-Bard   time as the autonomic activity. In this case the (*James-Lange/Cannon-Bard*) theory
                     is correct.

54. Regardless of what point in the emotional sequence bodily changes have their effect,
    they influence the *intensity* with which we experience emotion. Even though fear
    cannot be differentiated from anger on the basis of the kind of bodily changes that
    occur, the intensity with which we feel either emotion is dependent on the degree

bodily   of _____ changes or arousal.

55. People whose spinal cords have been injured so that they receive no sensations from
    the internal organs report that their experience of emotion is less intense than it
    was before their injury. Feedback from internal bodily changes is important to the

intensity   _____ of the emotional experience.

56. *Cognitive factors* also influence our conscious experience of emotion. We noted
    earlier that the label a person attaches to an emotion depends on the situation in
    which the physiological arousal occurs. The *cognitive-physiological theory* of emo-
    tion proposes that emotional states depend on the interaction of physiological

cognitive   arousal with cog_____ processes.

intensity   57. Physiological arousal is important to the _____ with which
cognitive   we experience an emotion. But _____ factors determine how
                    we interpret the emotional experience.

physiological   58. The cognitive-_____ theory of emotion assumes
                    that how we interpret the situation that causes physiological arousal will determine
                    the label we attach to the emotion.

cognitive   59. According to the _____-physiological theory, emotional states
cognitive   depend on the interaction of physiological arousal with _____
                    processes.

60. Studies have shown that a person's emotional response to a stressful situation (as
    measured by bodily changes) can be increased or decreased depending on the inter-
    pretation of the situation. This shows that emotional reactions are influenced by

cognitive   _____ factors.

James   61. The two theories of emotion discussed earlier, the _____-Lange and
Cannon   _____-Bard theories, are concerned with how the emotion-producing
                    stimuli and internal bodily changes interact to produce an emotional experience. A
                    third theory, which focuses on the way the individual interprets the emotion-

cognitive-physiological   producing situation, is the _____-_____
                    theory of emotion.

62. Some of the ways in which we express emotions are *innate,* appearing at birth or
    developing through *maturation.* As soon as infants are born they can cry. Crying is
    thus an innate expression of emotion. A six-month-old infant will laugh when

innate   mother smiles or makes funny faces. Laughing is thus an inborn, or _____,
maturation   expression of emotion. But it requires a period of mat_____
                    before it appears.

63. We are born with the capacity to cry and develop the ability to laugh through

maturation   _____, but we *learn* to modify our emotional expressions to conform to the patterns of our *culture*.

64. In our society women express sorrow by crying; men usually inhibit their tears.

culture   This is an example of the influence of one's c_____ on emotional expression.

65. As adults we are more apt to express our anger verbally than by hitting. This is

learning   another example of l_____ to modify our emotional expressions

culture   to conform to the patterns of our _____.

66. Some expressions of emotion are innate; they appear at birth or develop through

maturation, innate   _____. Crying and laughing are examples of _____

learning   emotional expressions. But _____ is important in modifying our emotional expressions.

67. How do emotions affect our performance? When they are mild, they keep us alert and interested in what we are doing. But intense emotions, whether pleasant or unpleasant, generally disrupt performance, making it less effective. If you are experiencing an intense emotion, your performance on a complex task will probably be

impaired   (*impaired/improved*).

68. Emotional states that are prolonged may lead to actual illness. A *psychosomatic illness* is one in which the symptoms are physical but the cause may lie in the person's *emotional* life. If continued worry over your job causes you to have high

psychosomatic   blood pressure, then this illness is considered psycho_____.

69. In psychosomatic illness the symptoms are physical but the cause may lie in the

emotional   person's em_____ life.

psychosomatic   **70.** Asthma, ulcers, and headaches are considered _____ when they are caused primarily by emotional stress.

TERMS AND CONCEPTS

psychological motives _____

_____

_____

_____

hierarchy of motives _____

_____

_____

_____

psychoanalytic theory of motivation _____

_____

_____

_____

life instincts _____

_____

_____

_____

death instincts _____

_____

_____

_____

repression _____

_____

_____

_____

unconscious motives _____

_____

_____

_____

social learning theory of motivation _____

_____

_____

vicarious learning _____

_____

_____

_____

models _____

_____

_____

_____

self-regulation _____

_____

_____

_____

instrumental aggression _____

_____

_____

_____

frustration-aggression hypothesis _____

_____

_____

_____

polygraph* _____

_____

_____

_____

James-Lange theory _____

_____

_____

_____

Cannon-Bard theory _____

_____

_____

_____

cognitive-physiological theory _____

_____

_____

psychosomatic illness _____

_____

_____

*Indicates terms used in Critical Discussions

SELF-QUIZ

_____ 1. Some psychologists distinguish between two forms of aggression. They would call assault committed during a robbery _____ aggression.
   a. instrumental
   b. secondary
   c. hostile
   d. conditioned

_____ 2. Freud believed in two opposing groups of instincts, which he felt were represented by behaviors that reflect
   a. dependency and sex
   b. sex and aggression
   c. dependency and aggression
   d. affiliation and dominance

_____ 3. According to social learning theorists, reinforcement has two basic sources, _____ and _____, which sometimes coincide and sometimes conflict.
   a. external, self-evaluative
   b. family, peers
   c. motives, incentives
   d. sexuality, aggression

_____ 4. In addition to taking a more generally cognitive position than strict behaviorists, social learning advocates stress the importance of _____ learning, that is, learning by _____.
   a. operant, reinforcement
   b. vicarious, observation
   c. latent, nonreinforced trials
   d. self-discovery, doing

_____ 5. According to Freud, motives that cannot be expressed openly are repressed and remain active as unconscious motives. Such unconscious motives are believed to be shown by
   a. slips of speech
   b. symptoms of mental illness
   c. dreams
   d. all of the above

_____ 6. The frustration-aggression hypothesis
   a. assumes that aggression is a basic instinct
   b. claims that frustration and aggression are both instinctive patterns
   c. assumes that frustration produces aggression
   d. was developed by social learning theorists

_____ 7. From a psychologist's viewpoint, much of the controversy over whether aggressive behavior should be displayed on television centers on the question of whether it is
   a. cathartic as opposed to stimulating aggressive acts
   b. frightening to children
   c. excessively violent
   d. justified by the circumstances

_____ 8. The James-Lange theory of emotion says that
   a. the thalamus has the central role in arousal
   b. we are afraid because we run
   c. perception of the emotion leads to physiological changes
   d. all of the above

_____ 9. Social learning theory proposes that aggression
   a. is instinctive
   b. results from an aggressive drive
   c. results from frustration
   d. is no different from any other learned response

_____ 10. Researchers studying the influence of television aggression on children found that watching violent television programs increased aggressive behavior in boys but not in girls. This difference may be related to the fact that
   a. girls in our socity are seldom reinforced for aggression
   b. most of the aggressive television models are male
   c. in general, girls in our society imitate aggression less than boys
   d. all of the above

_____ 11. Psychologists have in the past devoted much effort to trying to classify emotions. A classification that has proved useful is to divide emotions into _____ and _____.
   a. arousing, soothing
   b. innate, learned
   c. pleasant, unpleasant
   d. all of the above

_____ 12. Studies have shown that observation of _____ aggression greatly increases the likelihood of actual aggressive behavior.
   a. live modeled
   b. filmed

c. either a or b

d. neither a nor b

_____ 13. The facial expressions, postures, and gestures used by children blind from birth to express emotion

a. often develop appropriately through maturation

b. are unlike those of normal children

c. resemble the simple movements of an infant

d. must be carefully taught to them by others

_____ 14. Which of the following is *not* a true statement regarding emotional arousal level and performance?

a. The optimum level of arousal differs for different tasks.

b. Individuals are very similar in the extent to which their behavior is disrupted by arousal.

c. Intense arousal can seriously impair the performance of organized behavior.

d. Performance is optimal at moderate levels of arousal.

_____ 15. Most of the physiological changes that occur during intense emotion result from activation of the

a. sympathetic system

b. parasympathetic system

c. thalamic system

d. thalamus

_____ 16. Schachter's cognitive-physiological theory of emotion states that

a. cognitions give rise to the physiology of emotion

b. physiological responses create the cognitions in emotions

c. cognitions are involved in some emotions, physiological responses in others

d. cognitions and physiological responses interact to form emotions

_____ 17. In a psychosomatic illness,

a. continued emotional tension is the cause

b. the cause is primarily psychological

c. the symptoms are physical

d. all of the above

_____ 18. The concept of an aggressive drive is supported in the popular media by accounts of explosive outbursts in meek individuals such as Charles Whitman. Investigation of such episodes _____ this concept, noting that _____.

a. confirms, the stories are well founded

b. contradicts, these people have previously been aggressive

c. is unable to confirm or deny, the evidence is mixed

d. supports, more often than not it is an accurate summary

_____ 19. When veterans with spinal-cord injuries were interviewed about their emotions, it was found that the _____ the lesion, the more emotionality _____ following injury.

a. lower, increased

b. lower, decreased

c. higher, decreased

d. higher, increased

_____ 20. Maslow aided our understanding of the relationships among motives by

a. pointing out that psychological motives are based on physiological needs

b. describing them in terms of vicarious learning and self-control techniques

c. arranging them in a hierarchy, from biological ones to more complex psychological ones

d. showing the importance of instinctive aggressive patterns in more complex motives

KEY TO SELF-QUIZ

1. a p.319	6. c p.330	11. c p.320	16. d p.336
2. b p.317	7. a p.326	12. c p.324	17. d p.342
3. a p.317	8. b p.331	13. a p.339	18. b p.320
4. b p.318	9. d p.322	14. b p.341	19. c p.336
5. d p.315	10. d p.317	15. a p.330	20. c p.315

INDIVIDUAL EXERCISES

MEASURING MOTIVATION

Introduction

Psychologists study motivation in many ways. In laboratory studies, precise instruments that measure physiological responses in motivated behavior can be used. However, for classroom purposes it is difficult to make the necessary arrangements to measure physiological changes. For that reason the sentence-completion test that follows has been chosen. Many psychologists feel that it has clinical value in the study of personal adjustment.

Procedure

Below are 50 incomplete sentences. Take about 30 minutes to complete all the sentences. Try not to omit any item. Be sure to express your real feelings. The results will be more valuable if you write down thoughts that occur to you spontaneously, as soon as you see the first word or words of each item. You will be the only person to score the test and to see the results. Therefore, try to be frank and honest by writing the first thought that comes to mind.

After completing the test, score your sentences according to the directions given on page 297 of the Appendix.

1. College _____

_____

_____

2. I need _____

_____

_____

3. My nerves _____

_____

_____

4. Women _____

_____

_____

5. Secretly, I _____

_____

_____

6. My father _____

_____

_____

7. I wish _____

_____

_____

8. I'm afraid _____

_____

_____

9. People _____

_____

_____

10. The future _____

_____

_____

11. I worry about _____

_____

_____

12. Men _____

_____

_____

13. I know _____

_____

_____

14. At night _____

_____

_____

15. Marriage _____

_____

_____

16. My mother _____

_____

_____

17. If I could _____

_____

_____

18. My studies _____

_____

_____

19. My friends _____

_____

_____

20. I get annoyed _____

_____

_____

21. I daydream about _____

_____

_____

22. There are times when _____

_____

_____

23. My feelings _____

_____

_____

24. My goal _____

_____

_____

25. I find it difficult _____

_____

_____

26. Most of my friends _____

_____

_____

27. I know it is silly but _____

_____

_____

28. When I was a youngster _____

_____

_____

29. When I marry _____

_____

_____

30. My father thinks my mother _____

_____

_____

31. My family _____

_____

_____

32. I would do anything to forget _____

_____

_____

33. A real friend _____

_____

_____

34. Most of my friends don't know _____

_____

_____

35. I think a mother _____

_____

_____

36. I could be happy if _____

_____

_____

37. Ten years from now _____

_____

_____

38. Most of all, I _____

_____

_____

39. Sex _____

_____

_____

40. Compared with others, I _____

_____

_____

41. I can't understand _____

_____

_____

42. My father and I _____

_____

_____

43. Dating _____

_____

_____

44. My mother thinks my father _____

_____

_____

45. What I want most _____

_____

_____

46. My mother and I _____

_____

_____

47. My biggest fault _____

_____

_____

48. Sometimes I _____

_____

_____

49. My dreams _____

_____

_____

50. My appearance _____

_____

_____

Questions for Discussion

1. Does your score place you above or below the median? What does this mean?

2. Which items were most difficult for your to complete? Why?

3. Does your score correspond to your own evaluation of your adjustment?

4. Does the test reveal some of your current difficulties? Why or why not?

5. How might a clinical psychologist find your responses helpful in diagnosing your difficulties?

6. What are some of the cautions that should be observed in interpreting the results?

THE COIN-FLIP DECISION MAKER

Equipment Needed

A coin

Procedure

1. This procedure allows you to "focus" on your emotional responses when you are conflicted or confused about a decision. You have weighed the pros and cons but cannot decide on the evidence alone; you wonder just how you would really *feel* after deciding one way or the other. Next time you have this problem, try the coin technique, as follows.

2. Take out your coin and tell yourself that you will let a flip of the coin determine the decision. Put one choice on heads, the other on tails, and flip the coin.

3. The instant the coin lands and you realize what the outcome is, pay special attention to your own reaction. Do you hear a sigh of relief? Or a still small voice asking, "Two out of three?"

4. Frivolous as it may seem, such a technique may be useful. It appears to provide an instant role-playing situation, in which you sense how you would really feel if the decision had been made for you, rather than trying to predict your feelings through logic alone.

12
Mental Abilities and Their Measurement

LEARNING OBJECTIVES

12-1. Understand the distinction between aptitude and achievement tests.

12-2. Be able to specify the difference between reliability and validity and why each is necessary for a test to be trustworthy.

12-3. Know the assumptions underlying Binet's development of a mental-age scale of intelligence. Be able to describe how items are chosen for such a scale.

12-4. Understand the computation and interpretation of contemporary IQ scores, including the Stanford-Binet and Wechsler scales.

12-5. Be able to describe how factor-analysis techniques have been used by Spearman and Thurstone to separate the different abilities that contribute to intelligence.

12-6. Understand the difference between divergent and convergent thinking; show how this difference is important in the relationship between intelligence and creativity.

12-7. Be able to specify how intelligence scores change over a person's lifetime, including initial variability, later stability, and the possibility of subsequent decline.

12-8. Be familiar with the evidence for genetic and environmental contributions to intelligence. Understand what a heritability estimate does and does not tell you.

12-9. Be able to discuss the classification, causes, and treatment of the mentally subnormal. Be familiar with Terman's study of gifted children.

12-10. Know what the public concerns about psychological testing are and what psychologists think about these concerns.

PROGRAMMED UNIT

1. Individuals differ in *intelligence, knowledge,* and *skills.* In order to match the talents of each person to the appropriate job, we need some way of assessing or measuring his or her abilities. *Ability testing* is one way of assessing individual

   skills

   differences in intelligence, knowledge, and _____.

2. The study of individual differences in intelligence, knowledge, and skills is often

   ability testing

   carried on by means of _____ _____.

3. In attempting to appraise an individual's abilities, psychologists distinguish between what a person can do now and what the person might do if trained. Tests that identify what you can do now, or skills already accomplished, are *achievement tests.* Ben has had two years of typing instruction in high school. If a psychologist were interested in how fast and how accurately he can type *now,* he or she would ad-

   achievement

   minister an _____ test.

4. When you take your final examination in this course, your instructor will admin-

   achievement

   ister an _____ test to find out how well you have learned the various concepts and generalizations covered in the lectures and the textbook.

5. Tests designed to measure *capacity to learn*—that is, to predict what you can accomplish with *training*—are known as *aptitude tests.* Tests designed to measure skills already attained, or what a person can do now, are called

   achievement

   _____ tests.

6. Suppose a company has fifty unskilled applicants for a job as machinist and intends to train only ten of the fifty applicants to become machinists. An industrial psychologist employed by this company would probably administer an

   aptitude

   _____ test to determine which of the fifty applicants have the greatest capacity to learn to become machinists.

7. Tests designed to measure capacity to learn—that is, to predict what one can

   aptitude

   accomplish with training—are known as _____ tests.

   capacity   8. Aptitude tests are designed to measure _____ to learn, that is,

   training   to predict what one can accomplish with _____.

9. Before lawyers are admitted to the bar, they must pass a test of knowledge and

   achievement

   understanding of legal precepts. The test they take is an (*achievement/aptitude*) test.

10. If a law school can admit only forty out of several hundred applicants, an

    aptitude

    _____ test might be administered to determine which applicants have the greatest capacity to learn to become skilled lawyers.

    achievement   11. Tests designed to measure skills already attained are called _____ tests. Tests designed to predict what one can accomplish with training or to measure capacity to learn are called _____ tests.

aptitude

12. As the text points out, the distinction between an aptitude test and an achievement test is based on the *purpose* of the test, not on its contents. For example, the Law Scholastic Aptitude Test (LSAT), used to select applicants to law school, includes a test of reading comprehension, because this is a skill one must have to be an effective lawyer. Since a reading comprehension test measures how well one has learned to read, it is actually an (*aptitude/achievement*) test. But in this case it is used as part of an aptitude test.

achievement

13. The distinction between aptitude and achievement tests is based on their _____ .

purpose

14. If test scores are to be used for scientific purposes, they must be *trustworthy*. In scientific terms this means that they must meet two requirements: *reliability* and *validity*. Test scores that are not _____ are not likely to be regarded as useful by scientists.

trustworthy

15. If they are to be regarded as trustworthy, all test scores used for scientific purposes must meet two requirements. These two requirements are *reliability* and val_____ .

validity

16. By *reliability* we mean that the scores are dependable and reproducible, that they measure *consistently* whatever it is they measure. To be regarded as trustworthy, test scores must have both _____ and _____ .

reliability
validity (either order)

17. Test scores that measure consistently are said to have the characteristic of _____ , since the scores are dependable and reproducible.

reliability

18. Few of us would want to use a ruler made of rubber, because the measurements could vary considerably from one measurement to the next and would not give consistent and reproducible results. Such measurements would lack _____ .

reliability

19. A steel ruler, however, should give us consistent, dependable, and reproducible results from one measurement to the next and would therefore have the characteristic of _____ .

reliability

20. Psychologist X has developed a new intelligence test, which she had administered to a large group of students. She administered the same test twice to the same group of students and found that the pattern of scores on the second test compared quite closely to the pattern on the first test. Because her test gave consistent results, which are dependable and reproducible, her test presumably has _____ .

reliability

21. By reliability we mean that the scores are dependable and reproducible, that they measure _____ whatever it is they measure.

consistently

22. By *validity* we mean that the test scores measure what the tester *intended* to measure. For instance, if your instructor desires to measure what you have learned in this course and the test does measure your actual achievement, the test has the

validity   characteristic of _____.

23. If your instructor desires to measure knowledge achieved in the course, but the test measures your intelligence rather than your achievement, the test is not measuring

validity   what it is intended to measure and it therefore would lack _____.

24. By validity we mean that the test scores measure what the tester

intended   _____ to measure.

reliability)

25. By _____ we mean that the scores measure consistently

validity   whatever it is they measure; by _____ we mean that the scores measure what the tester intended to measure.

26. A test may be reliable but invalid. That is, a test may measure consistently yet not

intended   measure what the tester _____ to measure.

27. Suppose that a psychologist designed a new test test intended to measure intelligence. The same test was administered to the same subjects on two occasions and the scores for all subjects on both occasions were quite consistent; however, the test results correlated poorly with those of well-established intelligence tests. The new

validity   test has reliability but probably lacks _____ .

28. The psychologist, in attempting to learn how reliable the new test is, administered it twice to the same group of students. To compare the first and second sets of scores, we need to know the *degree of relationship* between the two sets of scores. This relationship is provided by the *correlation coefficient* (commonly abbreviated as r), a term already familiar to you as a measure of the degree of correspondence

coefficient   between two sets of scores. In this case, the correlation _____ between the two sets of scores is a *reliability coefficient*.

29. To estimate the degree of relationship between two sets of scores in order to find

reliability   out how reliable a test is, we need a re_____ coefficient.

30. Well-constructed psychological tests of ability commonly have reliability coefficients above $r = .90$. The psychologist who designed a new intelligence test should find an

.90 r of _____ or above for the test if it is to be considered as reliable as other well-constructed ability tests.

31. To measure *validity* we must also have two scores for each person taking the test, one being the test score and the other a score on a *criterion* of some sort. For instance, if we designed a test of ability to sell life insurance and obtained scores

criterion   for a number of persons, we would also need a _____ of some sort, which in this case might be the total value of insurance policies sold by those taking the test.

32. A criterion might be a standard selected as the goal to be achieved in a task, or a set of scores or other records against which the success of a predictive test is verified.

criterion	For instance, if effective life insurance salesmen sell at least $100,000 of insurance in a year, this figure might serve as a standard, or _____.
criterion	33. If we want to measure a test's validity, we need not only each person's score on the test, but also his or her score on a _____ of some sort.
validity	34. To measure validity we need to derive the *degree of relationship* between test scores and a criterion measure. This correlation coefficient is known as a *validity coefficient*. The correlation coefficient that tells us how well the test measures what it is supposed to measure is a (*validity/reliability*) coefficient.
validity	35. When we derive the degree of relationship between test scores and a criterion measure, we obtain a _____ coefficient.
mental	36. Alfred Binet invented the intelligence test as we know it and devised a scale of *mental age.* In Binet's system, *average* mental-age (MA) scores *correspond* to chronological age (CA), that is, to the age determined from the date of birth. Thus, a child of normal intelligence with a chronological age of 10 should have a _____ age of 10.
13	37. A child with a chronological age of 13 who has normal intelligence would also have a mental age of ____.
correspond	38. A child of normal intelligence has a mental age that will _____ to his or her chronological age.
Chronological	39. _____ age refers to the age determined from the date of birth.
below	40. A bright child's mental age is above his or her chronological age; one would expect, then, that a dull child's mental age would be _____ his or her chronological age.
mental	41. A retarded child has a _____ age below his or her chronological age.
	42. The *intelligence quotient* (IQ) is a convenient index of brightness. It expresses intelligence as a ratio of the mental age to chronological age:

$$IQ = \frac{\text{Mental Age (MA)}}{\text{Chronological age (CA)}} \times 100$$

100	The 100 is used as a multiplier to remove the decimal point and to make the average IQ have a value of 100. If a child with a chronological age of nine has a mental age of nine, the IQ, or intelligence quotient, is _____.
80	43. What is Tim's IQ if his mental age is eight and his chronological age is ten? _____
140	44. A child with an IQ *below 70* is considered *mentally subnormal*. A child with an IQ of *140 or above* is considered *gifted.* If Jill has a mental age of 14 and a chronological age of 10, her IQ would be _____.

45. Persons with IQs below _____ are considered mentally subnormal; those with IQs of _____ or above are considered gifted.

46. As the text points out, however, these cutoff points are quite arbitrary. Whether

subnormal

a person with an IQ below 70 is considered mentally _____ depends on his or her social skills and the complexity of the environment in which he or she lives. Whether a person with an IQ above 140, supposedly a

gifted

_____ individual, succeeds in using his or her ability depends largely upon social adjustment and motivation.

47. The most widely used intelligence tests are the *Stanford-Binet,* which is a revision

Binet

of the earlier test devised by Alfred _____, and the Wechsler scales—the *Wechsler Adult Intelligence Scale* (*WAIS*) and the *Wechsler Intelligence Scale for Children* (*WISC*).

Stanford

48. The _____-Binet Intelligence Test, like the earlier Binet tests, is a

mental

_____-*age scale.* It consists of a number of different items at each *age*

age

level. The number of test items passed at each _____ level determines the child's *mental-age score.*

Intelligence

49. The Wechsler scales, the Wechsler Adult _____

Children

Scale and the Wechsler Intelligence Scale for _____, are *not* mental-age scales. The individual obtains *separate* scores on twelve *subtests.*

50. Six of the subtests are *verbal,* testing such abilities as mathematical reasoning, vocab-

subtests

ulary, and recall of series of digits; the other six sub_____ are non-verbal, or *performance,* tests that involve assembling picture puzzles, manipulating blocks to form specific designs, or recognizing the missing detail in a picture.

Adult

51. The final IQ score on either the Wechsler _____ Intelligence Scale or the

Intelligence

Wechsler _____ Scale for Children is obtained

subtest

by averaging all the sub_____ scores. Separate IQ scores can be obtained for the sum of the verbal tests and the sum of the performance tests.

52. Since the Wechsler scales provide more information about a person's abilities than

age

just a single mental-_____ score, or IQ score, they are frequently used for diag-

verbal

nostic purposes. By analyzing the scores on both the _____

performance (either order)

subtests and the _____ subtests, it is possible to determine a person's special abilities and weaknesses.

mental-age

53. To recapitulate: the Stanford-Binet is a _____-_____ scale; it

does not

(*does/does not*) group test items according to type so as to permit a diagnostic analysis of different abilities. Tests that do provide separate scores for various

Wechsler

subtests are the _____ scales.

54. Christina is having trouble coping with the work in second grade. Her teacher suspects that she is quite bright but that difficulty in recognizing visual patterns hinders her reading. Of the intelligence tests we have discussed, the

Wechsler Intelligence Scale	_____ _____ _____ for
Children	_____ might provide more helpful information than the
Stanford-Binet	_____-_____.

55. What are the abilities that underlie intelligence? One method used to identify clusters of abilities that combine to make up the IQ scores obtained on tests such

Stanford-Binet   as the _____-_____ and the Wechsler scales is called *factor analysis.*

analysis   **56.** Factor _____ is a statistical procedure used to determine the *common factors* that contribute to a body of data. The same people are given a large number of tests, each individual test composed of similar items. The scores on all the tests are then intercorrelated. If two tests correlate highly with each other, they have a lot in *common* with each other. Tests that show high intercor-

common   relations have much in _____ with each other.

little   **57.** Tests that have low intercorrelations would have (*little/much*) in common with each other.

factor   **58.** This is the basic method of _____ analysis. It is a statistical procedure that provides a systematic way of finding a small number of *common factors* that can account for a large array of intercorrelations.

analysis   **59.** Factor _____ attempts to discover the underlying abilities that produce intelligence test results. In one study by Thurstone an analysis of more than sixty different tests yielded seven *primary abilities.* These primary abilities

common   were the _____ factors that emerged from the application of

factor   _____ analysis.

primary   **60.** Thurstone concluded that these _____ abilities were the basic abilities that comprise intelligence.

analysis   **61.** Other investigators, however, using factor _____ with different kinds of test items, have found many more abilities underlying intelligence than the

Thurstone   primary abilities discovered by Th_____. The number of abilities discovered depends partly on the kinds of test items used.

62. Most intelligence test items measure *convergent thinking,* that is, thinking that leads to, or "converges," on a specific *correct answer.* A test item such as "How many

convergent   eggs in a dozen?" measures con_____ thinking, since it requires a specific correct answer.

convergent   **63.** The question "What is the capital of Italy?" measures _____

correct   thinking, since it requires a specific _____ answer.

64. In problem solving, however, we often have to think of a number of *possible* solutions or answers before converging on the most appropriate one. The process of

possible   thinking of a number of p_____ solutions is called *divergent thinking*—our thoughts "diverge" along a number of different paths.

65. The question "How many uses can you think of for a paper clip?" asks for a

divergent

number of possible answers and is thus a measure of _____
thinking.

66. The item "Imagine all of the things that might happen if the force of gravity

divergent

suddenly disappeared" is a measure of _____ thinking.

correct

67. Convergent thinking is concerned with a specific _____ answer,

possible

while divergent thinking is concerned with many _____ answers.

convergent

68. Intelligence tests consist primarily of questions that require _____

convergent, divergent (either order)

thinking. Creative problem solving, however, requires both _____

and _____ thinking. We first have to think of a number of

possible

_____ solutions and then arrive at the correct one.

do not

69. You would be correct in assuming that intelligence tests (*do/do not*) provide a good
measure of creativity.

70. A question frequently debated is "How much of our intelligence is *inherited* and
how much is *acquired* through experience?" One way to find evidence on this
question is to compare the IQs of people who are *related genetically.* If people who

genetically

are related _____ are no more alike in IQ than total

acquired

strangers, then we would assume that intelligence is entirely (*inherited/acquired*).

71. Studies of this type generally have found that the closer the genetic relationship,
the more similar the IQ. Thus, the average correlation between the IQs of identical
twins is about .90, while the average correlation between the IQs of siblings who are
not twins is about .55. Since identical twins are closer genetically than ordinary
siblings (having developed from the same ovum), these results indicate that there

is

(*is/is not*) a genetic component to intelligence.

72. But if identical twins are reared from birth in different homes, the correlation between their IQs is not as high as if they were raised together. This finding points

environment

to the importance of (*heredity/environment*) in the development of intelligence.

73. Experts differ in the importance they attribute to genetic and to environmental factors in the determination of intelligence. But it is clear that

heredity

an individual's tested IQ depends on both h_____ and

environment

en_____ .

TERMS AND CONCEPTS

aptitude test _____
_____
_____
_____

achievement test _____
_____
_____
_____

intelligence test _____
_____
_____
_____

reliability _____
_____
_____
_____

validity _____
_____
_____
_____

reliability coefficient _____
_____
_____
_____

criterion of validity _____
_____
_____
_____

validity coefficient _____
_____
_____
_____

mental age _____
_____

_____

chronological age _____
_____
_____

Stanford-Binet test _____
_____
_____

culture-fair test* _____
_____
_____

basal mental age _____
_____
_____

intelligence quotient (IQ) _____
_____
_____

verbal scale _____
_____
_____

performance scale _____
_____
_____

individual IQ tests _____
_____
_____

*Indicates terms used in Critical Discussions

group IQ tests _____

_____

_____

_____

factor analysis _____

_____

_____

general intelligence factor (*g*) _____

_____

_____

special factors (*s*'s) _____

_____

_____

primary abilities _____

_____

_____

divergent thinking _____

_____

_____

_____

convergent thinking _____

_____

_____

threshold model of creativity _____

_____

_____

heritability _____

_____

_____

reaction range _____

_____

_____

mentally retarded _____

_____

_____

familial-cultural retardation _____

_____

_____

mentally defective _____

_____

_____

Down's syndrome _____

_____

_____

_____ 1. _____ developed the first tests designed to measure intelligence.
a. Alfred Binet
b. Lewis Terman
c. Sir Francis Galton
d. Louis Thurstone

_____ 2. A good test must be trustworthy, that is, it must be both reliable and valid. In considering these qualities we note that
a. a test cannot be reliable without being valid
b. valid scores are those that are reproducible
c. the reliability of scores is tested by use of criterion scores
d. scores are reliable if scores on half the test correlate highly with the other half

_____ 3. Psychologists who use the technique of factor analysis see intelligence as
a. a general capacity for comprehension and reasoning
b. a generally invalid concept
c. an array of relatively independent special abilities
d. all of the above

_____ 4. According to the intelligence quotient index suggested by Stern and adopted by Terman, IQ is computed as
a. $\frac{\text{Mental Age}}{\text{Chronological Age}} \times 100$

b. $\frac{\text{Chronological Age}}{\text{Basal Mental Age}} \times 100$

c. $\frac{\text{Basal Mental Age}}{\text{Chronological Age}} \times 100$

d. $\frac{\text{Mental Age}}{\text{Basal Mental Age}} \times 100$

_____ 5. In the contemporary versions of the Stanford-Binet tests, basal mental age is
a. set at 21 years for the adult tests
b. the level at which a child passes all items
c. computed by adding two months for every correct answer in the level above the child's own age
d. the mean level of performance for all children of a particular age

_____ 6. The Wechsler Intelligence Scales differ from the Binet tests by dividing the total test into

a. a performance scale and a verbal scale
b. an aptitude scale and an achievement scale
c. primary abilities and secondary abilities
d. convergent and divergent items

_____ 7. In studying the stability of IQ over time (that is, as one gets older), it has been found that IQ tests at age
a. 7 predict one's IQ at age 18 well
b. 2 do not predict one's IQ at age 7 well
c. 18 predict one's adult IQ well
d. all of the above

_____ 8. The proposed classification of mentally defective, as compared to mentally retarded,
a. means the same but sounds more medical
b. implies defective genetics are the cause of the problem
c. implies some identifiable defect in the nervous system
d. applies to those with IQs below 30

_____ 9. Thurstone objected to Spearman's conclusions but used his methodology, factor analysis. With it he identified
a. the general intelligence factor (g) involved in intelligence
b. seven primary mental abilities
c. 120 unique intellectual factors
d. over 30 special factors important in intelligence

_____ 10. It is important to note that heritability estimates for intelligence
a. are always above .65
b. apply to populations but not to individuals
c. imply that environmental conditions are not important
d. all of the above

_____ 11. The concepts of convergent and divergent thinking help our understanding of the complexities of intelligence testing. It has been found, for example, that
a. convergent thinking tests are a good measure of creativity
b. highly intelligent people are certain to show up as highly creative
c. divergent thinking is closely related to creativity
d. creativity is not related to intelligence

12. The most important criterion of whether an individual should be considered retarded is that individual's
   a. social competence
   b. mental age
   c. IQ
   d. ability to learn to speak

13. The National Merit Scholarship Qualifying Test
   a. is an achievement test, since it measures the effectiveness of prior schooling
   b. is an aptitude test, since it predicts success in college quite well
   c. illustrates the blurring of the distinction between aptitude and achievement tests
   d. all of the above

14. When IQ changes over a lifetime are examined for large numbers of adults, it is found that
   a. mental ability peaks at age 21, then steadily declines
   b. the decline after age 60 is very steep because most people show physical deterioration after that age
   c. some people show an increase in IQ after age 26
   d. mental abilities requiring speed tend to peak between ages 20 and 25

15. The intellectually gifted children studied by Terman were _____
   a. comparatively pale and sickly
   b. mostly ahead of their age group in school
   c. socially introverted
   d. all of the above

16. In considering public concerns about psychological testing, it is worth noting that
   a. ability tests are objective and may prevent discrimination in hiring
   b. intelligence tests are excellent predictors of success in life
   c. test scores are the only indications children have of their own intelligence
   d. all of the above

17. The assumptions of an intelligence test
   a. include the expectation that it predicts other important performances

b. can never be strictly met
   c. include the subject's familiarity with the standard language of the test
   d. all of the above

18. In seeking to understand the influence of genetics in IQ, we examine family members and environment in various combinations. When we do, we find that the correlation between the IQs of identical twins reared apart in separate homes is _____ the correlation between the IQ of siblings raised together.
   a. higher than
   b. about the same as
   c. less than
   d. only half as great as

19. In measuring abilities we need ways of considering both present and potential ones. Which of the following is *not* a true statement?
   a. Aptitude tests and achievement tests are both ability tests.
   b. Achievement tests measure accomplished skills.
   c. Aptitude tests measure capacity to learn.
   d. Intelligence tests are intended to be achievement tests.

20. A "threshold model" of creativity suggests that
   a. creativity is directly proportional to intelligence
   b. some minimum level of intelligence is necessary before a person can be creative
   c. creativity is not related to intelligence
   d. above a minimum level of intelligence, a person can be creative in any field

KEY TO SELF-QUIZ

1. c p. 349	6. a p. 354	11. c p. 360	16. a p. 372	
2. d p. 348	7. d p. 362	12. a p. 368	17. d p. 351	
3. c p. 357	8. c p. 369	13. d p. 372	18. a p. 364	
4. a p. 353	9. b p. 357	14. c p. 363	19. d p. 347	
5. b p. 353	10. b p. 370	15. b p. 365	20. b p. 361	

CLASS EXERCISE

INDIVIDUAL DIFFERENCES

Introduction

Despite the fact that humans resemble one another in some fundamental ways, they also differ from one another in many important characteristics, such as skills, attitudes, intelligence, aptitudes, interests, and personality. In many practical situations, as in the selection of employees, the measurement of these individual differences is important, especially if one wishes to select the best performers and eliminate the poor performers at a given task. This exercise is intended to show that individual differences exist even on relatively simple tasks.

Procedure

When your instructor gives you instructions to begin, immediately rearrange the following scrambled sentences to make meaningful sentences. Write your meaningful sentence in the space provided below each scrambled sentence. You will be permitted ten minutes for this task. You may not be able to finish in the time allowed, but do the best you can.

1. MEN THEM LIVES GOOD DO AFTER THE THAT

   _____

   _____

2. EYES YOU THEIR UNTIL SHOOT OF WHITES DON'T SEE THE

   _____

   _____

3. THE HUMAN WORLD IS THING MOST FREE VALUABLE THE MIND THE IN

   _____

   _____

4. TELL YOUR DEVIL GO THE TO STYLE YARN YOUR AND LET

   _____

   _____

5. IT MOMENTS WE THAT RARE LIVE ONLY IS AT

   _____

   _____

6. DO MUCH TOO KNOWING ANSWERS NOT BLAME ME FOR THE ALL NOT

   _____

   _____

7. THE FAULTS CONSCIOUS IS OF TO NONE OF GREATEST BE

   _____

   _____

8. MISUNDERSTAND BETTER IS UNDERSTAND LOT A THAN TO LITTLE A IT TO

   _____

   _____

9. THE BOASTING IT OF THAT MADE OF CAN SUCCESS BE USE WORST IS

   _____

   _____

10. BETTER FOOLISH FOOL THAN WIT A WITTY A

    _____

    _____

11. FIRST CURIOSITY OF LOT ONLY LOVE IS FOOLISHNESS AND A LITTLE A

    _____

    _____

12. THE LAUGHTER OF ASTONISHING IS POWER

    _____

    _____

13. MONEY UNHAPPINESS CURE CANNOT

    _____

    _____

14. FAILURE GROWS WITH REPUTATION YOUR EVERY

    _____

    _____

15. HOURS FOR MAN HIMSELF AND WILL HE ABOUT A LISTEN TO TALK

_____

_____

16. THE NOBODY BELIEVE WILL ONE IS THE THING TRUTH

_____

_____

17. MY TRUTH THE TO TELL OF JOKING IS WAY

_____

_____

18. LIVING IS MAKES WORTH THAT LIFE PLEASURE NOT IT

_____

_____

19. RIGHT BE RATHER PRESIDENT I HAD THAN

_____

_____

20. VERY MINDS COMPLEX OF IDEAS SIMPLE WITHIN LIE REACH THE ONLY

_____

_____

Total number unscrambled _____

Treatment of Data

1. The unscrambled sentences are given on page 298 of the Appendix; if your sentence is meaningful, it need not have precisely the same word order as that given in the Appendix. Count the number of meaningful sentences you wrote from the scrambled sentences. Enter your score where it reads "Total number unscrambled _____."

2. Your instructor will ask you to submit your score on a small slip of paper so that the data for the class as a whole can be plotted on the graph that appears on page 191.

Questions for Discussion

1. Is the curve symmetrical or skewed (see p. 575 of the text)?

2. Is there a clustering around the central tendency?

3. Which of the scrambled sentences took the longest time to unscramble? Why?

4. What conclusions can you draw regarding individual differences in performing a simple task such as this?

5. What would you conjecture about the particular abilities of those students who unscrambled the most sentences in the time allotted?

Number of students

1 2 3 4 5 6 7 8 9 10 11 12 13 14 15 16 17 18 19 20 21

Meaningful sentences

13

Personality and Its Assessment

LEARNING OBJECTIVES 13-1.   Be able to show, with examples, how inborn potential, common experiences, and unique experiences contribute to personality.

Be familiar with the following theoretical approaches to personality; be able to discuss the key concepts of each and to evaluate its contributions.

13-2.   Trait theory

13-3.   Social learning theory

13-4.   Psychoanalytic theory

13-5.   Phenomenological and humanistic theories

Be familiar with the techniques, advantages, and disadvantages of each of the following methods of assessing personality.

13-6.   Observational methods

13-7.   Personality inventories

13-8.   Projective techniques

13-9.   Be able to state the issues involved in the debate over consistency of personality; be familiar with the approaches to these issues that characterize the different personality theories.

13-10.   Understand how focusing on cognitive processes and social interactions may lead toward a more integrated view of personality.

PROGRAMMED UNIT

1. *Personality* is a difficult concept to define, but we will begin by referring to personality as the *characteristic patterns of behavior and modes of thinking* that determine an individual's adjustment to the environment. According to this definition, every person (*has/does not have*) personality.

   has

2. The characteristic patterns of behavior and modes of thinking that determine an individual's adjustment to the environment may be said to make up his or her

   personality   _____.

3. When we speak of Margaret's personality, we are referring to the characteristic patterns of _____ and modes of _____ that determine her adjustment to her environment.

   behavior, thinking

4. Some of the characteristics that influence personality are *innate,* that is, present at birth. Robert, a large, sturdy baby, lies placidly in his crib and is not easily upset.

   innate   These in_____ characteristics, physical size and emotional reactivity, may well influence his personality in later life.

5. Susan at three weeks of age is a small, frail infant who is fussy and continually active.

   innate, personality   These _____ characteristics may well contribute to her _____ as an adult.

6. The characteristics that are present at birth constitute the individual's *potential*—a potential that develops through maturation and learning as the person grows up. The experiences encountered in growing up shape or modify the innate

   potential   po_____. Some of these experiences are *common experiences,* shared by most individuals growing up in a certain *culture.*

7. If a particular culture emphasizes the value of cleanliness and early toilet training,

   common   then most individuals growing up in this culture will share _____ experiences in these areas.

8. If a culture expects females to be docile and submissive, then most of the girls grow-

   experiences   ing up in this culture will share some common _____ that tend
   innate   to develop these qualities. These experiences will *modify* the girls' _____ potential. A girl who is active and vigorous as an infant may become more placid as
   culture   her personality is shaped or modified by the _____.

   modify   9. Some of the experiences that shape or _____ the person's innate potential
   culture   are common to most individuals in a certain_____. Other experiences are *unique* or *individual;* they cannot be predicted from knowledge of the culture in which the person was raised.

   10. John grew up with a drunken father who badly mistreated him. This would be an

   unique   example of an individual or _____ experience for John—one that is not
   common   _____ to most children in his culture.

innate	11. Thus the _____ potential of the individual is shaped or modified by
common	_____ experiences (those shared by most members of the culture) as well
unique, personality	as by _____ or individual experiences to form the_____ we see in the adult.
	12. Many theories attempt to explain and describe personality, but most can be grouped into one of *four* types or classes: *trait, social learning, psychoanalytic,* and *pheno-*
four	*menological.* We will look at each of these _____ (*number*) types of theories in turn.
	13. Trait theories assume that people can be distinguished from one another on the basis of certain *measurable* and *persisting* characteristics called *traits*. A trait is a
measured	persisting characteristic that can be m_____.
	14. Thus, one may think of intelligence as a trait, since it is a measurable and relatively
persisting (or synonym)	_____ characteristic.
trait	15. Aggressiveness may also be considered a _____ to the extent that it is a measurable and persisting personality characteristic.
	16. When we attempt to describe a person in terms of certain persisting characteristics
trait	that can be measured, we are using a _____ theory.
	17. Trait theorists study personality by means of questionnaires or rating scales that are
traits	designed to measure persisting characteristics, or _____. If a psychologist asked your best friend to rate you on a scale describing degrees of such characteristics as friendliness, honesty, aggressiveness, conscientiousness, and so forth, he or
trait	she would be studying personality with the _____ approach.
	18. A second theoretical approach to the study of personality is *social learning theory.*
learning	Social _____theory assumes that personality is shaped by the *conditions of learning* a person encounters in the course of growing up.
	19. Thus, differences in personality from one person to the next can be explained in
learning	terms of differences in their l_____ experiences.
measurable	20. Trait theories assume that personality traits are consistent and m_____ characteristics of an individual. Social learning theorists maintain that many personality traits are not consistent but depend instead on the *specific situation* in which the behavior occurs.
	21. Harriet considers herself to be an "honest" person. She is careful to give the correct change when she works part time as a store clerk; she is scrupulous about filling out her income tax return, and she has never cheated on an examination. However, when she finds a wallet full of money on the sidewalk, she fails to return it, even though the owner's address is clearly indicated. This example points to the fact that
honesty	there is no unitary trait called h_____. Whether a person behaves in an
specific	"honest manner" depends on the _____ situation.

22. Social learning theorists assume that many personality traits are not consistent but depend on the specific _____ in which behavior occurs.

social

23. According to _____ learning theory, people behave in ways that are likely to produce *reinforcement.*

24. Ted's parents praise him whenever he acts aggressively toward his classmates and wins a fistfight, but they punish him whenever he shows any aggression toward them. Social learning theory would predict that Ted will display aggression only in

reinforcement

those situations where he has received r_____. He will not show aggression in all situations.

is not

25. Thus, according to social learning theory, aggression (*is/is not*) a trait; it is a learned response to a specific situation.

26. So far we have discussed two approaches to personality. One, which describes people

trait

by measuring their persisting characteristics, is called _____ theory. The other,

social

which emphasizes learned responses to specific situations, is called _____

learning

_____ theory. A third, and quite different, approach to personality is provided by *psychoanalytic theory,* as formulated by Sigmund Freud.

27. Freud conceived of personality as composed of three major systems: the *id,* the *ego,* and the *superego.* The id represents the innate instinctual drives (including sex and aggression). The id seeks immediate gratification of impulses without regard for the consequences. A person who acts impulsively, without concern for more remote

id

consequences, is likely to be expressing the _____ portion of his or her personality.

28. In psychoanalytic theory, the pleasure-seeking, impulsive portion of personality is

id

called the _____. It is manifested in early childhood but is never completely out-grown, so that behavior stemming from this part of the personality can be found in the most sober of adults.

29. It is obvious that if the id were given full rein we could never have a civilization. We need a part of the personality that will exert control in such a way as to make our behavior conform to reality and social constraint. This is called the *ego.* The aspect of personality that takes into account the real consequences of our search for plea-

ego

sure is, then, the _____.

ego

30. The id is the pleasure-seeking aspect of personality that ignores reality; the _____ is the more rational portion that tries to take reality into account.

id

31. Because it seeks immediate pleasure, the _____ is said to be controlled by the

ego

pleasure principle; because it conforms to environmental realities, the _____ is said to be controlled by the *reality principle.*

32. The third part of the personality, according to psychoanalytic theory, is the *super-ego,* an aspect that develops out of the ego's experiences with social reality and parental prohibitions. Parental commands become part of the individual, who then feels guilt if he or she violates this internalized code. The common word for the *superego* is *conscience.* If the ego proposes a course of action that is in violation of

ego, superego   one's conscience, the _____ will be opposed by the s_____ .

33. Let us set up a hypothetical situation involving a young boy, in which his thoughts may be attributed to these three aspects of personality. The boy is angry at one of his classmates and thinks, "I'd sure like to beat him to a pulp!" This statement

id   would be an expression of the _____. Next the boy thinks, "But he's bigger than I

ego   and might beat *me* up." This is the _____ at work. Finally the boy thinks, "Well,

superego   fighting is wrong anyhow." This would be the judgment of the _____ .
A person's approach to such problem situations reflects the way in which that individual has learned to cope with the conflicting demands of the three parts of his or her personality. (The text also discusses the developmental aspects of the psychoanalytic theory of personality, which are concerned with the form the id impulses take during the various stages of psychosexual development and some of the personality characteristics that develop if a person becomes fixated at any of these stages.)

trait   34. So far we have discussed three approaches to the study of personality: _____,

social learning, psychoanalytic   _____ _____ , and _____ theories. A fourth approach emphasizes the individual's *subjective experience.* This approach is called *phenomenological* because it is concerned with the individual's own *perception* and *interpretation of events,* or *phenomena.*

subjective   35. Phenomenological theories emphasize _____ experience—the

interpretation   individual's own perception and _____ of events.

36. Ruth is playing a game with some of her nursery school classmates. Suddenly she hits out in anger, knocking another child to the floor. A social learning theorist might analyze the situation in terms of the aggression-provoking actions of the

reinforcement   other child and Ruth's past history of r_____ for aggressive behavior. A psychologist taking the phenomenological approach would ask

interprets   Ruth how she perceives and _____ the situation—what it means to her.

37. The individual's subjective experience, rather than the objective situation, is the

phenomenological   focus of _____logical theories of personality.

phenomenological   38. The phenomeno_____ approach to personality includes some theories that have also been called *humanistic* because they emphasize those characteristics of people that are uniquely *human,* not shared by lower animals.

humanistic   39. Some phenomenological theories are called h_____ because, in

subjective   addition to their focus on _____ experience, they emphasize people's uniquely human characteristics. One of the most important of these is *self-actualization*—an innate tendency toward growth and fulfillment (actualization) of all of one's potentials.

40. According to humanistic theories, self-actualization, the innate tendency toward

growth, potentials   g_____ and the fulfillment of one's p_____ , is the basic force motivating behavior.

actualization

41. The basic force motivating behavior, according to humanistic theories, is self-_____.

subjective

42. The phenomenological approach to personality emphasizes _____

perception, interpretation

experience, the individual's own _____ and _____

humanistic

of events; it includes some theories that are also called _____ be-

self-

cause of their focus on such uniquely human characteristics as _____ -

actualization

_____ .

43. One of the most influential of the psychologists whose approach to personality is both phenomenological and humanistic is Carl Rogers. His theory of personality

Rogers

centers on the *concept of the self.* The self, according to Carl _____,
consists of all the *ideas, perceptions,* and *values* that characterize "I" or "me."

values

44. Your self-concept includes all of the ideas, perceptions, and _____ that

concept

characterize you. Your self-_____ influences both your perception of the world and your behavior. If you do something that is not consistent with your

self-concept

s_____ -_____ , you feel uncomfortable and may even distort or deny your actions to preserve your self-concept.

45. Rogers proposes that we all have an *ideal self* in addition to our self-concept. An ideal self is the kind of person we would like to be. The closer our self-concept is to

ideal

our i_____ self, the more fulfilled and happy we will be.

ideal self

46. The person we would like to be is the _____ _____ . If we are close to our ideal self and have fulfilled most of our potential, then we have come close to self-actualization.

47. Self-actualization is the basic force motivating behavior according to

humanistic

h_____ theories of personality.

48. Each of the theoretical approaches we have discussed looks at personality from a slightly different viewpoint. Can you identify each of these approaches from their main emphasis?

psychoanalytic

a. A three-component personality: _____ theories

social learning

b. Reward and punishment: _____ _____ theories

phenomenological
humanistic (either order)

c. Subjective experience: _____ and _____ theories

trait

d. Consistent and enduring personality characteristics: _____ theories

49. Regardless of one's theoretical approach, in order to study personality we need methods of *assessing* personality. The many methods used to assess

personality

_____ can be classified under three headings: *observational methods, personality inventories,* and *projective tests.*

50. If you watch a child in a classroom, making notes on behavior as he or she studies

observational   and interacts with teacher and classmates, you are using an ob_____
method of assessing personality.

51. If you interview an individual for a job, noting responses to questions and the person's manner of interacting with you, you are also using an observational method

assessing   of _____ personality.

52. The impressions gained from an interview or from observing behavior in a natural setting, such as a classroom, can be put into *standardized form* by means of *rating*

scale   *scales.* A rating _____ is a device for recording impressions about a personality trait.

53. A rating scale records your impressions about a personality trait in a

standardized   s_____ form. A sample item from a rating scale is given below.

Place a check at the point that describes the individual's poise.

Nervous and ill at ease	Somewhat tense; easily upset	Average poise and security	Self-confident	Very composed; adapts well to crises

54. In this example you would record your impression of the individual's poise by plac-

scale   ing a check at the appropriate point on the s_____.

55. In rating personality traits it is important to avoid the *"halo effect."* The halo

effect   _____ refers to the tendency to rate someone high on all traits because of a good impression on one or two traits, or to rate the person low throughout be-

traits   cause of a poor impression on one or two_____.

56. Jim has a very friendly and pleasant manner. His employer rates him high on his ability to get along well with others; she also rates Jim high on honesty and efficiency although she has little information on which to base her judgment of the

halo effect   latter two traits. This example shows how the _____ _____ interferes with objectivity in rating others.

rating   **57.** The halo effect is a possible source of error in the use of _____

scales   _____. Another possible source of error is the tendency of raters to be influenced by *social stereotypes.*

58. Unless the raters know the persons being rated fairly well, they may base their

stereotypes   judgments as much on social _____, how they *believe* a "housewife" or a "high school athlete" or a "long-haired college student" acts and thinks, as on observations of actual behaviors.

halo   **59.** Two possible sources of error in the use of rating scales are the _____

effect, social   _____ and _____ stereotypes.

scales   **60.** Rating_____ are most often used when one person assesses the traits of another, but they can also be used for self-ratings. If you were asked "How well do you control your emotions?" and were requested to rate yourself by placing a check mark at the appropriate place on a line that runs from "tend to be unresponsive" to "tend to be overemotional," you would be using a _____ _____ to evaluate your own personality traits.

rating

scale

61. Another method of personality assessment, which relies on an individual's *self-observations*, is the *personality inventory*. A personality in_____ is essentially a questionnaire in which the person reports reactions, feelings, and attitudes.

inventory

62. The questions on a p_____ inventory are designed to measure certain *traits.* The same questions are asked of each person and the answers are given in a form that can be easily scored. An individual's scores can be compared with the scores of other people to see how he or she compares on certain _____.

personality

traits

63. A method of personality assessment in which people respond to a number of questions about themselves is a _____ _____.

personality inventory

64. One of the most widely used personality inventories, the Minnesota Multiphasic Personality Inventory (abbreviated MMPI), was designed at the University of Minnesota to measure various phases of personality—thus the word *"multiphasic."* The Minnesota Multiphasic Personality Inventory (abbreviated _____) measures a number of different personality characteristics or _____.

MMPI

traits

65. One method of assessing personality is to record impressions about a person on a _____ _____. Another method uses a personality inventory such as the Minnesota _____ Personality Inventory.

rating scale

Multiphasic

66. The two methods of personality assessment we have discussed so far,_____ _____ and _____ _____, are fairly *structured;* they ask specific questions or require judgments about specific traits. A third method, *projective tests,* is much less structured and allows the individual to express him or herself more freely.

rating

scales, personality inventories
(either order)

67. Projective tests are (*more/less*) structured than rating scales or personality inventories. They present an *ambiguous stimulus* to which the person may respond as he or she wishes. Because the stimulus is am_____ and does not require a specific response, the individual is said to *project* his or her personality onto the stimulus.

less

ambiguous

68. A projective test presents an _____ _____ to which the individual responds with an imaginative production rather than a specific answer. The person is said to p_____ his or her personality onto the stimulus.

ambiguous stimulus

project

69. For example, in the *Rorschach Test* a person is shown a series of irregularly shaped inkblots and asked to tell what they suggest. Since the inkblots are _____ stimuli, the Rorschach Test is a _____ test.

ambiguous

projective

70.

projective

Tests composed of relatively unstructured and ambiguous stimuli that elicit projections of the personality are called _____ tests.

Rorschach

71. One example of a projective test is the R_____ Inkblot Test. Another projective test, the Thematic Apperception Test, consists of a series of pictures about which the person tells stories. In so doing the subject may say things about the characters in the stories that apply to him or herself. The Rorschach Test utilizes

inkblots

_____ as stimuli, whereas the Thematic Apperception Test utilizes a series of pictures.

Thematic

72. The _____ Apperception Test utilizes a series of pictures to which the subject responds with stories. Certain themes that recur in the person's imaginative productions are analyzed by the psychologist to arrive at basic motives and conflicts.

73. The Thematic Apperception Test is so called because certain "themes" recur in the imaginative productions of a person. "Apperception" means a readiness to perceive in certain ways, based on prior experience. Hence, the person interprets an ambigu-

picture

ous stimulus, in this case a _____, according to his or her apperceptions and elaborates the stories in terms of preferred themes that reflect personality characteristics.

Rorschach

Thematic Apperception

projective

74. Both the _____ Test, which utilizes inkblots, and the _____ _____ Test, which utilizes pictures, are _____ tests of personality.

trait, psychoanalytic (either order), social learning, phenomenological humanistic

observational

rating scales

personality inventories

projective tests

75. Let's have a final review. We have discussed four theoretical approaches to personality: _____, _____, _____ _____ and _____ or _____ theories. We have also mentioned three general methods for assessing personality: _____ methods, which may involve the use of _____ _____ for recording impressions of personality characteristics; _____ _____, which are essentially questionnaires; and _____ _____, which allow more freedom of expression than either of the other methods. The text discusses how assessment methods are used to investigate the *consistency* of personality characteristics across different situations and over the span of a lifetime.

TERMS AND CONCEPTS

personality _____

_____

_____

_____

introvert _____

_____

_____

_____

extravert _____

_____

_____

_____

trait _____

_____

_____

_____

factor analysis _____

_____

_____

_____

vicarious learning _____

_____

_____

_____

person variables _____

_____

_____

_____

id _____

_____

_____

_____

primary process thinking _____

_____

_____

ego _____

_____

_____

_____

secondary process thinking _____

_____

_____

_____

superego _____

_____

_____

_____

conscience _____

_____

_____

_____

ego-ideal _____

_____

_____

_____

psychosexual stages _____

_____

_____

_____

oral stage _____

_____

_____

_____

anal stage _____

_____

_____

_____

phallic stage _____

_____

_____

genital stage _____

_____

_____

_____

self-actualization _____

_____

_____

_____

self _____

_____

_____

_____

ideal self _____

_____

_____

_____

halo effect _____

_____

_____

_____

stereotype _____

_____

_____

_____

observational methods _____

_____

_____

_____

rating scale _____

_____

_____

_____

personality inventory _____

_____

_____

_____

MMPI _____

_____

_____

_____

empirical construction _____

_____

_____

_____

projective test _____

_____

_____

_____

Rorschach Test _____

_____

_____

_____

Thematic Apperception Test (TAT) _____

_____

_____

_____

"Barnum effect"* _____

_____

_____

_____

*Indicates terms used in Critical Discussions

_____ 1. Freud's major contribution to our understanding of personality is probably
    a. the recognition that unconscious needs and conflicts motivate much of our behavior
    b. the recognition that sexual conflicts cause most personality disturbances
    c. his definition of psychosexual stages
    d. his definition of defense mechanisms

_____ 2. Social learning theorists believe that
    a. reinforcement is not necessary for learning
    b. much human learning is vicarious
    c. reinforcement is crucial for performance of learned behavior
    d. all of the above

_____ 3. Personality is defined in the text as the characteristic _____ and _____ that determine a person's adjustment to the environment.
    a. thoughts, emotions
    b. patterns of behavior, modes of thinking
    c. desires, behaviors
    d. systems of beliefs, ways of perceiving

_____ 4. In Freud's theory of personality
    a. the ego obeys the reality principle
    b. the id operates by secondary process thinking
    c. the superego obeys the pleasure principle
    d. the ego operates by primary process thinking

_____ 5. Social learning theorists focus on several "person variables" that determine what an individual will do in a particular situation. These do _not_ include
    a. competencies
    b. subjective value of outcome
    c. traits
    d. cognitive strategies

_____ 6. While type theories have a certain appeal, they are misleading because
    a. they do not give enough weight to genetic factors
    b. most people fall on a continuum between types
    c. they place too much emphasis on early development
    d. most people fit one of the types, leaving only a few to be sorted into the other types

_____ 7. Freud compared the human mind to an iceberg. In this analogy the portion below the water was the _____.
    a. conscience
    b. id
    c. superego
    d. unconscious

_____ 8. Although cultural and subcultural measures impose some personality similarities, an individual personality is never completely predictable from a knowledge of the group in which the person was raised because
    a. individuals differ in their inherited characteristics
    b. a given culture is not applied uniformly to all members of it
    c. individuals have different life experiences
    d. all of the above

_____ 9. The personality inventory called the MMPI
    a. is based on the method of empirical construction
    b. only works if those who take it answer truthfully
    c. is based on factor analysis
    d. was originally designed as a college admission test

_____ 10. Which of the following is _not_ a criticism of the TAT or the Rorschach?
    a. Little research has been done.
    b. Ability to predict behavior is poor.
    c. Interpretation of responses is too subjective.
    d. Test reliability is poor.

_____ 11. The halo effect typically causes problems in
    a. the Sixteen Factor Personality Questionnaire
    b. the MMPI
    c. rating scales
    d. personality inventories

_____ 12. In Carl Rogers' theory of personality, one's "perceived self"
    a. influences one's perception of the world
    b. consists of unsymbolized feelings
    c. is similar to Freud's ego-ideal
    d. always conforms closely to reality

_____ 13. In the development of his personality theory, Abraham Maslow did _not_ make major use of
    a. peak experiences
    b. the experience of being

c. self-actualization

d. antisocial needs

_____ 14. Two dimensions found consistently in factor-analytic studies of personality form the basis of Eysenck's personality theory; they are
a. responsible-undependable and calm-anxious
b. introversion-extraversion and stability-instability
c. cooperative-negativistic and adventurous-cautious
d. intellectual-unrefined and goodnatured-irritable

_____ 15. The basic concept of any projective test is the presentation of a stimulus that is deliberately ambiguous, to encourage the subject to
a. reveal hidden psychopathology
b. display creativity
c. reveal his or her personality
d. accept the tester's interpretations

_____ 16. A social learning theorist would *not* accept

_____ as a reason for the apparent consistency of our friends' behavior.
a. our own presence in the situations when we see our friends
b. our "implicit personality theories"
c. stable personality traits
d. constant physical qualities of people, such as voice tone

_____ 17. According to Freud
a. defense mechanisms defend against repression
b. repression reduces anxiety

c. individuals are similar in their balance of id, ego, and superego systems

d. all of the above

_____ 18. Future personality theories will probably concentrate on two areas:
a. self-actualization and situational factors
b. cognitive processes and social interactions
c. intellectual abilities and traits
d. aggressive instincts and social needs

_____ 19. _____ theories assume that people vary on a number of continuous dimensions or scales.
a. Type
b. Psychoanalytic
c. Trait
d. Social learning

_____ 20. Current research on anxiety and hostility suggests that the greatest amount of variability may result from
a. individual differences in traits
b. variations in environmental conditions
c. different modes of response
d. interactions among the above

KEY TO SELF-QUIZ

1. a p. 392	6. b p. 382	11. c p. 399	16. c p. 407	
2. d p. 385	7. d p. 389	12. a p. 394	17. b p. 390	
3. b p. 377	8. d p. 379	13. d p. 395	18. b p. 410	
4. a p. 389	9. a p. 400	14. b p. 384	19. c p. 382	
5. c p. 387	10. a p. 405	15. c p. 403	20. d p. 409	

CLASS EXERCISE

A PROJECTIVE TEST

Introduction

The Rorschach Test, introduced by Dr. Hermann Rorschach in 1921, consists of a series of complex inkblots. Subjects are asked to tell what they see in each inkblot, and their responses are then scored and interpreted by experienced testers (see pp. 403–06 of the text).

In this demonstration we will use an inkblot like those used in the Rorschach Test (see p. 207). The exercise is designed to demonstrate that people looking at the same blot will see different things. No attempt at interpretation will be made by your instructor.

Procedure

Your instructor will ask six volunteers, preferably three men and three women, to leave the room. While they are out of the room, write below what the blot looks like to you. They will be called in one at a time and will be asked to relate what the blot looks like to them or what it makes them think of. You are to write each student's response in the space provided on page 206.

Your own impression:

Student 5:

Student 1:

Student 6:

Student 2:

Questions for Discussion

1. Were there differences in the responses of the six subjects? If so, can you think why?

2. Although the sample used was small, did there seem to be sex differences in perception?

3. Do you think people "project" aspects of their personality in responding to such a blot?

Student 3:

4. What are the advantages of using stimuli as unstructured as this to assess personality? The disadvantages?

5. How does this test differ from the Thematic Apperception Test?

6. Would it be easy to derive objective scoring methods for a test of this type?

Student 4:

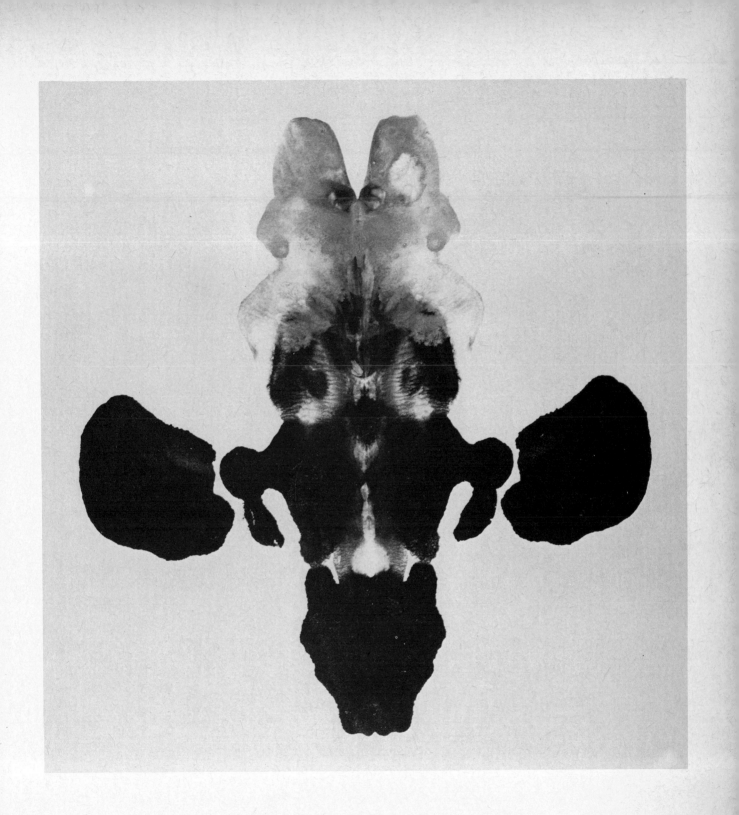

14
Conflict and Stress

LEARNING OBJECTIVES

14-1. Understand how conflict situations can lead to frustration; be familiar with the major types of conflict that produce ambivalent attitudes.

14-2. Be able to explain scapegoating as an example of displaced aggression; show how this differs from direct aggression.

14-3. Be familiar with the research on learned helplessness as a form of apathy reaction. Be able to give examples of frustration-produced regression.

14-4. Understand how the concept of anxiety helps explain reactions to frustration. Be able to compare the psychoanalytic and learning theory views of anxiety.

14-5. Be able to define the defense mechanisms of denial and repression; show how they represent reactions to external and internal threats.

14-6. Be able to define the defense mechanisms of reaction formation and projection. Show how they would differ in their defense against an undesired personal trait.

14-7. Be able to define the defense mechanisms of rationalization and intellectualization. Show how they differ from rational and intellectual thinking.

14-8. Be able to define the defense mechanism of displacement and show why it is said to be the most successful of the defense mechanisms in aiding adjustment to everyday problems.

14-9. Be familiar with the research on stress-induced ulcers in animals and the implications for psychosomatic disorders.

14-10. Be able to discuss the factors that influence the severity of stress; give examples of how to reduce the impact of each.

209

1. No matter how resourceful we may be in coping with problems, we are bound to encounter *frustration* and *conflict*. Frustrating situations vary all the way from petty annoyances to major defeats and disappointments. Frustration occurs when progress toward a *desired goal* is blocked or delayed. You have only a few minutes to catch a plane and you find yourself snarled in a traffic jam at the entrance to the airport. Since your progress toward a desired goal is blocked, you are experiencing

frustration   _____.

goal   2. Frustration occurs when progress toward a desired _____ is blocked or delayed.

3. There are many barriers to the attainment of goals. The physical environment presents such obstacles as floods and snowstorms; the social environment presents obstacles through the restrictions imposed by other people. All of these are possible

frustration   sources of _____.

4. Sometimes we are kept from reaching a desired goal because of our own *limitations*. You may want to become a professional musician, yet you don't have the ability. In

limitations   this case, the source of frustration is your own l_____.

frustration   5. If you set goals beyond your ability, then _____ will result. Another source of frustration is a *conflict* between two *opposing goals* or

conflict   *motives*. When two motives _____, frustration will result.

goal   6. Frustration refers to the blocking of progress toward a _____. It may result

environment   from obstacles in the physical or social en_____, from per-

limitations, conflict   sonal l_____, or from c_____

between two goals.

7. Sometimes the conflict is between a motive and a person's *internal standards* of

goals   behavior rather than between two external _____. Frank needs to pass chemistry in order to graduate, and since he feels unsure of his ability, he is tempted to cheat on the exam. But he is deterred by the knowledge that he would feel ashamed if he did so. His conflict is between his desire to succeed and his internal

standards   _____ of what constitutes acceptable behavior.

8. Most conflicts involve goals that are simultaneously desirable and undesirable, goals about which we feel *ambivalent*. You want to go to the movies but are worried about the consequences of lost study time. Your attitude toward a possible evening

ambivalent   at the movies is am_____.

9. Conflicts   involving   goals   that   are   simultaneously   desirable   and

undesirable   un_____ are called *approach-avoidance* conflicts.

avoidance   10. One's attitude toward the goal in an approach-_____

ambivalent

dislike

conflict is _____. To be ambivalent is to both like and

_____ something at the same time.

disliked

11. In an approach-avoidance conflict the goal is both liked and

dis_____ at the same time. Approach-avoidance conflicts tend to result in *vacillation*. At some distance from the goal the positive aspects predominate and the person approaches; nearer to the goal the negative aspects become influential and the tendency is to withdraw. These conflicting tendencies may

vacillation

result in a period of _____ before a final decision is reached.

conflicts

12. Frustration—whether it is the result of obstacles, personal limitations, or

c_____—may have a number of immediate consequences. One common response to frustration is *aggression;* the person feels angry and wants to attack the source of frustration.

aggression

13. If Tommy kicks his older sister when she takes his ball away from him, he is dis-

playing _____ toward his sister as the source of frustration.

direct
is not

14. When a frustrated person directly attacks the frustrating object or person, we say he or she is displaying *direct* aggression. If after Tommy's sister takes the ball away

from him, he kicks her, he is displaying _____ aggression. If he kicks the door instead, he (*is/is not*) displaying direct aggression.

displaced

15. If we cannot satisfactorily express our aggression against the source of frustration, we may shift, or *displace,* the aggression toward an innocent person or object. Sandra, who is angry with her father, pulls the cat's tail. She is probably exhibiting

_____ aggression.

displaced

16. The football player who has caught and then dropped a pass stamps the ground.

This is an example of _____ aggression.

apathy

17. Sometimes when frustrated we may simply act indifferent or attempt to withdraw from the situation—that is, we may react with *apathy.* Ann, who has been told that she cannot attend a movie with her friends, does not display active aggression but goes to her room and sulks. Her behavior could be described as

_____, which is the opposite of aggression.

aggression, displaced

apathy

18. People react differently to frustrating situations. While a common response is

_____, either direct or dis_____, another

response is _____. Perhaps the person whose efforts (aggressive or otherwise) to satisfy his or her needs were never successful may have *learned* to be helpless, or apathetic, when faced with frustrating situations.

19. The concept of *learned helplessness* grew out of some experiments with dogs. The dogs were placed in a situation in which they were helpless to avoid an electric shock. Later, when shock could be easily avoided by means of a simple response, the dogs made no attempt to make the avoidance response; they had learned to

helpless   be h_____ .

20. By being placed in a situation where nothing they did could avoid shock, the dogs

learned, helplessness   I_____ to be helpless; this learned _____
generalized to subsequent situations where avoidance was possible.

learned helplessness   21. The concept of _____ _____
may explain why some people react with apathy when faced with frustrating situations.

aggression   22. Frustration may cause people to respond with _____ or

apathy (either order)   _____ . It may also cause them to behave in an immature or childish manner. Returning to behavior patterns characteristic of an *earlier stage* of development is called *regression*.

23. A young child who is frustrated returns to thumb-sucking or to bed-wetting. Since these are behavior patterns that were characteristic of the child at a younger age, we

regression   can say that the child's responses to frustration illustrate _____ .

24. Adults sometimes resort to yelling, cursing, or fighting when frustrated. Since these are immature forms of behavior for an adult, they would be examples of

regression   _____ .

25. Regression refers to a return to behavior patterns characteristic of an

earlier   _____ stage of development.

26. Three reactions that may occur in response to frustration are

aggression, apathy   _____ , which may be direct or indirect, _____ ,

helplessness   which may reflect learned _____ , and

regression   _____ .

27. In order to explain these reactions to frustration (as well as reactions to other forms of stress) psychologists use the concept of *anxiety*. Any situation that threatens a person's well-being is assumed to produce a state of anxiety. Conflicts and other types of frustration threaten a person's feeling of well-being and thus create a

anxiety   state of _____ .

28. Threats of physical harm or threats to one's self-esteem are also sources of anxiety,

being   since they threaten a person's well-_____ .

anxiety   29. Any situation that threatens a person's well-being can produce _____ .
By anxiety we mean that unpleasant emotion characterized by the terms "worry," "apprehension," and "fear" that we all experience at times.

emotion   30. Because anxiety is an unpleasant _____ that threatens our well-

being   _____ , we are motivated to do something to alleviate it.

31. One way of coping with anxiety is to take *direct action* to deal with the anxiety-producing situation. If you are anxious because you are about to fail a course, you can cope with your anxiety directly by finding out what you need to do to improve your grade and devising a plan for doing it. This (*direct/indirect*) method of handling anxiety is called a *coping strategy.*

direct

32. Behaviors that a person uses to deal directly with stressful situations are called

coping

c_____ strategies.

33. Another way of handling anxiety in this situation would be to refuse to acknowledge the possibility of failure or to convince yourself that the course is worthless, so it doesn't matter if you fail or not. Both of these alternatives are attempts to

anxiety

defend yourself against an_____ without dealing directly with the anxiety-producing situation. These indirect methods of handling anxiety are called *defensive strategies.*

strategies

34. Defensive _____ do not deal with the anxiety-producing situation in any way; they only defend the person against feelings of

anxiety

_____.

35. Another way to handle your concern about failing the course would be to deaden anxiety with alcohol, tranquilizers, or marijuana. Since these actions reduce anxiety but do not deal with the anxiety-producing situation, they would be considered

defensive

_____ strategies.

coping strategies

36. Direct methods of handling anxiety are called _____ _____; indirect methods that do not change the anxiety-producing situation, but simply

anxiety, defensive

defend against _____, are called _____ strategies.

coping, defensive
(either order)

37. People often use a combination of _____ and _____ strategies in dealing with stressful situations.

do not

38. Defensive strategies often *distort reality* in some way. They (*do/do not*) alter the objective situation, but they may change the way the person thinks about it.

39. If you reduce anxiety by refusing to acknowledge the possibility of failing a course,

distorting

even though the signs are clear, you are dis_____ reality.

reality

40. Freud called the defensive strategies that involve distortion of _____ *defense mechanisms,* and he assumed that they were unconscious processes. Some

mechanisms

of these defense m_____ occur often enough to have been given names.

mechanisms

41. Two basic defense _____ are *denial* and *repression*. Denial of reality is a defense against external threat; the person tries to block out disturbing realities by refusing to acknowledge them.

42. A woman whose husband is unfaithful may refuse to admit to herself that anything is wrong even though she has ample evidence to the contrary. By denying reality

anxiety

she tries to defend herself against an_____.

43. The mother of a child who is fatally ill may refuse to admit that there is anything seriously wrong with her child even though she has been fully informed of the diagnosis and the expected outcome of the illness. In this case, the defense mechanism of _____ protects her against intolerable anxiety.

denial

44. Repression is similar to denial but it refers to an *internal* threat. Impulses or memories that might cause unbearable _____ are excluded from conscious awareness.

anxiety

45. Denial is a defense against external threat, while _____ is a defense against internal threat.

repression

46. A young woman feels intensely hostile toward her mother. But because such feelings are totally inconsistent with her concept of herself as a loving daughter, they would cause anxiety if she were aware of them. Consequently, her feelings of hostility are re_____ and banished from memory.

repressed

47. A young boy was partially responsible for his brother's death. As an adult he has no memory of the events surrounding the tragedy. This is another example of _____.

repression

48. Both denial and repression defend against anxiety by _____ reality. Denial usually refers to an individual's defending against an _____ threat by refusing to acknowledge some disturbing aspects of reality; repression usually refers to an individual's defending against an _____ threat by banishing anxiety-producing impulses or memories from conscious awareness.

distorting

external

internal

49. George is frequently criticized by his employers for poor workmanship, but he fails to perceive their dissatisfaction or to admit to himself that there is anything wrong with his work. This would most likely be considered an example of (*denial/repression*).

denial

50. Lucy felt very jealous and resentful of her younger sister and often wished something fatal would happen to her. If, as an adult, Lucy has no memory of these feelings, one would assume that _____ has occurred.

repression

51. Repression and denial are the two basic defense _____. The text discusses five additional defense mechanisms that may be used to aid denial or repression. They help keep anxiety-producing thoughts from awareness by distorting re_____ in some way. They include (1) *rationalization,* (2) *reaction formation,* (3) *projection,* (4) *intellectualization,* and (5) *displacement.*

mechanisms

reality

52. Assigning logical reasons or plausible excuses for what we do impulsively is known as *rationalization.* The statement, "I'd have been here on time but my alarm clock didn't go off," might very well be a _____.

rationalization

53. A young boy refuses to share his candy with his younger sister and gives as the reason, "If I give her some candy, it will only make her teeth decay." If the boy is giving a "good" reason but not the "true" reason for not sharing, he is using the defense mechanism of _____.

rationalization

rationalization 54. In _____ we give "good" reasons but not "true" reasons for our behavior.

55. In *reaction formation* we *conceal a motive* from ourselves by giving strong expression to its *opposite.* The mother who unconsciously resents the demands and restrictions that result from having a child may be excessively fussy and particular in her care of the child. She conceals her real feelings through the mechanism

formation of reaction _____.

hiding → *a need or desire that cause a person to act*

56. Concealing a motive by giving strong expression to its opposite describes the de-

reaction formation fense mechanism known as _____ _____.

57. Mrs. Z, once an alcoholic but now a teetotaler, is an ardent prohibitionist and engages in a personal crusade to convert everyone from drinking any kind of alcoholic beverage. She may be displaying a defense mechanism called

reaction formation _____ _____.

58. In *projection* we protect ourselves from recognizing our own *undesirable* qualities by assigning them in an exaggerated amount to other people. If a man says, "You can't trust people any farther than you can throw them," he may be untrustworthy himself and may be attempting to keep himself from acknowledging this trait by

projection using the mechanism of _____.

projection 59. In the defense mechanism known as _____, we attribute to others traits we find undesirable in ourselves.

60. Sally is overly critical but does not readily acknowledge this as one of her traits. She is overheard saying that her roommate is a very critical person. Sally is attributing to another individual an undesirable trait that she herself possess. This illustrates

projection the mechanism of _____.

61. In projection we protect ourselves from recognizing our own

undesirable _____ qualities by assigning them in an exaggerated amount to other people.

62. *Intellectualization* is an attempt to gain *detachment* from an emotionally threatening situation by dealing with it in abstract, intellectual terms. A young man watches his mother slowly die from cancer. In talking about her death to a friend he focuses on the medical details of her condition and treatment. He is using

intellectualization intell_____ to defend against very stressful emotions.

detachment 63. In intellectualization the person tries to gain de_____ from an emotionally threatening situation by dealing with it in abstract,

intellectual _____ terms.

64. The defense mechanism whereby we assign logical reasons or plausible excuses

rationalization for what we do impulsively is known as _____.

65. Individuals who attribute to others qualities that they find undesirable in them-

projection selves are engaging in _____.

66. When we try to detach ourselves from an emotionally threatening situation by dealing with it in abstract, intellectual terms, we are using

intellectualization

_____ as a defense mechanism.

67. Concealing a motive by giving strong expression to its opposite is known as

reaction formation

_____ _____.

anxiety

68. All of these mechanisms are ways of protecting oneself against _____

reality

by distorting _____ to some extent. They may be used as aids to

repression

the basic defense mechanisms of denial and re_____, which block the anxiety-producing feelings completely from awareness.

69. In repression, an impulse or memory that might provoke feelings of *anxiety* or *guilt* is completely banished from awareness. A ten-year-old boy has strong feelings of hostility and resentment toward his father. Yet he has been brought up to feel that one should love one's parents. To protect himself from anxiety he has succeeded in burying these feelings of hostility and is not aware they exist. The defense

repression

mechanism known as _____ is operating in this case.

70. Refusal to acknowledge an unpleasant or anxiety-producing situation is similar to repression, in that it keeps the unpleasant thoughts out of awareness. In this case,

denial

the mechanism is called _____ because it defends against external rather than internal threat.

71. An additional defense mechanism discussed in the text is *displacement*. In displacement, a motive whose gratification is blocked in one form is *displaced* or directed into a different, more *socially acceptable* channel. If one's hostile impulses are expressed in boxing or wrestling, this is an example of

displacement

dis_____. Sexual impulses that cannot be expressed directly may be expressed indirectly in such creative activities as art and music.

displacement

This is another example of _____.

72. Freud felt that displacement was the most satisfactory way of handling blocked aggressive and sexual impulses, because it allowed these impulses to be expressed

acceptable

indirectly in more socially _____ forms.

73. To the extent that defense mechanisms help a person through difficult times until he or she can learn more *mature* and *realistic* ways of coping with

anxiety

_____-producing situations, they contribute to satisfactory adjustment.

74. If, however, the individual continues to rely upon defense mechanisms so that he

mature

or she is never forced to learn more m_____ and realistic ways of behaving, then such mechanisms would constitute a barrier to satisfactory adjustment.

TERMS AND CONCEPTS

frustration _____

_____

_____

_____

conflict _____

_____

_____

_____

ambivalent attitude _____

_____

_____

_____

approach-avoidance conflict _____

_____

_____

_____

avoidance-avoidance conflict _____

_____

_____

_____

displaced aggression _____

_____

_____

_____

apathy _____

_____

_____

_____

learned helplessness _____

_____

_____

_____

regression _____

_____

_____

anxiety _____

_____

_____

objective anxiety _____

_____

_____

neurotic anxiety _____

_____

_____

_____

unconscious conflict _____

_____

_____

_____

coping strategies _____

_____

_____

_____

defensive strategies _____

_____

_____

_____

defense mechanisms _____

_____

_____

_____

denial _____

_____

_____

_____

repression _____

_____

_____

rationalization _____

_____

_____

_____

reaction formation _____

_____

_____

projection _____

_____

_____

_____

intellectualization _____

_____

_____

_____

displacement _____

_____

_____

_____

psychosomatic medicine _____

_____

_____

_____

biofeedback* _____

_____

_____

_____

relaxation training* _____

_____

_____

_____

*Indicates terms used in Critical Discussions

SELF-QUIZ

_C_ 1. One example of a defense mechanism as a helpful coping device is the use by doctors of the mechanism of
   a. repression
   b. displacement
   c. intellectualization
   d. rationalization

___ 2. Freud was one of the first theorists to focus on the importance of anxiety. He
   a. differentiated between objective anxiety and neurotic anxiety.
   b. viewed neurotic anxiety as synonymous with fear
   c. felt objective anxiety stemmed from an unconscious conflict
   d. all of the above

___ 3. "Scapegoating" as an outcome of frustration illustrates a response called _____ aggression.
   a. direct
   b. frustrated
   c. instrumental
   d. displaced

___ 4. The text points out three important precautions to be kept in mind when considering defense mechanisms. Which of the following is _not_ one of them?
   a. All of them are found in everyday behavior of normal people.
   b. A label for behavior is not an explanation of it.
   c. There is no experimental evidence for any of them.
   d. Defense mechanisms are hypothetical constructs.

___ 5. The common element in defense mechanisms is
   a. primitivation
   b. self-deception
   c. covert aggression
   d. displacement

___ 6. When subjects respond to a posthypnotic suggestion, they sometimes feel so embarrassed that they _____ the behavior.
   a. repress
   b. rationalize
   c. project
   d. displace

___ 7. According to social learning theory, a lifelong fear of dogs that stems from a frightening experience with a dog in childhood persists because
   a. it occurred during a critical period of development
   b. it was reinforced by later experiences with snarling dogs
   c. by avoiding dogs the person never learns that most dogs are friendly
   d. people can fool themselves into thinking they are afraid

___ 8. The defense mechanism that best serves its function of reducing anxiety while still allowing some gratification of the unacceptable motive is
   a. displacement
   b. rationalization
   c. intellectualization
   d. reaction formation

___ 9. In Freud's view, defense mechanisms "defend" by
   a. keeping certain impulses out of awareness
   b. gratifying the id's impulses
   c. strengthening the superego
   d. all of the above

___ 10. Studies of wartime prisoners show that a common reaction to frustrating conditions of long duration from which there is no hope of escape is
   a. scapegoating
   b. fantasy
   c. apathy
   d. stereotyping

___ 11. The "executive" monkeys who developed ulcers attracted a lot of attention. Further research with rats showed that an important factor in _preventing_ ulcers is
   a. immediate feedback
   b. ability to make an effective response
   c. both a and b
   d. neither a nor b

___ 12. Amnesia is a phenomenon that illustrates some aspects of the defense mechanism called
   a. displacement
   b. undoing
   c. reaction formation
   d. repression

_____ 13. When a goal is both wanted and not wanted, our attitude toward it is
 a. likely to become increasingly negative
 b. likely to become increasingly positive
 c. termed ambivalent
 d. expressed in terms of frustration gradients

_____ 14. The unconscious mechanism by which we assign exaggerated versions of our own undesirable qualities to other people is called
 a. displacement
 b. projection
 c. reaction formation
 d. undoing

_____ 15. Two common responses to frustration are aggression and apathy; which of them occurs in a given situation is probably the result of
 a. innate differences in temperament
 b. learned differences in reactions
 c. differences in the situations
 d. whether or not aggression is apt to be successful in that situation

_____ 16. A person who shows a reaction formation is one who
 a. assigns his or her undesirable qualities to others
 b. completely blocks from awareness an anxiety-producing impulse
 c. conceals a motive by strongly expressing its opposite
 d. develops repetitive and ritualistic behavior

_____ 17. Studies show that novice skydivers experience the most fear
 a. the night before the jump
 b. at the point of final commitment to jump
 c. during free fall before the chute opens
 d. just before landing

_____ 18. Freud believed that neurotic anxiety resulted from a(n)
 a. unconscious conflict between id impulses and ego constraints
 b. exaggerated fear of some part of the environment
 c. realistic fear of the environment
 d. conscious fear of failing to live up to society's standards

_____ 19. The particular psychosomatic symptoms that a person develops in response to stress depend on the
 a. genetic or illness-caused vulnerability of certain organs
 b. person's early learning experiences
 c. individual differences in the reactivity of the autonomic nervous system
 d. all of the above

_____ 20. Which of the following does *not* reduce the effects of stress?
 a. being unable to predict when a stressful event will occur
 b. having control over the duration of a stressful event
 c. having friends who share the worry but are supportive
 d. feeling competent about one's own abilities

KEY TO SELF-QUIZ

1. c p.430	6. b p.428	11. c p.433	16. c p.429
2. a p.425	7. c p.425	12. d p.427	17. b p.419
3. d p.421	8. a p.430	13. c p.418	18. a p.425
4. c p.427	9. a p.426	14. b p.429	19. d p.434
5. b p.426	10. c p.422	15. b p.423	20. a p.434

INDIVIDUAL EXERCISES

REACTIONS TO FRUSTRATION

Introduction

People react differently to stress and frustration. The text discusses some of the immediate reactions to, and ways of coping with, frustrating situations. This exercise should help you analyze your own responses to frustration.

Procedure

1. Think back over the past two months and list any occasions on which you were frustrated either by other people or by circumstances. Some of these events may be trivial (for example, you were late to class because you failed to awake in time or your car wouldn't start); others may be major disappointments (for example, you failed a test in an important course

or were rejected by someone you love). If you can't recall any frustrations during the past two months, you lead a blessed life or are good at repressing unpleasant experiences. Whatever the reason, keep going back in time until you have listed five to ten frustrating experiences. Write down a few phrases to identify each episode. Don't read further until you have recalled at least five or more events.

2. Now think about each event and try to recall your immediate reactions (for example, anger, tension, feelings of helplessness) and your method of coping with your feelings (for example, tried to forget about the situation, went out for a milkshake and pizza, went to a movie, sought the comfort of friends, took some action to remedy the situation). You may have had more than one reaction to each situation; if so, list all your reactions.

3. Examine your list of reactions. Do you discern a characteristic way of handling frustration?

4. As a final step, keep a record for the coming week, listing any frustrating situations and your reactions as they occur.

Questions for Discussion

1. Was it difficult to recall past reactions to frustration? If so, why do you think this is the case?

2. Did you notice any difference in reactions recorded for earlier events and those recorded for the past week? If so, what factors might contribute to this difference?

3. Does your increased awareness of your reactions to frustration make it easier to change the way you respond?

RATIONALIZATION

Complete each of the following sentences with the first answer that comes to mind. Work quickly without pondering your responses. No one else need see them.

1. My grades would be higher if _____

_____

_____

2. I would feel more comfortable in social situations if

_____

_____

_____

3. I would be more popular with the opposite sex if

_____

_____

_____

4. I would have done better in my last exam in this course if _____

_____

_____

5. I would have achieved more honors and recognition for extracurricular activities if _____

_____

_____

6. Sometimes my grades are lower than they should be because _____

_____

_____

7. I could work better if _____

_____

_____

8. I do not engage in many extracurricular activities because _____

_____

_____

9. I would have more friends if _____

_____

_____

10. I could manage my finances better if _____

_____

_____

Someone else looking at your answers might discern some evidence of rationalization—the tendency we all have to give "rational" and "good" explanations rather than "true" reasons. (See page 428 in the text for some examples of rationalization.) Examine each of your answers carefully and objectively, as if you were an outside observer. Do you find any evidence of rationalization—instances where the reasons you give are not exactly the real ones? In which, if any, areas of your life are you more likely to use this defense?

15

Abnormal Psychology

LEARNING OBJECTIVES

15-1. Know the four criteria that may be used in defining abnormality, as well as the characteristics that are considered indicative of normality. Be able to distinguish between neuroses, psychoses, and personality disorders.

15-2. Be able to define and give examples of the five common neurotic reactions discussed in the text; understand the problems involved in classifying such reactions.

15-3. Understand the characteristics of psychoses that distinguish them from neuroses. Know the difference between organic and functional psychoses.

15-4. Be familiar with the various forms of affective disorders; show how they illustrate the problems of separating psychoses from neuroses.

15-5. Be able to compare the psychoanalytic and learning theory views of depression; be familiar with the evidence for genetic and biochemical factors.

15-6. Know the defining characteristics of schizophrenia and give examples of each.

15-7. Be familiar with the research on the causes of schizophrenia; be able to discuss the probable contributions of genetic, biochemical, and psychological factors.

15-8. Know the defining characteristics and probable cause(s) of psychopathic personalities; be able to show how these illustrate the general category of personality disorders.

15-9. Be familiar with the observed patterns of alcoholism and drug abuse, including when physical dependence and psychological dependence are involved.

15-10. Be able to discuss the overall prevalence of mental disorders, class differences in specific disorders, and trends in hospitalization in the United States.

abnormal

1. This chapter discusses a variety of *abnormal* behaviors. But what do we mean by abnormal? The word itself, ab_____, means "away from the norm." So one definition of abnormality is any behavior that is *statistically infrequent* or deviant from the norm.

infrequent

2. But this definition is not completely satisfactory. People who are very gifted intellectually or unusually well adjusted deviate from the norm in the sense of being statistically (*frequent/infrequent*), yet we would not consider them abnormal.

abnormal

3. A second method of classifying behavior as normal or abnormal is by determining whether the behavior is in accord with *society's standards*. Anthropological studies have revealed, however, that what is considered normal in one society may be considered abnormal in another. Therefore, this definition of abnormality, which really constitutes a *social* definition, also has its limitations. For example, homosexuality is considered normal behavior in some cultures, but in other cultures it is considered _____.

statistical

social

4. A definition of abnormality in terms of st_____ frequency is not satisfactory because some very desirable traits may fall outside the normal range. Likewise, we cannot be content with a _____ definition of abnormality, since the standards of normality and abnormality vary from one culture to the next or even from time to time within the same culture.

maladaptive

5. A third definition of abnormality is based on *maladaptiveness of behavior*. Behavior is abnormal if it is *maladaptive;* that is, if it has adverse effects either for the individual or for society. According to this definition a man who is so fearful of enclosed places that he cannot enter an elevator or a windowless room would be considered abnormal because his behavior is mal_____; it has adverse effects for him.

society

6. A woman whose anger explodes in assaultive attacks on others would also be considered abnormal by this definition, because her behavior has adverse effects for s_____.

abnormal

7. A fourth criterion looks at abnormality from the viewpoint of people's subjective feelings—their *personal distress*—rather than their behavior. According to this criterion a person who functions very effectively at his or her job and whose behavior appears quite normal to observers, may still be considered _____ if the individual feels acutely miserable most of the time.

distress

8. A fourth definition looks at abnormality in terms of the individual's personal _____ rather than his or her behavior.

frequency, society

behavior, distress

9. Our four definitions of abnormality take into account statistical f_____, the standards of _____, maladaptiveness of _____, and personal _____. In most instances all four criteria are used in diagnosing abnormality.

abnormality

10. Normality is even more difficult to define than _____.
Some of the characteristics discussed in the text as possessed to a *greater degree* by normal individuals than by those diagnosed as abnormal include an *efficient perception of reality, self-knowledge* and *self-acceptance,* ability to *control's one's behavior* and to *form affectionate relationships,* and *productivity.* These characteristics do not distinguish sharply between the mentally healthy and the mentally ill; they are

greater

simply traits that the normal person possesses to a _____ degree than one diagnosed as abnormal.

11. The major *diagnostic categories* of abnormal behavior, based on *behavioral signs,* include *neuroses, psychoses,* and *personality disorders.* Each of these is further divided

behavioral

into a number of subcategories, also based primarily on _____ signs.

12. A major distinction is made between the *neuroses* (singular, *neurosis*) and the psychoses (singular, *psychosis*). The *neurotic* disorders are less severe than the *psychotic* disorders; they do *not* involve *personality disintegration* or *loss of contact with reality.* People who are so disturbed that they cannot distinguish their

psychotic

own fantasies from reality would be classed as (*neurotic/psychotic*).

13. The neurotic disorders may be viewed as exaggerated forms of the normal *defense mechanisms* used in an attempt to resolve a persistent conflict. When a person cannot achieve a realistic solution to a persistent conflict but instead habitually resorts to exaggerated forms of defense mechanisms to relieve his or her problems,

neurotic

the individual may be considered _____tic.

14. The neuroses are characterized by the habitual use of exaggerated forms of the

defense

normal _____ mechanisms in response to a persistent conflict.

15. Unresolved conflicts create *anxiety.* Consequently, it is not surprising that the chief

anxiety

sign of neurosis is an _____.

16. We noted in the preceding chapter that defense mechanisms serve to protect our

anxiety

self-esteem and to defend against _____. A person who cannot resolve a persistent conflict either remains in a state of anxiety or resorts to habit-

defense mechanisms

ual use of one of the _____ _____, often in exaggerated form, to defend against anxiety.

17. Everyone resorts to defense mechanisms at one time or another. It is only when these defenses become the dominant method of handling problems that the person

neurotic

is called _____.

neuroses
(or neurotics)

18. Anxiety is the chief sign of the _____. Sometimes the anxiety is very obvious—the individual appears tense, restless, and may be unable to eat or sleep. *Anxiety reactions* are a type of neurosis in which the chief sign,

anxiety

_____, is obvious.

anxiety

19. In the type of neurosis called _____ reactions the person habitually appears tense and restless, and reacts to even the slightest difficulty with strong feelings of anxiety.

20. Since the unresolved conflicts that underlie a neurosis are frequently *unconscious,* persons suffering from anxiety reactions usually have no clear idea of why they feel so tense and apprehensive. The reasons behind their anxieties are often

unconscious   un _____ .

21. When people feel tense and anxious much of the time without being able to specify

anxiety reactions   exactly what they are afraid of, they are suffering from _____

_____ .

22. Another type of neurosis is the *obsessive-compulsive* reaction. An obsessive-

compulsive   _____ reaction may take three forms: (1) *obsessive thoughts,* (2) *compulsive acts,* and (3) a *combination* of obsessive thoughts and com-

obsessive   pulsive acts. You might guess that a person with _____ thoughts has persistently unwelcome, disturbing thoughts and that a person with a compulsion has an irresistible urge to repeat a certain stereotyped or *ritualistic*

act   _____ .

23. *Obsessive thoughts* frequently involve aggressive or sexual impulses that are quite unacceptable to the conscious feelings of the person who has them. Because these unacceptable impulses would cause great anxiety if the person acknowledged them as his or her real feelings, they are repressed and appear as

obsessive   _____ thoughts that the individual experiences as not being really his or her own.

impulses   **24.** Obsessive thoughts thus involve unacceptable _____ that the person cannot acknowledge as his or her own.

25. A young mother had frequent thoughts of murdering her two small children. She professed nothing but love for them and maintained that "these awful thoughts that pop into my head" had nothing to do with her real feelings. In this case

obsessive   _____ thoughts protected the mother from the anxiety she would feel were she to acknowledge these impulses as her own.

26. *Compulsive acts* are stereotyped or ritualistic acts that are designed to protect the individual from feelings of anxiety or guilt. A young boy who suffered guilt feelings whenever he masturbated felt compelled to scrub his hands many times a

compulsive   day. In this case the _____ act served to relieve his feelings of guilt.

27. Obsessive thoughts and compulsive acts thus serve to protect the individual against

anxiety, obsessive- _____ or guilt. They are characteristic of an _____-

compulsive   _____ reaction.

28. *Phobias* constitute a third type of neurosis. Phobias are *excessive fears* of certain objects or situations in the *absence of real danger.* Jane is so fearful of closed places that she will never take the elevator to her ninth-floor office but insists on climbing

phobia   the stairs instead. She has a _____ .

29. Tom is so fearful of fire that he cannot stay in a room in which there is a fire burning in the fireplace. Since Tom's fear is excessive in a situation in which there is no

phobia

real danger, it is another example of a _____.

absence

30. Phobias are excessive fears in the _____ of real danger. Some phobias may be maladaptive responses that are learned, while others may develop as a defense against impulses that the individual feels may become dangerous. The text discusses both of these possibilities.

anxiety

31. So far we have discussed three kinds of neuroses: (1) _____ reactions, in which feelings of tension and anxiety are predominant; (2)

obsessive-compulsive

_____-_____ reactions, in which the individual has persistent, unpleasant thoughts or feels the need to perform a ritualis-

phobias

tic act of some sort; and (3) _____, which are excessive fears in the absence of real danger.

32. In a fourth type of neurosis, called *conversion reaction,* physical symptoms appear without any underlying organic cause. Freud believed that anxiety was being

conversion

"converted" into *physical symptoms,* hence the term _____ reaction.

physical

33. In conversion reactions there are _____ symptoms that appear to have no organic cause. While Freud believed that such reactions represented a con-

anxiety

version of _____ into physical symptoms, most psychologists now interpret conversion reactions as a means of avoiding a stressful situation by unconsciously adopting *sick-role behavior.*

34. A pilot becomes afraid to fly following an emergency landing in which he nearly lost his life. He develops a paralysis of the right arm that prevents him from returning to his job. Since the doctors can find no physical cause for the paralysis, it is

conversion reaction

probably a _____ _____.

35. A woman is afraid that her husband may leave her. She suddenly loses her sight so that she is totally dependent on his care. Since no physical cause can be found for her blindness, this appears to be another case of a

conversion reaction

_____ _____.

sick-role

36. In conversion reactions the person unconsciously adopts _____-_____ behavior as a means of avoiding a stressful situation. It should be emphasized, however, that the individual is not faking. The physical disability seems quite real to the person, and the purposes served are largely un_____.

unconscious

37. We have discussed four types of neuroses, all of which are related to anxiety:

anxiety

(1) _____ reactions, in which the tension is very obvious; (2)

obsessive-compulsive

_____-_____ reactions, in which ritu-

phobias

alistic acts serve to ward off anxiety-producing impulses: (3) _____, in which excessive fears are focused on particular objects or situations and anxiety

conversion

is reduced by avoiding them; and (4) _____ reactions, in

which anxiety-producing situations are avoided by unconsciously adopting sick-role behavior.

depression

38. A fifth type of neurosis is *neurotic depression.* In neurotic de_____ the person reacts to a distressing event with more than the usual amount of sadness and fails to recover within a reasonable amount of time.

39. After losing her job Barbara spends all her time lying in bed and crying. She has no interest in anything, feels worthless, and contemplates suicide. Since her depression seems out of proportion to the precipitating event and shows no signs of improving,

neurotic

it would be classed as _____.

40. If, in addition to the above symptoms, Barbara becomes so immersed in her own thoughts and fantasies that she can no longer distinguish her fantasies from what is going on in the real world, she would be diagnosed as *psychotic* rather than

neurotic

n_____.

41. *Psychotic* disorders are much more serious than neuroses. The personality is disorganized and normal social functioning is greatly impaired. The psychotic individual often requires hospitalization. While the neurotic tries to cope with anxiety in order

psychotic

to continue functioning, the p_____ is no longer able to function adequately and has lost contact with reality so that he or she can no longer distinguish fantasies from what is actually happening.

42. Some psychoses are due to *physical* damage or malfunctioning. These are called the *organic* psychoses. Others are called *functional* psychoses because no

physical

ph_____ basis for them has been demonstrated so far. Functional

psychoses

_____ are presumed to be primarily psychological in origin, although genetic and other biological factors may play a significant role.

43. A person who showed signs of psychosis following a head injury would be diag-

organic

nosed as suffering from an _____ psychosis.

44. Disorders with no demonstrable physical basis in which environmental conditions

functional

are assumed to play a major role are called _____ psychoses.

45. One category of functional psychoses is the *affective disorders,* which are disturbances of *affect,* or mood. The person may be severely *depressed, manic* (wildly

depression

elated), or may alternate between periods of mania and d_____.

affect

These changes of mood, or _____, are often so extreme that the individual requires hospitalization.

disorders

46. People suffering from affective _____ may be either severely

depressed

_____ or elated. Or they may alternate cyclically between

manic, depressed
(either order)

_____ and _____ states, with a period of normal behavior in between. This pattern is called a *manic-depressive psychosis.*

manic-depressive

47. One type of affective disorder is a _____-_____ psychosis.

affective	**48.** One category of functional psychoses includes the _____ disorders; another group of functional psychotic disorders is labeled *schizophrenia*.
affect (or mood)	Whereas affective disorders are characterized by disturbances of _____, schizophrenia is characterized by disturbances of *thought*.
	49. A person suffering from schizophrenia may speak in a jumble of words and phrases that seem unrelated. This "word salad" reflects the disturbance of
thought	_____ that is characteristic of schizophrenia.
schizophrenia	**50.** The thought disturbances that are characteristics of schizo_____ seem to reflect difficulty in *"filtering out" irrelevant stimuli.* Whereas normal individuals are able to selectively focus attention, people suffering from schizo-
irrelevant	phrenia appear unable to filter out _____ stimuli; they are responsive to many stimuli at the same time and have difficulty focusing
attention	at _____ on the relevant ones.
	51. The thought disturbances observed in cases of schizophrenia seem to stem from a
filtering	difficulty in _____ out irrelevant stimuli.
schizophrenia	**52.** Another common symptom of the psychosis called sch_____ is *withdrawal from reality.* The individual tends to withdraw from interaction with others and becomes absorbed in his or her inner thoughts and fantasies.
reality	**53.** In some cases this withdrawal from _____ progresses to the point where the person is completely unresponsive to external events, remaining silent and immobile for days at a time.
withdrawal	**54.** The disturbed thought processes and _____ from reality characteristic of schizophrenia may be accompanied by *delusions* and *hallucinations*.
	55. Delusions are *false beliefs* that are maintained despite contradictory evidence or experience. Patient X thinks that he is God and has returned to earth to save us.
delusion	He is evidently experiencing a _____, since he is maintaining a false belief.
beliefs	**56.** Whereas delusions are false _____, hallucinations are false sensory perceptions—that is, sense experiences occurring in the absence of appropriate external stimuli.
	57. Patient Y hears voices talking to her and threatening her that no one else hears.
hallucination	She is probably experiencing a _____.
beliefs	**58.** Delusions are false _____, whereas hallucinations are false sensory
perceptions (or experiences)	_____.
	59. We have mentioned several signs of schizophrenia. These include disturbed
thought	_____ processes, which may reflect difficulty in filtering out
stimuli, reality	irrelevant _____; withdrawal from _____; false
delusions	beliefs, or _____; and false sensory perceptions, or

hallucinations

_____. Another characteristic of schizophrenia is a *disturbance of affect;* the individual's affect, or emotion, is inappropriate to the thoughts being expressed or the situation being experienced.

60. Patient Y smiles as he describes the death of a friend. Since the emotion is inappropriate to the thoughts being expressed, this indicates a disturbance of

affect

_____.

61. Although disturbed thought processes constitute one of the major signs of schizo-

affect

phrenia, there may also be disturbances of _____. The text discusses some of the psychological and biological factors that may lead to schizophrenia and points out that the label probably includes a *group* of disorders, which may turn out to have different causes.

affective

62. We have discussed two major classes of psychosis: _____ disorders, which are characterized by extreme changes in mood; and

schizophrenia

_____, characterized by thought disturbances and withdrawal from reality.

63. A third category of abnormal behavior that differs from either the

neuroses, psychoses

n_____ or the p_____ is called *personality disorders.* This category includes a wide variety of disorders that are often *long-standing patterns of maladaptive behavior* rather than reactions to conflict or stress.

disorders

64. Personality _____ are often longstanding patterns of

maladaptive

_____ behavior. *Psychopathic personality,* for example, is a form of personality disorder in which the individual has a lifelong history of socially deviant behavior.

psychopathic

65. One type of personality disorder is the psych_____ personality. The chief characteristic of individuals diagnosed as psychopathic personalities is a *lack of conscience.* They have no sense of morality or concern for others; their behavior is determined entirely by their own needs.

66. The chief characteristic of individuals with psychopathic personalities is a lack of

conscience

_____. They cannot tolerate frustration and seek immediate gratification of their needs, regardless of the welfare of others.

67. "I want what I want when I want it" sums up the behavior of the individual with

psychopathic

a _____ personality.

68. The characteristics of psychopathic personalities frequently bring them into conflict with the law. They are likely to be found in a (*prison/hospital*). The text

prison

discusses some of the biological and psychological factors that may be responsible for the psychopathic personality.

69. Other behaviors that are included under the category personality

disorders

_____, although it is questionable whether they belong there, are *alcoholism* and *drug dependence.* Many factors can lead to dependence on

drugs

alcohol and other _____; to call them personality disorders oversimplifies the problems.

alcohol

70. Dependence on _____ or other drugs can be *psychological* and/or *physical*. Psychological dependence means that the person has *learned* to use the drug as a means of coping with stressful situations. Physical

dependence

_____ refers to what was formerly called *addiction*.

physical

71. Dependence on drugs may be either _____ or

psychological (either order)

_____, or both. Physical dependence, synonymous

addiction

with _____, is characterized by *tolerance*—with continued use the person must take more and more of the drug to achieve the same effect—and *withdrawal*—if use is discontinued the individual experiences unpleasant physical symptoms.

72. After sniffing heroin a number of times, Helen discovers that she has to inject the drug under her skin to achieve the same effect. She is showing (*tolerance/with-*

tolerance

drawal), which is one sign of _____ dependence.

physical

73. After several years of heavy alcohol consumption, Mark finds that he feels irritable and shaky if he does not have a drink by late afternoon. He is showing the symp-

withdrawal

toms of _____, which is another characteristic of

physical

_____ dependence.

tolerance

74. The two characteristics of physical dependence are _____ and

withdrawal (either order)

_____. A person who has learned to use a drug to cope with

psychological

stress (a condition called _____ dependence) may progress to physical dependence with continued usage. The text discusses some of the factors involved in alcoholism and drug dependence.

anxiety

75. Let's review. The chief symptom of the neuroses is _____. See if you can identify the five major types of neuroses.

phobias

a. Excessive fears in the absence of danger: _____

anxiety reaction

b. Continual tension and anxiety: _____ _____

obsessive-compulsive

c. Persistently disturbing thoughts or urges: _____ _____

reaction

_____

conversion reaction

d. Physical symptoms with no organic cause: _____ _____

depression (or neurotic
depression)

e. Prolonged sadness out of proportion to the precipitating event:

_____

76. The psychoses are more severe disorders. One characterized by withdrawal from

schizophrenia

reality and thought disturbances is called _____.
Another type of psychosis, characterized by extreme mood changes, is the

affective disorders

_____ _____.

77. Longstanding patterns of maladaptive behavior, such as the psychopathic person-

personality disorders

ality, are classified as _____ _____.

drug dependence

Also included in this category are alcoholism and _____ _____.

TERMS AND CONCEPTS

neuroses _____

_____

_____

_____

psychoses _____

_____

_____

delusion _____

_____

_____

hallucination _____

_____

_____

_____

personality disorders _____

_____

_____

medical model of abnormality* _____

_____

_____

psychoanalytic model of abnormality* _____

_____

_____

social learning model of abnormality* _____

_____

_____

_____

sociocultural model of abnormality* _____

_____

_____

_____

"neurotic paradox" _____

_____

_____

anxiety reaction _____

_____

_____

_____

acute anxiety attack _____

_____

_____

"free-floating" anxiety _____

_____

_____

_____

obsessive-compulsive reaction _____

_____

_____

_____

phobia _____

_____

_____

conversion reaction _____

_____

_____

neurotic depression _____

_____

_____

*Indicates terms used in Critical Discussions

organic psychoses _____

_____

_____

_____

functional psychoses _____

_____

_____

_____

affective disorders _____

_____

_____

_____

manic state _____

_____

_____

_____

manic-depressive psychosis _____

_____

_____

_____

schizophrenia _____

_____

_____

_____

autism _____

_____

_____

_____

paranoid _____

_____

_____

_____

monozygotic (MZ) twins _____

_____

_____

_____

dizygotic (DZ) twins _____

_____

_____

_____

concordance rate _____

_____

_____

_____

schizoid _____

_____

_____

_____

dopamine hypothesis _____

_____

_____

_____

endorphins _____

_____

_____

_____

psychopathic personality _____

_____

_____

_____

physical dependence _____

_____

_____

_____

tolerance _____

_____

_____

_____

withdrawal _____

_____

_____

_____

_____ 1. The three major diagnostic categories of abnormal behavior considered in this chapter are
a. neuroses, personality disorders, psychoses
b. neuroses, psychoses, conversion reactions
c. schizophrenias, personality disorders, neuroses
d. psychoses, psychophysiological disorders, personality disorders

_____ 2. A study of children born to schizophrenic mothers but raised in foster homes found that
a. all of them became schizophrenic eventually
b. the incidence of schizophrenia was no higher than for controls
c. 66 percent became schizophrenic
d. many more became schizophrenic than controls

_____ 3. Normal people are characterized in the text as possessing a series of traits to a greater degree than individuals diagnosed as abnormal. Which of the following is _not_ one of these characteristics of the psychologically healthy individual?
a. self-esteem and acceptance
b. social conformity
c. productivity
d. self-knowledge

_____ 4. A major defining characteristic of personality disorders is that they
a. are maladaptive more from society's view than from that of the persons who have them
b. reflect a lack of contact with reality
c. are comparatively easy to treat
d. are frequently short-term responses to stress

_____ 5. A person who has to some extent lost contact with reality is termed
a. psychopathic
b. neurotic
c. psychotic
d. paranoid

_____ 6. One notable aspect of the behavior of neurotics has been called the "neurotic paradox." This refers to the fact that they
a. can behave normally and simultaneously experience anxiety
b. are often successful yet belittle themselves
c. show chronic lack of energy yet drive themselves too hard
d. cling rigidly to self-defeating behavior patterns and do not recognize this

_____ 7. Which of the following statements is _not_ true of individuals diagnosed as schizophrenics? They
a. occupy about half of all neuropsychiatric hospital beds
b. often experience hallucinations
c. exhibit multiple personalities
d. are characterized by thought disorders

_____ 8. Each of the criteria for defining abnormal behavior has both advantages and drawbacks. The only useful criterion for some neuroses, for example, is
a. personal distress
b. adaptiveness of behavior
c. social standards
d. statistical frequency

_____ 9. The person characterized as a psychopathic personality
a. typically comes from a home marked by intense conflict or disturbed relationships
b. is best characterized by "lovelessness" and "guiltlessness"
c. has been said to have an overreactive autonomic system
d. suffers from anxiety attacks.

_____ 10. Studies of the family background of schizophrenics have found that
a. schizophrenics are more likely than normals to have lost a parent early in life
b. disturbed home life is much more common for schizophrenics than normals
c. no single pattern of family interaction leads to schizophrenia
d. all of the above

_____ 11. The college student described in the text as fearful of many things, including leaving his dorm room, represents a
a. typical college student
b. phobia
c. conversion reaction
d. schizophrenic reaction

_____ 12. It has been hypothesized that class differences in the incidence of psychoses result from
a. differences in child-rearing practices
b. lowered class status as a result of psychoses
c. a tendency for the pressures of poverty to cause psychoses
d. all of the above

13. The woman described in the text as spending most of her waking hours checking the doors and windows and taking showers is displaying a(n)
   a. anxiety reaction
   b. obsessive-compulsive reaction
   c. phobic reaction
   d. conversion reaction

14. Unusual types or amounts of substances found in the blood of hospitalized schizophrenics
   a. may be either a cause or a result of their problem
   b. are called psychotomimetic substances
   c. have been shown to cause certain symptoms
   d. probably have no relationship to schizophrenia

15. A(n) _____ is an apparent physical problem that in fact is an unconscious means of avoiding a stressful situation.
   a. psychosomatic illness
   b. compulsive ritual
   c. obsessive reaction
   d. conversion reaction

16. The "split" in schizophrenia refers to a
   a. split between the person and his or her mind
   b. splitting into multiple personalities
   c. fragmenting of thought processes
   d. split between the person and his or her environment

17. Psychoanalytic theories of depression interpret depression as
   a. akin to learned helplessness
   b. a result of reduced reinforcement

   c. anger turned inward
   d. all of the above

18. _____ refers to a learned need for a drug.
   a. Psychological dependence
   b. Addiction
   c. Physical dependence
   d. Tolerance

19. A person whose pacing, shouting, and general disorientation fit our popular notion of a "raving maniac" is technically diagnosed as
   a. having an extreme anxiety reaction
   b. being in an acute manic state
   c. having a psychopathic personality
   d. suffering from an obsessive-compulsive reaction

20. The chronic tension of a person with an anxiety reaction is often interrupted by periods of
   a. comparative relaxation
   b. loss of contact with reality
   c. acute anxiety
   d. extreme withdrawal

KEY TO SELF-QUIZ

5. c p. 455	10. d p. 470	15. d p. 453	20. c p. 448
4. a p. 471	9. b p. 471	14. a p. 468	19. b p. 457
3. b p. 443	8. a p. 442	13. b p. 450	18. a p. 475
2. d p. 467	7. c p. 462	12. d p. 482	17. c p. 459
1. a p. 444	6. d p. 447	11. b p. 452	16. c p. 462

INDIVIDUAL EXERCISE

CLASSIFYING ABNORMAL BEHAVIOR

Descriptions of individuals displaying various kinds of abnormal behavior are given below. In each instance, attempt to classify the disorder on the basis of the behavioral symptoms, using the descriptions in Chapter 15 as a guide. Remember that the *neuroses* include anxiety reactions, obsessive-compulsive reactions, phobias, conversion reactions, and neurotic depression. The *psychoses* include the two functional psychoses—affective disorders, which include manic and depressed states, or a cyclical alternation between the two, and schizophrenia. *Psychopathic personality* is a *personality disorder* and is not included under the neuroses or psychoses.

It is important to remember that clinical cases in real life show a wide variety of symptoms and seldom fit as neatly into categories as do our hypothetical cases. The correct diagnoses are given on page 298 of the Appendix.

CASE 1

John, a patient at the state mental hospital, appears to be happy and elated. He frequently makes humorous remarks, laughs at them himself, and is successful in making others laugh too. In expressing his thoughts he jumps from one topic to another without following any particular course. If, while he is talking about his family, the psychologist suddenly interjects a comment about the weather, John immediately switches his conversation to the weather or any other topic the psychologist introduces. Furthermore, he is hyperactive. He is either drumming with his fingers, playing with a pencil, or engaging others with his rapid talk. There is no deterioration of intellectual and emotional faculties, however. His present illness will probably be followed by several years of "normal" behavior.

CASE 2

Jack has been hearing for several months the same voice, which makes derogatory accusations about his being a sexually immoral pervert. This same voice often commands him to do such things as throw furniture out of the window. His speech is monotonous except when he is talking about his troubles, at which time it becomes quite animated and vehement. His sentence structure is often shattered and his statements are usually incoherent, since they consist of a sequence of apparently unconnected words. An example of his "word-salad" is "The pipe tail on the bed, the TV said, a brown came out of the lawn, the flowers are board walk." He also coins new words such as "lapicator," which he said was an important chemical that will be used to purify the world.

CASE 3

Jim, a soldier, is in an Army medical hospital. He complains of a loss of sensation in his fingers. He also complains that he cannot see, although a competent occulist examined his eyes and found nothing wrong. It seems strange that Jim is calm about his disorder even to the point of feeling indifferent about it. Except for this, his personality seems intact.

CASE 4

Jane has been referred to a psychiatrist by her local physician, who can find nothing physically wrong with her. She complains, however, of feeling that something terrible is going to happen to her or to her family. She realizes that her fear is irrational, but she can't seem to help it. She has also become fearful of doing things she formerly did without any apprehension whatsoever, such as going to dances and driving her car. One might describe her as being in a state of apprehension about practially everything. Jane herself is not certain what she fears, and she seems to lack insight into the etiology of her present condition.

CASE 5

Margaret, an eighteen-year-old girl, is afraid to be alone at home or to go alone more than one block away from home. She is particularly afraid of being in a room by herself. She becomes becomes panicky when alone and reports she has the feeling that the walls are closing in on her.

CASE 6

Bill is an extremely orderly, clean, stubborn, and stingy person. He expects everything in the house to be spotless at all times. He insists that every chair, napkin, ashtray, and book be in its proper place. His wife loves him but finds it very difficult to keep the house in the rigid order he demands. He tends to have some time-consuming rituals connected with dressing and personal care, such as arranging his toilet articles in a particular order, rinsing his face exactly five times after shaving, laying out all of his clothes in a fixed sequence and making sure that he puts them on in that order.

CASE 7

Ralph is a highly impulsive person who has difficulty making plans or sticking to a job for any length of time. He has been fired from several jobs because he was caught stealing or because of frequent absences due to periodic drinking and gambling sprees. He always blames his employer for his dismissal and will not admit that his own behavior is responsible for his poor job history. Women tend to find him charming and personable, but they soon tire of his irresponsible behavior, frequent financial sponging, and general lack of consideration. His quick temper and disregard for social regulations have brought him into frequent brushes with the law, but he usually manages to charm his way out and has never been convicted of a crime. He appears to feel little guilt or anxiety regarding his behavior.

CASE 8

Following the breakup of her engagement to Fred, Martha has become very despondent. She shows little interest in her job (which previously she found stimulating and exciting) and often calls in sick. She spends a great deal of time alone in her room, sitting idly by the window or listening to the radio. When friends call to invite her out she usually refuses, pleading illness or fatigue. She complains that she feels continually tired, has to force herself to undertake such simple tasks as getting dressed or fixing a meal, and cannot concentrate enough to read a newspaper or magazine. Tears flow at the slightest provocation, and she feels worthless and inadequate. Her condition does not improve after several months have passed.

Questions for Discussion

1. Which of the symptoms shown by neurotic patients are most common (in less extreme form) among mentally healthy people?

2. In what way do neurotic individuals differ from those classed as psychotic?

3. In what way does the psychopathic personality differ from individuals classed as psychotic or neurotic?

16
Methods of Therapy

LEARNING OBJECTIVES 16-1. Be familiar with the historical background and current trends in the treatment of abnormal behavior.

16-2. Be able to specify the backgrounds and professional roles of the different specialists involved in psychotherapy.

Be able to describe the following approaches to psychotherapy, including the therapist's techniques and the patient's or client's experiences that are presumed to yield improvement.

16-3. The psychoanalytic approach.

16-4. The behavioral approach.

16-5. The client-centered form of the humanistic approach.

16-6. Be familiar with the techniques, advantages, and disadvantages of group therapy and family therapy. Understand what is meant by an eclectic approach to therapy.

16-7. Be able to discuss the difficulties involved in evaluating the success of psychotherapeutic techniques.

16-8. Be familiar with the techniques, advantages, and disadvantages of the three forms of biological therapy.

16-9. Be familiar with the variety of community resources being explored as techniques for enhancing mental health.

16-10. Understand what the experiences of therapists suggest that you can do to promote your own emotional well-being.

PROGRAMMED UNIT

1. What can be done to help people who are seriously disturbed emotionally or who show signs of abnormal behavior? One method of treatment is *psychotherapy.* If you know that "therapy" means treatment, you can guess that psychotherapy is

psychological

   treatment by _____ methods.

2. The use of psychological methods for treating abnormal behavior is called

psychotherapy

   _____. This is in contrast to *biological therapy,* which uses drugs, electroshock, and brain surgery to treat some types of abnormal behavior.

psychotherapy

3. The professionals involved in the practice of psycho_____ include *psychiatrists, clinical* or *counseling psychologists, psychiatric social workers,* and, in hospitals, *psychiatric nurses.*

4. A psychiatrist is the only member of this group with an M.D. degree. Since the only person who can assume *medical* responsibility for a patient is a physician, this is

psychiatrist

   one function of the _____ .

5. Some psychiatrists are psychoanalysts and follow the therapeutic methods formulated by Freud, but most psychiatrists are not trained in psychoanalysis. They use

biological

   other methods of psychotherapy and may also use bio_____ therapies, such as drugs.

6. A psychoanalyst is almost always a psychiatrist, but a psychiatrist is not always a

psychoanalyst

   _____ .

7. The clinical psychologist has a Ph.D. degree in psychology and has special training in the fields of diagnostic testing, psychotherapy, and research. Clinical psycholo-

medical

   gists are not trained in medicine, however, and cannot assume m_____ responsibility for their patients.

clinical

8. Counseling psychologists receive training somewhat similar to that of cl_____ psychologists, although they usually deal with less serious problems—such as problems of social adjustment or educational goals.

9. Psychiatric social workers have a Master's or Ph.D. degree in social work with special training in interviewing, compiling case histories, and carrying treatment procedures into the home and community. Neither psychiatric social workers nor clinical or counseling psychologists have medical training, however, and therefore they (*can/*

cannot

   cannot) assume medical responsibility for their patients.

10. You will remember that psychoanalysis was discussed as a theory of personality. We will now consider psychoanalysis as a method of psychotherapy. One of the basic techniques of this method is called *free association:* the patient is told to say, without selection or editing, everything that enters his or her mind. In order to bring repressed thoughts into awareness, the psychoanalyst asks the person to talk, to ramble, not to think too much about what he or she is saying, and not to sup-

free association

   press anything. This is the technique of _____ _____ .

11. One word will be associated, through past experience, with other words. For instance, if the person says "father," the word "stern" may come to mind. If this type of association is allowed to continue freely, without censorship, repressed

free   thoughts and feelings may enter awareness through the technique of _____

association   _____ .

free association   12. The technique of _____ _____ assumes that as people continue to talk without editing their words, they will utter thoughts and feelings that are associated with their problems and that these will give the analyst, and eventually the patient, the information necessary to understand and work through the problems.

13. Thoughts, feelings, and impulses of which a person is unaware are assumed to be repressed into the unconscious. The psychoanalyst uses the technique of free association to help the person bring to conscious awareness that which is

unconscious   un_____ .

14. People often repress thoughts and feelings that make them feel uncomfortable. It is natural, therefore, to *resist* their recall during psychoanalysis. You might guess that

resistance   one of the tasks of the analyst is to help people overcome their _____ance, so that they can deal with these unconscious thoughts and feelings.

15. Patient C is late for her appointment and when she does show up, she states that she cannot recall something she wishes to share with the analyst. This is an example

resistance   of _____ . That is, consciously the patient wishes to recall, but unconscious blocks hinder recall. And the fact that she was late for her appointment

resistance   might also be interpreted as _____ .

16. In order to help Patient C to overcome resistance and to better understand herself, the psychoanalyst will make *interpretations* of her behavior. The analyst may, for instance, call the patient's attention to her resistance to treatment by pointing out to her that she was late for her appointment and that she cannot recall what she

interpretation   wishes to share with the therapist. Psychoanalysts use _____ to help people overcome resistance to treatment and to help them understand themselves better.

17. The psychoanalyst helps people understand some of the deeper meanings of their free associations as well as their dreams by helping them make interpretations. For instance, a man may recall the manifest content of a nightmare he had the previous night, but he cannot understand the dream's latent content—what the dream means or implies. With the help of the analyst, however, he may be able to make an

interpretation   _____ of what the dream really means.

resistance   18. It is not unusual for a person to have some _____ to therapy, since symptoms are often less painful than the reality of some of the person's conflicts and feelings. To help the individual deal with what has been repressed, the

free, interpretations   analyst may use _____ association and make _____ of the deeper meanings of the person's associations and dreams.

19. On a conscious level the person wishes to solve his or her problems and feel better.

resistance

But on an unconscious level, the person may show _____ to therapy by coming late for appointments and by frequent blocking of what he or she wishes to relate to the analyst.

20. During psychotherapy people often *transfer* to the analyst emotional reactions they have had to other people important in their lives. This tendency is called

transference

tr_____ence. By analyzing these reactions, which often are not appropriate to the actual relationship of the analyst and the patient, the analyst gets clues to the patient's difficulties.

21. If a woman acts toward an analyst in the way she used to act toward her father or mother or some other significant person in her life, we would call this a manifesta-

transference

tion of _____ .

22. Sometimes a patient acts in a hostile manner toward the analyst when the latter has

transference

provided no reason to do so. This is interpreted as _____ , since the patient is responding emotionally toward the analyst as though the analyst were someone else.

23. In the permissive atmosphere of the therapist's office it is sometimes possible for a patient to relive a past situation that had strong emotional aspects and to express this emotion *freely,* as he or she had been unable to do in the original situation. This process, called *abreaction,* often brings the patient some relief from tension. If a woman relives a situation in which her father treated her unfairly and freely expresses the anger that she could not express then, she is experiencing

abreaction

_____ .

emotion
abreaction

24. A free expression of _____ that was felt but not expressed in an earlier situation is known as _____ .

25. At the time of his father's funeral Peter suppressed his feelings of anguish because they might be regarded as unmanly. Now that Peter is in therapy and relating the experience to an uncritical listener, the former suppressed feelings are expressed and he sobs freely. We would say Peter is now experiencing what psychoanalysts

abreaction

call _____ .

freely

26. Abreaction is like catharsis in that pent-up feelings are _____ly expressed in a permissive setting.

abreaction

27. A form of emotional cleansing, called _____ by psychoanalysts, sometimes takes place in therapy; by itself, it does not eliminate the causes of conflict, though the patient may feel some relief from tension.

28. When people understand the roots of their conflicts, they have achieved *insight.* For instance, Sue now understands the relationship between some of her current problems and some early life experiences. In other words, she has achieved some measure

insight

of _____ into her difficulties.

29. Stan now understands that he forms an immediate dislike of anyone in a supervisory capacity over him because the first authority figure in his life, his father, continually bossed and belittled him. We would say that Stan now has some

insight

_____ into his hatred for authority figures.

30. As a patient gains insight, he or she goes through a process known as *working through.* In this process, the person examines the same conflicts over and over again as they have appeared in a variety of situations throughout life, and learns to face

Working _____ them in a more mature way. _____through is part of the process of learning to face reality.

31. Since the patient will often face his or her conflicts over and over again outside the

working through _____ therapist's office, it follows that the _____ _____ process will continue in many situations in everyday life.

32. Psychoanalysis is a method of _____ therapy that focuses on unconscious

psychotherapy _____ conflicts. A quite different form of psychotherapy is *behavior therapy,* which is based on learning theory. The assumption behind this kind of therapy is that if

unlearned _____ *maladaptive behavior* is *learned,* it can also be un_____ by having the person learn new or more appropriate responses in place of the maladaptive responses.

33. Whereas psychoanalysis is concerned with understanding how one's past conflicts

behavior _____ influence behavior, behavior therapy focuses on the actual b_____ itself.

34. For example, behavior therapists view anxiety as a learned response to certain situations, rather than as the result of unconscious conflicts (which is the

psychoanalytic _____ _____ view). Since anxiety is a maladaptive response, the behavior therapist would try to have the person learn a more appropriate response to the situation.

35. Behavior therapists attempt to have the person learn more appropriate responses to

maladaptive, behavior _____ replace mal_____ ones. One technique used by _____ therapists is called *systematic desensitization:* a maladaptive response is weakened by strengthening an incompatible, or *antagonistic,* response. Since it is difficult to be relaxed and anxious at the same time, relaxation is a response that is

antagonistic _____ an_____ to anxiety.

36. In the technique of systematic _____ a person is

desensitization _____ systematically desensitized to an anxiety-producing situation by learning to relax in response to that situation.

37. The behavior therapist starts the procedure of _____ desensiti-

systematic _____ zation by having people list the sorts of situations that are anxiety producing for them. The situations are ranked in a sort of *hierarchy* from least to most anxiety provoking. Such a list is called an *anxiety hierarchy* because the situations are

most _____ ranked from the least to the _____ anxiety provoking.

38. When a behavior therapist ranks from low to high those situations that a particular

anxiety _____ person finds anxiety producing, he or she is establishing an_____ hierarchy.

39. Once the anxiety _____ is established, the individual is trained in a

hierarchy _____ procedure of muscle relaxation. We noted that relaxation is a response that is

antagonistic _____ _____ to anxiety.

40. The person is instructed to relax while visualizing or imagining the least anxiety-provoking situation in his or her _____ _____. If the individual remains relaxed and appears not to be anxious, the therapist proceeds to the next situation in the _____ hierarchy.

anxiety hierarchy

anxiety

41. Therapy continues in this manner until the situation that originally provoked the most anxiety now elicits only relaxation. Thus, the individual has learned to respond with _____ to situations that initially produced a response of anxiety.

relaxation

42. While this method of systematic _____ through imagined scenes has proved effective in reducing anxiety, it is *less* effective than desensitization through actual encounters with the anxiety-producing situations.

desensitization

43. Thus, if you want to overcome your anxiety about speaking in public, giving speeches before progressively larger audiences while practicing relaxation techniques would be (*more/less*) effective than imagining speech situations while relaxing.

more

44. Systematic desensitization is a technique used by _____ therapists in which a maladaptive response is weakened by _____ an incompatible, or antagonistic, response. Relaxation is one response that is _____ to anxiety; another is an approach, or *assertive,* response.

behavior

strengthening

antagonistic

45. Some people feel anxious in social situations because they do not know how to assert themselves—to "speak up" for what they feel is right or to "say no" when others take advantage of them. In *assertive training* the therapist helps the person practice _____ responses that might be used in situations where the individual tends to be passive.

assertive (or approach)

46. Two methods used by behavior therapists to help the individual substitute adaptive responses for maladaptive ones are _____ desensitization and _____ training. The text discusses some additional behavior therapy methods that are based on learning principles. These include positive reinforcement of adaptive responses, extinction of maladaptive ones, modeling adaptive behavior, and learning to regulate, or control, one's own behavior.

systematic

assertive

47. A third approach to psychotherapy that differs from either psychoanalysis or _____ therapy includes the *humanistic therapies,* which focus on the individual's natural tendency toward *growth* and *self-actualization.*

behavior

48. The humanistic therapist does not interpret a person's statements and behavior (as would a _____) or try to modify behavior (as would a _____ _____). Instead, the therapist tries to facilitate the individual's own tendency toward _____ and self-actualization.

psychoanalyst

behavior therapist

growth

49. We noted in earlier chapters that self-_____ refers to the realization, or actualization, of an individual's *potentials.* The job of the humanistic therapist is to help the individual realize his or her _____.

actualization

potentials

humanistic   **50.** One of the most widely used h_____ therapies was developed by *Carl Rogers;* it is called *client-centered therapy.* Rogers assumes that the patient, or client, can work out his or her own problems if the therapist provides the right psychological atmosphere.

centered

psychoanalyst   **51.** The client-_____ therapist neither instructs the person to free associate nor interprets the client's statements as would a _____ . Instead the therapist attempts to understand and reflect the individual's feelings and to see things from the individual's point of view, or *frame of reference.*

    52. The client-centered therapist tries to see things from the client's frame of

reference _____ . The therapist *accepts* the client and his or her feelings and

accept statements so that the client may begin to acc_____ him or herself.

client-centered   **53.** In _____-_____ therapy, the therapist mainly accepts and reflects the views of the client so that the client can understand him or herself better.

client-centered   **54.** An assumption basic to _____-_____ therapy is that each individual has the capacity to deal with his or her problems; the therapist's task is

growth simply to facilitate the individual's natural tendency toward _____ and

self-actualization _____-_____ .

    55. One of the main tenets of client-centered therapy is that the therapist must try to

reference adopt the frame of _____ of the client. That is, the therapist must

client try to see things as the patient, or _____, sees them.

    56. Let's review. We have discussed three approaches to psychotherapy; see if you can identify them in terms of their techniques.

psychoanalytic a. Uses free association to arrive at unconscious conflicts: _____ therapy.

client-centered b. Tries to adopt the patient's frame of reference: _____-_____ therapy.

behavior c. Uses learning principles to modify behavior: _____therapy.

    57. Since most emotional problems stem from difficulties in relating to other people, it makes sense sometimes to practice therapy in *groups.* Such therapy is called, appro-

group priately enough, gr_____ *therapy.*

    58. When therapy is carried out with a therapist and more than one client, we call it

group _____ therapy. Group therapy saves time, gives the individual the feeling that his or her problems are not unique—that others are "in the same boat"—and provides opportunities to learn better ways of interacting with other people. All the methods of psychotherapy that we have discussed have been used, often in modified form, in group therapy.

    59. *Encounter groups* are a popular offshoot of group therapy. The main difference is

encounter that en_____ groups are aimed at teaching people how to relate more openly to one another rather than at solving emotional problems or treating behavior disorders.

groups 60. Encounter _____, also known as *T-groups* or *sensitivity groups,* emphasize learning how to express one's feelings more openly. They may help people achieve a better understanding of how to interact with others, but they are not designed to

disorders treat emotional problems or behavior _____ .

encounter 61. T-groups and sensitivity groups are other names for _____

groups _____ .

62. Psychotherapy is the treatment of abnormal behavior or emotional disorders by

psychological psych_____ means. *Biological therapies* use physiological methods such as *electroshock, psychosurgery,* and *drugs* to modify emotions and behavior.

biological 63. Electroshock therapy, which is one type of _____ therapy, is sometimes used to relieve severe depression. Psychosurgery, a controversial procedure in which certain nerve fibers in the limbic system or hypothalamus are destroyed, has also been used to treat severely depressed and suicidal individuals.

therapy 64. The most successful biological _____, however, has been the use of *tranquilizers* and other drugs to modify behavior.

65. Tranquilizers, such as reserpine and chlorpromazine, have been very effective in calming disturbed and anxious patients, making them more amenable to treatment

psychotherapy by psychological means, or _____ .

66. Another group of drugs, called *antidepressants,* help to elevate the mood of de-

tranquilize pressed individuals. They energize rather than tr_____, apparently by affecting the amount of certain neurotransmitters in the brain.

drugs 67. The most successful biological therapy has been the use of _____ to modify behavior. Drugs that are effective in calming anxious patients are

tranquilizers _____ ; those that elevate the mood of depressed

antidepressants individuals are _____ .

68. While drug therapy has successfully reduced the seriousness of many types of abnormal behavior, particularly the psychoses, there are limitations. The drugs can have undesirable side effects, and they may alleviate symptoms without requiring the individual to face the problems that are creating maladaptive

behavior(s) _____ . Since the attitudes and response patterns that have developed over a lifetime cannot be changed suddenly by taking a drug, psycho-

drug therapy is usually needed along with _____ therapy.

TERMS AND CONCEPTS

psychiatrist _____

_____

_____

_____

psychoanalyst _____

_____

_____

_____

clinical psychologist _____

_____

_____

_____

counseling psychologist _____

_____

_____

_____

psychiatric social worker _____

_____

_____

_____

psychiatric nurse _____

_____

_____

_____

psychotherapy _____

_____

_____

_____

psychoanalysis _____

_____

_____

_____

free association _____

_____

_____

interpretation _____

_____

_____

_____

transference _____

_____

_____

_____

abreaction _____

_____

_____

_____

insight _____

_____

_____

_____

working through _____

_____

_____

_____

behavior therapy _____

_____

_____

_____

systematic desensitization _____

_____

_____

_____

anxiety hierarchy _____

_____

_____

_____

assertive training _____

_____

_____

modeling _____

_____

_____

_____

self-regulation _____

_____

_____

insight therapists* _____

_____

_____

_____

symptom substitution* _____

_____

_____

_____

humanistic therapies _____

_____

_____

_____

client-centered therapy _____

_____

_____

_____

self-congruent person _____

_____

_____

_____

group therapy _____

_____

_____

_____

encounter groups _____

_____

_____

_____

eclectic approach _____

_____

_____

_____

hello-goodbye effect _____

_____

_____

placebo effect _____

_____

_____

_____

spontaneous remission _____

_____

_____

_____

biological therapies _____

_____

_____

_____

electroshock therapy _____

_____

_____

_____

psychosurgery _____

_____

_____

_____

placebo* _____

_____

_____

_____

double-blind procedure* _____

_____

_____

_____

*Indicates terms used in Critical Discussions

_____ 1. There are several professions involved in psychotherapy and sometimes the situation seems more complicated than it really is. One complexity is that a _____ is almost always a _____ but not vice versa.
   a. psychotherapist, psychiatrist
   b. clinical psychologist, psychiatric nurse
   c. psychoanalyst, psychiatrist
   d. psychiatric social worker, psychiatrist

_____ 2. In the use of behavior therapy for the relief of snake phobias the most effective approach was
   a. symbolic modeling
   b. live modeling with participation
   c. desensitization
   d. positive reinforcement

_____ 3. A consensus regarding the effectiveness of psychotherapy is difficult to reach. Nevertheless some things do seem clear. Which of the following is _not_ one of them?
   a. Only those patients treated by the psychotherapy most appropriate to their problems show much improvement.
   b. Psychotherapies do help patients.
   c. All psychotherapies share common features, such as a warm relationship in a special setting.
   d. There is little evidence, except for phobias and specific anxieties, that one form of therapy produces better results than another.

_____ 4. The "basic rule" of _____ is to say everything that enters your mind, without selection or editing.
   a. interpretation
   b. transference
   c. abreaction
   d. free association

_____ 5. A psychotherapist who maintains an eclectic approach might include _____ in the treatment of an anxiety neurotic.
   a. tranquilizers and relaxation training
   b. a discussion of the patient's history
   c. education techniques
   d. any of the above

_____ 6. The text offers several suggestions for bettering your emotional well-being. Which of the following is _not_ one of them?
   a. Seek always to solve your own problems, turning to professionals only as a last resort.
   b. Discover occasions that provoke emotional overreaction, so as to be able to guard against it.
   c. Learn to accept your feelings as something natural and normal.
   d. If emotional expression is blocked by circumstances, learn to seek permissible outlets.

_____ 7. During the past 20 years the emphasis in treatment of the mentally ill has shifted from
   a. client-centered therapy to psychoanalytic therapy
   b. somatotherapy to psychotherapy
   c. professionals to amateurs
   d. hospital treatment to community treatment

_____ 8. When systematic desensitization is used as a therapeutic technique,
   a. maladaptive responses are weakened or eliminated by strengthening antagonistic responses
   b. anxiety is increased to effect an alteration in behavior
   c. the patient is placed in a restricted environment with no anxiety-provoking stimuli
   d. modification of behavior depends on the patient's understanding of unconscious motives

_____ 9. An important concept in psychoanalysis is transference. This refers to the tendency of patients to
   a. transfer emotional responses to the therapist
   b. transfer their own responsibilities to the therapist
   c. show reduced resistance as therapy progresses
   d. free associate less freely as therapy progresses

_____ 10. Carl Rogers has described what he believes to be a consistent pattern of change in encounter groups. Which of the following is _not_ characteristic of such groups? Members
   a. initially tend to be confused and frustrated
   b. often begin the expression of their feelings with negative comments about others
   c. express their feelings openly at the beginning
   d. become impatient with defensiveness, by the final session

_____ 11. Behavior therapists believe that insight is
   a. a worthwhile goal
   b. not sufficient for behavior change
   c. not necessary for behavior change
   d. all of the above

12. The first advocate of humane treatment of the mentally ill was
    a. Clifford Beers
    b. Hippocrates
    c. Phillippe Pinel
    d. Sigmund Freud

13. The course of improvement during psychoanalytic therapy is commonly attributed to three main experiences of the patient. Which of the following is *not* one of these?
    a. insight
    b. abreaction
    c. transference
    d. working through

14. The purpose of client-centered therapy is to_____ the client's feelings.
    a. direct
    b. clarify
    c. judge
    d. elaborate on

15. In recent studies described in the text, former drug addicts, prison inmates, and college students have all
    a. been found to suffer depressive episodes
    b. functioned as psychotherapists
    c. been relieved of phobias by modeling techniques
    d. been found to need assertive training

16. Some of the problems of assessing cure in psychotherapy are seen in the "hello-goodbye effect," in which
    a. therapists see the patients' problems as more severe when they enter therapy than when they leave
    b. patients exaggerate their problems at the beginning of therapy

    c. patients try to minimize their problems at the beginning of therapy
    d. patients exaggerate any of their problems that still remain at the end of therapy

17. "Token economies" have been developed by behavior therapists on the basis of principles of
    a. modeling
    b. aversive conditioning
    c. operant conditioning
    d. classical conditioning

18. For Carl Rogers, the most important element of a therapeutic relationship is
    a. a "self-congruent" therapist
    b. abreaction
    c. the "shaping" of behavior
    d. transference

19. Electroshock therapy is currently used successfully with
    a. a wide variety of mental problems
    b. most psychoses
    c. severely depressed patients
    d. no one

20. The most successful biological therapy is
    a. psychosurgery
    b. electroshock therapy
    c. insulin-shock therapy
    d. drug therapy

KEY TO SELF-QUIZ

1. c p. 490	6. a p. 513	11. d p. 494	16. b p. 506	
2. b p. 497	7. d p. 489	12. b p. 487	17. c p. 496	
3. a p. 507	8. a p. 494	13. c p. 493	18. a p. 502	
4. d p. 491	9. a p. 492	14. b p. 501	19. c p. 508	
5. d p. 505	10. c p. 503	15. b p. 512	20. d p. 509	

INDIVIDUAL EXERCISE

FREE ASSOCIATION

Introduction

This is a very simple exercise, but it will give you a better feeling for what goes on in therapy and a better understanding of why certain kinds of therapy take so long.

The main technique in psychoanalytic therapy is free association. The therapist instructs the client to say whatever comes into his or her mind. There should be no attempt to censor any material that comes to consciousness—it should all be verbalized, no matter how irrelevant, unimportant, or embarrassing it may seem.

Equipment Needed

None required, but if a tape recorder is available it would be useful.

Procedure

The technique of free association appears to be very simple. It is, however, harder to do than it might seem. In order to get some idea of what it is like, first go to a place in which you know you will not be disturbed or overheard; go to any lengths you feel necessary in order to find such a place. Some students have waited until they were at home and their family was away. Then, when you are *sure* that you are alone and no one else can hear you, try to follow the rules for free association. Say everything *aloud* in a clear tone.

If possible, it would be instructive to tape record your free associations so that you can analyze them later.

Questions for Discussion

1. Was it easy to do? If not, why do you think it was not?

2. Can you imagine what it would be like to do this in the presence of another person?

3. How long do you think it would take you to be able to do this in the presence of another person?

4. Can you trace some of the cues that made one thought lead to another?

17
Social
Psychology

LEARNING OBJECTIVES

17-1. Be able to define social psychology in terms of its two major emphases.

17-2. Be familiar with the factors that influence whether or not a bystander will intervene in an emergency situation. Be able to differentiate between "pluralistic ignorance" and "diffusion of responsibility."

17-3. Be able to name, and to explain the differences between, three processes of social influence. Be familiar with the Asch and Milgram studies, including factors that increased or decreased compliance. Be able to state the general conclusion that social psychologists draw from these studies.

17-4. Understand how the theory of cognitive dissonance applies to the internalization of beliefs or attitudes; show how this explains the one dollar-twenty dollar study.

17-5. Know what is meant by identification with a reference group. Be familiar with the Bennington study and be able to show how its findings may be relevant to Patty Hearst's "conversion."

17-6. Be able to differentiate between primacy and recency effects in our judging of others. Know which effect is likely to occur when.

17-7. Be familiar with the factors that promote interpersonal attraction, and with some of the difficulties encountered by researchers seeking to specify such factors.

17-8. Understand what is meant by the attribution process. Be able to differentiate between dispositional and situational attributions. Be familiar with the covariance and discounting rules.

17-9. Be able to explain the theory of self-perception and know how it may be applied to a variety of situations.

17-10. Be able to define the fundamental attribution error. Be able to explain some of its implications and to show how social psychology's emphasis on situational factors acts as an antidote to it.

1. *Social psychology* studies the ways in which a person's *thoughts, feelings,* and *behaviors* are *influenced by other persons.* Since most of our lives are spent in the presence of other people, we might conclude that almost all of psychology is

social   s_____ psychology.

2. But social psychologists tend to look at social influence from a somewhat different perspective than other psychologists. First, they are more apt to focus on the current or ongoing *situational influences* on behavior than on developmental or personality factors. Social psychologists are more interested in current or ongoing

situational   _____ influences on behavior than they are in the influences of factors in the individual's past that may have shaped his or her personality.

3. Thus, if the leader of a teenage gang assaults a police officer, the social psychologist

influences   is more interested in the situational _____ (for example, What was the provocation? Were other gang members present?) than in experiences in the individual's past that predisposed him or her to be aggressive.

4. The social psychologist is more interested in situational factors than in developmental or personality influences on be_____.

behavior

5. A second emphasis of social psychology is on the individual's *phenomenology,* that is, on the *individual's own point of view* or *subjective definition of the situation,* as opposed to some objective measure of the circumstances. In other words, phenomenology refers to the study of phenomena from the individual's own point

view   of _____.

6. Thus, if the gang leader attacked the police officer because he or she believes all police officers are hostile, this perceived hostility *is* the cause of the individual's behavior—regardless of what the objective situation may be. Social psychologists

definition (or view)   are interested in the individual's subjective _____ of the situation.

phenomenology   7. For social psychologists the important thing is the individual's phen_____ rather than some objective measure of the situation.

8. Social psychology differs from other areas of psychology in two ways: its focus on

situational   the ongoing _____ influences on behavior and its emphasis on the individual's _____.

phenomenology

9. Situational variables and the way individuals interpret them have a profound influence on what people do in an emergency. The term "bystander apathy" has been used to explain why people often fail to intervene in an emergency situation. Studies have shown, however, that it is not simple indifference to the fate of the

emergency   victim that prevents people from intervening in em_____ sit-

is not

uations, but a host of other variables. Thus, the term bystander apathy (*is/is not*) really accurate.

10. One situational variable is the *presence of other people.* The presence of other

people

_____ decreases the probability that any given person will intervene by (a) *defining the situation as a nonemergency* and (b) *diffusing* the *responsibility* for acting.

11. Suppose you are sitting in a theater and think you smell smoke; you even imagine you see wisps of smoke coming from behind the curtain. But everyone else appears to be unconcerned. You might take action if you were alone. But the presence of other people who remain calm serves to define the situation as a

nonemergency

_____ .

12. Suppose that while walking down a crowded street, you observe a woman fall to the pavement, striking her head severely. In this case it is difficult to define the situation as a nonemergency, but the presence of other people diffuses the

responsibility

_____ for acting. If you were alone you might go to her aid. But in a crowd you do not feel responsible. You assume that someone else will take care of her.

13. Two factors that help explain "bystander apathy" are defining the situation as a

nonemergency, responsibility

_____ and diffusion of _____ .

14. One factor that will *increase* the probability of an individual's helping in an emergency is having watched someone else help in a similar situation. If you pass a car with a flat tire and notice that someone has stopped to help, you will be (*more/less*)

more

likely to stop and help the next disabled driver you pass.

15. When bystanders mislead one another about an emergency situation, their influence on one another is unintentional. But more often, *social influence* is *intentional*. When you persuade a friend to go with you to the movies or to vote for your favor-

intentional

ite candidate, your influence is _____ .

16. Psychologists have identified three basic processes of social influence: *compliance, internalization,* and *identification.* These are ways in which our *attitudes, beliefs, or*

people

behaviors are changed through the influence of other _____ .

17. Compliance occurs when we conform outwardly to the wishes of an influencing agent but do not really believe in the attitudes we express or the behavior we dis-

attitudes (or beliefs)

play. The agent has influenced our behavior but not our _____ .

18. You are offered 10 dollars to vote for a man who is running for mayor. You think he is a poor candidate, but you vote for him anyway. This is an example of

compliance

_____ .

19. Your girlfriend tells you that your beard looks awful and that she will not go out with you unless you shave it off. You do so even though you think you look much

compliance

less attractive without it. This is another example of _____ .

attitudes

20. When social rewards and punishments induce us to comply, they often do so without changing our _____ .

influence

social

21. Compliance is one of the basic processes of social _____ . Another form of _____ influence is *internalization,* which occurs when we incorporate new beliefs and attitudes into our value system. In this case we

behavior

change more than just our _____ .

22. When social influence leads us to incorporate new beliefs and attitudes into our value system and our behavior changes accordingly, the process is called

internalization

_____ .

internalized

23. If individuals express an attitude because they really believe it and have incorporated it into their value system, the attitude is said to be _____ .

compliance

24. When people are persuaded to engage in behavior they do not really believe in, the process is called _____ . But under certain circumstances compliance can lead to internalization; that is, inducing people to engage in behav-

attitudes (or beliefs)

ior they do not really believe in can lead them to change their _____ .

25. In general, if people are offered a large sum of money to change their behavior or comply with a request, they are more apt to do so than if offered a small sum. Similarly, a severe threat of punishment is more apt to result in compliance than a mild threat. Although large rewards or severe threats of punishment are effective in

behavior

producing changes in _____ , they are usually less successful in getting people to believe in what they have been induced to do; that is, to change

attitude

their _____ .

26. For example, in one study, college students were given some dull, repetitive tasks to perform, and after completing them were bribed to go into the waiting room and tell the next subjects that the tasks had been fun and interesting. For some of the students the bribe was only one dollar; for others it was twenty dollars. Later the students were asked their actual opinion of the tasks. If small reward are more suc-

$1

cessful than large rewards in inducing attitude change, then we would expect that the (*$1/$20*) subjects would be more likely to say at a later time that they really enjoyed the tasks.

27. And this is what happened. Subjects who were paid one dollar to convince someone that the tasks were interesting, actually came to believe that they were; subjects

twenty

who were paid _____ dollars did not change their attitude. All subjects complied with the request, but only those who were given a minimum bribe changed

attitude

their _____ .

compliance

28. In other words, the large reward produced only _____ , while

internalization

the small reward resulted in _____ .

more

29. What explains the fact that attitude change is (*more/less*) likely to occur when inducements are minimal? One theory, called *cognitive dissonance theory,* assumes

that people strive for *consistency* among their various beliefs and attitudes and between their beliefs and their behaviors. When people engage in behavior they do not believe in, they will be uncomfortable because their behavior is not

consistent   con _____ with their beliefs.

dissonance   **30.** Cognitive _____ theory assumes that people want their behaviors and beliefs to be consistent. The feeling of inconsistency that occurs when people engage in behavior they do not believe in is called cognitive

dissonance   _____; cognitions are dissonant with each other or with behavior.

dissonance   **31.** People seek to resolve this _____, and one way is to change

behavior   their beliefs so they are consistent with their _____.

32. In the one dollar-twenty dollar study, the student tells another person the tasks were interesting when actually he or she considered them dull. Since this behavior is inconsistent with the person's true attitude, we would expect this situation to

cognitive   produce _____ dissonance.

33. The students who were paid twenty dollars have a good reason for making the false statements. They can justify their behavior ("I did it for the money"), so there is

attitudes (or opinions)   no "dissonance pressure" for them to change their _____ about the tasks.

34. The students who were paid only one dollar cannot justify their behavior by convincing themselves that they made false statements for the money. They thus ex-

cognitive dissonance   perience _____ _____ until they change

consistent   their opinions to be more _____ with their behavior. They decide they must have enjoyed the tasks.

35. Cognitive dissonance theory explains why internalization is more likely to occur

small   when inducements are (*small/large*).

compliance   **36.** So far we have discussed two processes of social influence, _____,

internalization   which does not involve attitude change, and _____, which does. A third form of social influence, called *identification,* occurs when we change our beliefs, attitudes, or behavior in order to be like a person or group we admire.

37. The change may be temporary; that is, the new beliefs, attitudes, or behaviors may

value   not be incorporated into our _____ system. Hence, identification

internalization   differs from _____.

38. A group of people that we refer to in deciding what to believe and how to act is called a *reference group.* When we identify with a reference group and change our attitudes or behavior to be like the group members, the process is called

identification   _____.

39. Any group that influences our attitudes and behavior—either through the use of social rewards and punishments, or by providing us with a frame of reference for

reference   interpreting events—is called a _____ group.

40.   Since our families have certain attitudes about the world and provide us
      with a frame of reference for interpreting events, they would be considered a

reference   _____ group.

41.   The society in which we live also prescribes certain attitudes and behaviors that are
      considered "correct" and punishes us with social disapproval (or worse) when we

reference group   stray from them. Thus, society would be another _____ _____.

42.   Any group that influences us, either through the use of social rewards and

punishments, reference   _____ or by providing a frame of _____
                   for interpreting events, is called a reference group.

43.   We "refer" to such groups in order to evaluate our beliefs, attitudes, and behaviors;

identify   if we seek to be like them, we are said to id_____ with them.

44.   Most of us identify with more than one reference group, and this often leads to

behaviors   conflicting pressures on our beliefs, attitudes, and _____ .

45.   College students often find that the attitudes of their classmates differ on a number
      of issues from those of their parents. These differences between the peer reference

reference group   group and the family _____ _____ may lead to
                   conflict.

46.   Studies have shown that students become more politically liberal during their college
      years, moving away from the conservative views of their parents. If the students
      revert to their former conservatism after graduation, then the changes in attitude

identification   would be considered a temporary id_____ .

47.   If, on the other hand, the more liberal attitudes are maintained in later life, we can
      assume that the new attitudes have been incorporated into the individuals' value

internalization   systems. This is the process of _____ .

48.   Most of our beliefs and attitudes are initially based on identification. When we
      start to identify with a new reference group, we "try on" the new set of atti-
      tudes and beliefs they prescribe. We may eventually discard them; or we may
      incorporate them into our value system. In the latter case, identification has led to

internalization   _____ .

49.   We have discussed a number of ways in which we are influenced by other people,
      both intentionally and unintentionally. Another topic of interest to social psy-
      chologists is our perception of other people—what factors influence our impressions

people   of other _____ .

50.   First impressions are important because we are biased toward *primacy effects*; that
      is, we tend to give too much weight to initial information and too little to later

information   in_____ that may be contradictory.

much

51. Primacy effects refer to the tendency to give too (*much/little*) weight to the initial information we receive about a person.

52. Agnes did very well on her first psychology test but poorly on later tests; Mark received a low score on his first test but improved markedly on subsequent tests. The instructor still thinks of Agnes as a better student than Mark. The instructor is

primacy

biased by _____ effects.

53. The tendency to stick to our initial impression of a person and to ignore later con-

primacy effect

tradictory information is called the _____ _____.

54. Studies have shown that if sufficient *time* intervenes between the initial informa-

primacy

tion and the subsequent contradictory information, then the _____ effect may be reversed. That is, the initial information may *dim in memory* so that we give greater weight to the *more recent* information. This is known as the *recency effect.*

55. As the name implies, the recency effect refers to the tendency to bias our judg-

recent

ments toward the more _____ information.

56. One variable that determines whether the recency effect will be more influential

time

than the primacy effect is the _____ interval between the two sets of information.

primacy

57. If the two sets of information occur close together, then _____ effects will be important; if there is a sufficient time lapse between the two sets of

recency

information, then _____ effects may occur because the initial in-

memory

formation has dimmed in _____ .

58. Suppose a trial jury hears all of the prosecution lawyer's arguments in one block and then immediately hears the arguments of the defense. Since the two sets of information come close together, we would predict that the jury would be more

prosecution

influenced by the arguments of the (*defense/prosecution*) lawyer in arriving at its verdict. A short time interval between two sets of information favors the

primacy

_____ effect.

59. If there is a large time interval between the two arguments, then we would expect

recency
last

the jury to be biased by _____ effects. In this case the advantage would go to the defense lawyer, whose case was present (*first/last*).

60. Social psychologists are also interested in interpersonal attraction. Research has uncovered a number of factors that determine whether people will be *attracted* to each other. These include *physical appearance, competence, similarity, reciprocal liking,* and *familiarity.* All of these factors help determine whether two people will

attracted

be _____ to each other.

61. Although people usually do not *rate* physical attractiveness as important in their liking of others, studies indicate that appearance is more important than personality characteristics or similar interests in determining whom college students choose to date. And people tend to attribute more positive personality characteristics to photographs of attractive individuals than they do to photos of unattractive individuals. Despite what we prefer to believe, physical _____ is an important determiner of liking.

appearance (or attractiveness)

62. We also tend to be attracted to people who appear competent, are similar to us in attitudes and values, and who like us. Thus, competence, _____, and reciprocal liking are variables influencing interpersonal attraction.

similarity

63. Familiarity is also a determiner of liking. Even if your roommate is quite different from you in attitudes and values, you may like him or her better at the end of the year than a new acquaintance who is more similar to you. In this instance _____ is operating to promote interpersonal attraction.

familiarity

64. Other variables that influence interpersonal attraction, in addition to familiarity, are _____ appearance, c_____, s_____, and r_____ liking.

physical, competence

similarity, reciprocal

65. We have seen that first impressions can be important and have noted some of the factors that determine whether or not we will like someone. In sizing up people, we observe their behavior and attempt to interpret it. The process by which we attempt to interpret and explain the behavior of other _____ is called *attribution*.

people

66. If, while observing a person's behavior, we attempt to interpret it—to infer the causes of the individual's actions—we are engaged in the process of at_____.

attribution

67. To what do we *attribute* the individual's behavior? We may attribute it to forces or pressures in the environment, or we may _____ it to the individual's own personality and attitudes.

attribute

68. If we decide that something about the person is primarily responsible for the behavior, we are making a *dispositional attribution*. (A person's beliefs, attitudes, and personality characteristics are sometimes called dispositions.) If we decide that some external force (such as money, threats, or social pressure) is primarily responsible for the behavior, then we are making a *situational* _____.

attribution

69. A young man stands on a street corner giving an eloquent speech in support of a bill to legalize prostitution. To what do we attribute his behavior? To the fact that he fervently believes in legalized prostitution? That he or his wife is a prostitute and they need more money? That he is being paid to give the speech? That he is fulfilling an assignment for his public-speaking class? If you attribute his behavior to either of the first two possibilities, you are making a _____ attribution. If you attribute his actions to either of the last two possibilities, you are making a _____ _____.

dispositional

situational attribution

70. We make a dispositional attribution when we infer that the cause of behavior lies in the individual's attitudes or _____ characteristics.

personality

71. We make a situational disposition when we attribute the cause of behavior to some

external (or environmental) _____ force.

72. The attribution process refers to our attempts to infer the causes of an individual's

behavior _____ .

73. Research shows that there are some systematic biases in our attributions; we tend to give too much weight to personality variables as determinants of behavior and to underestimate the situational factors that caused the person to behave as he or she did. That is, we tend to give too much importance to (*dispositional/situational*)

dispositional factors.

74. In one study subjects heard an individual give a speech either favoring or opposing racial segregation. They were informed in advance that the speaker has been *told* which side of the issue to take and the specific arguments to use. Despite this knowledge, the subjects inferred that the speaker believed to some degree the point of view

dispositional he or she was arguing. This illustrates our bias toward _____ attributions.

75. Because another person's behavior is such a dominant aspect of any situation we

situational observe, we tend to weight it too heavily and to underestimate _____ factors that may have led the individual to act as he or she did. This tendency to

dispositional give too much weight to _____ factors and too

situational little to _____ variables is known as the *fundamental attribution error.*

76. In the beginning of this chapter we noted that social psychology differs from other

phenomenology areas of psychology in two ways: its focus on the individual's phen_____

situational and its emphasis on the ongoing _____ influences on behavior. Social psychology's emphasis on the situational causes of behavior may help counterbalance our normal tendency to overestimate the influence of dispositional

error factors, that is, our bias toward the fundamental attribution _____ .

TERMS AND CONCEPTS

phenomenology _____

_____

_____

_____

bystander apathy _____

_____

_____

pluralistic ignorance _____

_____

_____

diffusion of responsibility _____

_____

_____

compliance _____

_____

_____

internalization _____

_____

_____

cognitive dissonance theory _____

_____

_____

identification _____

_____

_____

reference group _____

_____

social perception _____

_____

_____

primacy effect _____

_____

_____

recency effect _____

_____

_____

attribution problem _____

_____

_____

dispositional attribution _____

_____

_____

situational attribution _____

_____

_____

self-perception theory _____

_____

_____

fundamental attribution error _____

_____

_____ 1. Social psychologists may be distinguished from other psychologists in at least two ways: their emphasis on the individual's "phenomenology" and their focus on _____ causes of behavior.
   a. situational
   b. developmental
   c. personality
   d. systematic

_____ 2. Self-perception theory relates behavioral compliance and attitude change by a rather surprising proposal; it claims that we
   a. base our interpretations of others' behavior on what we would do in similar circumstances
   b. assume that situational forces are very powerful and attribute too little effect to our own motives
   c. try to behave according to the way that we feel but are often unsuccessful
   d. infer our attitudes by observing our own behavior as if it were that of someone else

_____ 3. When superior persons commit embarrassing blunders we tend to like them more, provided we have
   a. low self-esteem
   b. average self-esteem
   c. feelings of superiority
   d. proof that they feel humiliated

_____ 4. Studies such as the "college bowl" study have helped to define the fundamental attribution error. One important finding of these studies is that dispositional attributions
   a. tend to be made even when the situational forces are clear
   b. are not made if the situational forces are clear and unambiguous
   c. can be reversed by providing new information
   d. are less likely to be made than are situational attributions

_____ 5. Asch's studies on compliance, in which a subject was asked to judge the length of a line after pseudosubjects had intentionally misjudged it, have since been replicated and extended. Which of the following statements is *not* true about this research?
   a. In the basic study about 3/4 of the subjects conformed on at least one trial.

   b. If even one confederate broke with the majority, conformity dropped sharply.
   c. Conformity was reduced by a nonconforming confederate only when the confederate gave the correct answer.
   d. Subjects in the basic study conformed about 1/3 of the time (that is, on 1/3 of the critical trials).

_____ 6. When we receive mixed information about a person, we tend to base our impression on the information that is
   a. favorable
   b. received first
   c. unfavorable
   d. received last

_____ 7. When subjects who believed themselves to be in a group discussion via intercom heard one of the "group members" supposedly have a seizure,
   a. "pluralistic ignorance" kept many of them from responding appropriately
   b. those who did not report the seizure showed more distress than those who did
   c. the "diffusion-of-responsibility" effect kept subjects from defining the situation as an emergency
   d. the concept of "bystander apathy" was shown to be appropriately named

_____ 8. Research shows that physical appearance is important in determining
   a. whether blind dates like each other
   b. whether five-year-old children are popular with their peers
   c. adults' predictions of a child's personality
   d. all of the above

_____ 9. Milgram's compliance studies not only utilized a phony "shock machine" but shock us with their results. We can take some comfort, however, from the finding that
   a. once the "learner" no longer answered at all, few subjects continued the shocks
   b. the obedience rate dropped when subjects were made to feel more responsible for their actions
   c. none of the subjects continued to administer shocks when the experimenter left the room and gave instructions by telephone
   d. all of the above

_____ 10. A study of helping behavior, carried out in the New York subway, attempted to minimize the processes that prevent people from intervening in emergency situations. This study found that
a. an apparently ill victim received help in over 95 percent of the trials
b. people on the subway were even more reluctant to intervene than subjects in the laboratory
c. black "drunk" victims were aided only by black passengers
d. "diffusion of responsibility" played a major role in the results

_____ 11. A number of experiments based on cognitive dissonance theory have been used to examine the relationship(s) of behavioral compliance and attitude change. One general conclusion from this area of research is that
a. behavioral compliance never leads to attitude change
b. the less the inducement for compliance, the more attitude change
c. the greater the inducement for compliance, the more attitude change
d. most behavioral compliance yields some attitude change

_____ 12. "Pluralistic ignorance" refers to the fact that
a. few of us know what to do in a real emergency
b. most people are simply not attentive enough to notice the signs of an emergency
c. the presence of other people diffuses the responsibility for action
d. collective inaction in a group convinces each member that no emergency exists

_____ 13. Which of the following best summarizes the data on marriage and personal similarities?
a. Married couples develop similar tastes.
b. Complementary traits are more important than similar attitudes.
c. People like those similar to them.
d. Opposites attract.

_____ 14. Psychologists studying the influences of reference groups have noted that
a. individuals must belong to the reference group if its influence is to be effective
b. most individuals identify with a single reference group
c. reference groups serve to both regulate behavior and interpret events for their members
d. all of the above

_____ 15. The "attribution problem" refers to the question of why
a. one theory wins out over another
b. primacy effects are more powerful than recency ones
c. reference groups are so powerful
d. a person performs any action

_____ 16. One important finding of the Bennington study has general relevance for the development of personal convictions during college. Stated in formal terms it is that
a. internalization precedes identification
b. reference groups obtain primarily overt compliance
c. identification often leads to internalization
d. choosing the correct reference group allows one to avoid conflict

_____ 17. If we hear that a well-known athlete has endorsed a product, but we are not convinced of her sincerity because of the high fee we suspect she received, we are applying the attribution rule of
a. discounting
b. covariance
c. consistency
d. distinctiveness

_____ 18. The power of the primacy effect can be reduced by
a. warning people about biases in judgment before giving them any information
b. inserting another activity between the two contradictory descriptions
c. warning people about biases in judgment in between the two contradictory descriptions
d. any of the above

_____ 19. A dispositional attribution would be appropriate if a person's actions were motivated by a
a. financial reward
b. social norm in favor of the action
c. belief in the correctness of the action
d. threat of punishment

_____ 20. Studies of repeated requests have found results called "foot-in-the-door" and "door-in-the-face" effects. According to these findings, if an initial request is agreed to, a second request is
a. more likely to be accepted, even if it is more demanding than the first
b. less likely to be accepted, even if it is less demanding than the first
c. as likely to be accepted as the first
d. not affected in any consistent way by the first

INDIVIDUAL OR CLASS EXERCISE

CONFORMITY TO RULES

Introduction

In order to function effectively and to provide for the safety and welfare of its people, any society must establish certain rules and regulations governing behavior. Social psychologists are interested in the factors that produce conformity to society's rules. The purpose of this exercise is to investigate some of the variables that influence motorists' conformity to the rule requiring them to stop at a stop sign.

Equipment Needed

Clipboard and pencil.

Procedure

Select a four-way stop intersection (marked by stop signs, not a traffic light) with a moderate flow of traffic. It should be an intersection where you can watch the traffic from all four directions without being too conspicuous.

For a 45-minute period observe each car that approaches the intersection and record the information specified on the data sheet on page 266. You will need to decide first whether the car (1) comes to a full stop at the intersection, (2) slows down but does not make a complete stop, or (3) makes little or no attempt to slow down. You should spend a few minutes observing the cars before starting your recording period in order to get an idea of how to classify the various degrees of "stopping." Exclude from your records those cars that are forced to stop because they were either behind another car or blocked by cross traffic.

After deciding on the appropriate conformity category, note the sex of the driver, approximate age (under or over

25), and whether or not the driver is traveling alone. Place a tally mark in the appropriate box on the data sheet. For example, if the driver was a female, over 25, traveling with two children, and she made no attempt to slow down, you would place a tally mark in the bottom row in the box to the far right. If the driver was a male, under 25, traveling alone, and he came to a full stop, your tally mark would go in the top box of the extreme left-hand column. Obviously, if the car does not stop you will have to make some quick judgments as to age, sex, and companion.

Treatment of Data

Either you may analyze only your own data or the instructor may collect the data sheets from the entire class and provide you with the class totals in each category for your analysis.

1. Compute the overall percentage of individuals who made a full stop (that is, those who were rated as falling in conformity category 1).

    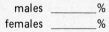 %

2. Compute the percentage of males who made a full stop, and do the same for females.

    males _____ %
    females _____ %

3. Compute the percentage of individuals under 25 who made a full stop, and do the same for those over 25.

    under 25 _____ %
    over 25 _____ %

4. Compute the percentage of times a full stop was made when the driver was alone, and the percentage when he or she was accompanied by one or more riders.

    alone _____ %
    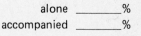
    accompanied _____ %

DATA SHEET

			Conformity categories		
			1. Full stop	2. Considerable slowing but not full stop	3. Little or no slowing
Alone	Under 25	Male			
		Female			
	Over 25	Male			
		Female			
With others	Under 25	Male			
		Female			
	Over 25	Male			
		Female			

Questions for Discussion

1. Do most people comply with the regulation requiring a full stop at stop signs?

2. Does the degree of compliance or conformity depend on the age and sex of the drivers? Is compliance influenced by whether or not the driver is alone?

3. In calculating our percentages, only conformity category 1 was considered. Do we gain any additional information by examining the percentage of drivers that fell in categories 2 and 3?

4. What other variables besides those recorded in this study seemed to predict conformity behavior? For example, did you get the impression that factors such as type or condition of the car or the apparent socioeconomic status of the driver were related to conformity?

5. How accurate do you think your judgments were concerning stopping behavior and the other variables? Would it have been worthwhile to have had several judges rather than a single observer making ratings?

6. If you were to make a large-scale study of this type of conformity behavior, what changes would you make in the research procedure?

18

Psychology and Society

LEARNING OBJECTIVES

18-1.　Be able to explain how stereotypes develop and how they can lead to prejudice and discrimination.

18-2.　Be familiar with the five factors that are necessary elements in the "contact hypothesis" of prejudice reduction.

18-3.　Be able to describe the characteristics of an authoritarian personality. Be familiar with the background and current status of this concept.

18-4.　Understand how prejudice may reflect social norms. Be familiar with the effects on social norms, and thus on prejudice, of legislation and court decisions.

18-5.　Be familiar with the factors that contribute to the limited effectiveness of media persuasion on individuals' beliefs and attitudes.

18-6.　Be able to discuss the procedures, results, and implications of the Stanford Heart Disease Prevention Program.

18-7.　Be familiar with research on the psychological effects of noise, including the influence of predictability and control.

18-8.　Be familiar with research on the psychological effects of crowding.

18-9.　Be able to show, with both historical and contemporary examples, how society and behavioral scientists mutually influence each other's assumptions and decisions.

18-10.　Know the aspects of science that provide an "objectivity" beyond that achievable by any individual researcher.

1. Because it is not possible to deal with every new person we meet as if he or she were unique, our initial impression of an individual is often based on a *stereotype.*

stereotype   A stereo_____ is a belief about a group of people that has been *overgeneralized* and *applied too broadly* to *every member* of the group.

2. The only Mexicans that Roy has encountered are the itinerant workers on his father's farm. When his freshman roommate turns out to be Mexican, Roy assumes that the young man is from a poor family and is attending the university on a

stereotype   minority scholarship. His initial impression is based on a _____.

3. A stereotype is a belief about a group of people that has been

overgeneralized, every   over_____ and applied too broadly to _____ member of the group.

4. When we treat people as members of a group rather than as individuals, we are

stereotypes   usually operating on the basis of _____.

stereotypes   5. Some of our overgeneralizations, or _____, may lead to *prejudice—negative attitudes* toward individuals based solely on their *group membership.*

negative   6. If we are prejudiced against people, we hold _____ attitudes

group   toward them on the basis of their _____ membership.

attitudes   7. Prejudice refers to negative _____. Such attitudes can, in turn, lead to *discrimination—unfair treatment* of individuals based solely on their group membership.

attitudes   8. While prejudice refers to (*attitudes/behavior*), discrimination refers to (*attitudes/*

behavior, unfair   *behavior*)—specifically, _____ treatment of individuals because of their

stereotypes   group membership. Both can result from the use of _____.

9. Frank believes that all Puerto Ricans are lazy. This is an example of

prejudice   _____ stemming from a stereotype. He refuses to hire any

discrimination   Puerto Ricans. This is an example of _____.

attitudes   10. In seeking to reduce prejudice (negative _____) and discrimi-

treatment   nation (unfair _____), one approach has been to provide increased contact between the groups involved. The *contact hypothesis* assumes

reduced   that prejudice and discrimination can be (*increased/reduced*) by greater intergroup contact.

11. But a little reflection should raise doubts about the validity of the contact

hypothesis   _____. For example, contacts between black ghetto resi-dents and white police officers seem to increase rather than reduce prejudice, sug-

is not   gesting that increased contact by itself (*is/is not*) sufficient to reduce prejudice.

contact

12. The _____ hypothesis appears to hold only under certain conditions. For example, studies have shown that in order for increased contact to reduce prejudice, the *participants* must be of *equal status.*

13. If white professionals always interact with blacks who are in low-status occupational roles, the contacts will probably only reinforce the stereotypes each group holds of the other. For contact to reduce prejudice, the participants should be of

equal

_____ status.

14. Another condition that increases the probability that intergroup contact will reduce

prejudice

_____ is the *potential* for *personal acquaintance.* If members of each group have frequent but only casual contact and never get to know each other as individuals, there is less chance that prejudice will decrease.

personal

15. There must be a potential for _____ acquaintance in the contacts, if we expect them to reduce prejudice.

16. However, even if we do not have a chance to get to know individuals from another group on a personal basis, we may revise our prejudices if we meet individuals who *do not conform to our stereotypes.* If, for example, a man meets a number of efficient and capable female executives, he may revise his stereotypes about women's abilities and become less prejudiced against females in business. Exposure to indi-

conform

viduals who do not _____ to the stereotype may reduce prejudice.

17. We have mentioned three conditions under which intergroup contact is likely to

status

lead to a reduction of prejudice: equal _____ of participants, potential

personal

for _____ acquaintance, and exposure to individuals who do not

stereotype

conform to the _____. A fourth condition is a *social envi-ronment* that *favors equality and fair treatment.*

18. For example, if neither parents nor teachers are pleased that their school has been desegregated, the increased contact between black and white students is less likely to lead to a reduction of prejudice than if desegregation occurs in a social

environment

_____ that favors equality and fair treatment.

equality

19. A social environment that favors _____ and fair

treatment

_____ is an important factor in reducing prejudice.

20. A fifth, and perhaps the most potent, factor is participation in a *cooperative effort.* One study found that when Anglo, Chicano, and black schoolchildren were required to work together to attain a desired goal, they came to like each other much

cooperative

better. Participation in a _____ effort helps to reduce

favors

prejudice, as does a social environment that _____ equality.

21. Intergroup contact under the five conditions that we have discussed presumably

stereotypes

reduces prejudice by reducing the s_____ that groups hold about one another. Another possibility is that these conditions also foster interaction that is rewarding in itself, motivating the participants to interact further in the future.

22. Are there certain personality factors that predispose an individual to be prejudiced? Research on anti-Semitism in the 1940s identified a type of "prejudiced personality" called the *authoritarian personality*. The authoritarian _____

personality

refuses to acknowledge any personal weaknesses and, instead, *projects* such undesirable traits onto members of minority groups, using such groups as *scapegoats* for his or her own frustrations.

23. Projection of one's own undesirable traits onto members of minority groups is said

authoritarian

to characterize the prejudiced, or _____, personality.

projects

24. The authoritarian personality _____ undesirable personal traits

scapegoats

onto members of minority groups, using them as _____ for his or her own frustrations.

25. While there may be prejudiced personality types, such as the

authoritarian personality

_____ _____, evidence indicates that most prejudice and discrimination stem from *conformity to social norms*.

26. A community's implicit rules specifying the beliefs, attitudes, and behaviors "appro-

norms

priate" for its members are called social _____. If the attitudes of the community favor prejudice, then the community member who expresses prejudiced

social norms

attitudes is probably simply conforming to the local _____ _____.

27. The social norm explanation of prejudice sees prejudice as stemming from

group

(*individual/group*) characteristics.

28. In the 1950s southern Americans expressed much stronger anti-black attitudes than northern Americans, but they were not more anti-Semitic. This suggests that the

social norms

most important factor in prejudice is (*social norms/personality characteristics*).

29. Southerners who affiliated with a political party during the 1950s were more anti-black than political independents; no such differences appeared in the North. If we assume that political party members are more conforming than independents,

social

then these results suggest that racial prejudice is based largely on _____

norms

_____.

30. Thus we have two explanations for prejudice. One focuses on the

authoritarian

_____ personality, while the other emphasizes the

social norms, second

importance of _____ _____. The (*first/second*) factor is considered the more important of the two.

31. The history of racial desegregation shows that legislation, by changing social

norms

_____, can change people's *attitudes*. When the Supreme Court ruled in 1954 that segregated public schools were unconstitutional, only a small percentage of the white population favored integration. Some ten years later, a majority of the population was favorable. These data indicate that legislation can lead to

attitude

_____ change.

norms
attitudes

32. Since most racial attitudes are rooted in social _____, changing the norms of the community changes racial _____ as well.

33. Another social issue of concern to psychologists is the effect of the mass media on our attitudes. Despite the millions of dollars spent on TV advertising and political messages, research indicates that media persuasion is not as effective in changing

attitudes

our _____ as we might suppose. The main problem lies in reaching the intended audience; people expose themselves mainly to opinions they already agree with. This is known as *selective exposure.*

34. Democrats listen mainly to speeches by Democrats; Republicans listen mainly to

exposure

speeches by Republicans. This is an example of selective _____.

35. Liberals read *The New Republic* but are unlikely to read the *National Review.* This

selective

is another example of _____ exposure.

36. But even if we are exposed to a persuasive message, we are more likely to "tune in" to communications that support our views than to those that do not. This is called *selective attention.* For example, if you strongly favor legalizing marijuana you are more apt to adjust the radio dial to remove static from messages supporting legali-

attend

zation than from messages opposing it. You selectively _____ to the message you agree with.

37. The message of the would-be persuader may not reach us because of selective

exposure, attention
(either order)

_____ or selective _____. Even if we do attend to the message, we are likely to interpret it in the context of our own beliefs and attitudes. This is called *selective interpretation.*

38. A politician delivers a rather ambiguous speech on the problem of national health care. Those listeners who favor socialized medicine are apt to view the politician as supporting their position more than he or she actually did; those opposed are apt to interpret the speech as more in line with their views than it actually was. This is

interpretation

an example of selective _____.

39. When we listen to a message that is at all ambiguous, we tend to

interpret

_____ it in the context of our own beliefs and attitudes.

40. Three obstacles that operate to prevent the mass media from influencing us are

exposure, attention

selective _____, selective _____,

interpretation (any order)

and selective _____.

41. A quite different social problem, the quality of the environment, is the research focus of *environmental psychologists.* Two of the main concerns of environmental

psychologists

_____ are the psychological effects of living under noisy and crowded conditions.

42. Studies have shown that people can *adapt* to a wide range of *noise levels.* If subjects are exposed to short bursts of very loud noise while performing a fairly easy task, they are initially disturbed. But after a few minutes they manage to do as well as

adapt

subjects who are not exposed to noise. They are able to _____ to the noise.

43. If the task becomes more complicated, however, loud noise does interfere with per-

adapt

formance. Thus, there are limits to our ability to _____ to noise.

44. Studies have shown that noise level itself is less important than its *predictability*. Noise that occurs at regular intervals has a much less detrimental effect on a subject's subsequent performance than noise that occurs at random, unpredictable

predictability

intervals. Thus, the _____ of the noise is more important than its level.

more

45. Unpredictable noise is (*more/less*) disruptive than predictable noise.

noise

46. Predictability is one variable that reduces the negative effects of _____; another variable is *control*. If people know that they can turn off the noise if it gets too annoying (even if they do not actually do so), its effects are much less disruptive.

control

47. Two variables that influence the negative effects of noise are _____

predictability (either order)

and _____.

environmental

48. Noise is one research focus of _____ psychologists; another is *crowding*. Crowding refers to the *subjective feeling* that too many people are packed too closely.

subjective

49. Crowding is a _____ feeling, but *density* refers to the number of people in a given area.

50. A number of variables—temperature, noise level, cultural norms, whether the other people are friends or strangers—influence our feeling of being crowded. Thus,

density

crowding is only partially a function of d_____.

51. You may feel more "crowded" in a hot room with twenty-five strangers than in a cool room with an equal number of friends. Variables other than sheer

density

_____ of people influence your feelings of being crowded.

52. Some researchers distinguish between two kinds of density: *inside density*—the number of *people within a residence;* and *outside density*—the number of

people

_____ *per square mile*.

53. Studies comparing people who live in large cities with those living in towns or rural areas (using the number of people per square mile as a criterion for classifying)

outside

would be looking at the effects of _____ density.

54. Such studies have found that, in general, people in large cities are just as happy as

outside

those in small towns and rural areas. This suggests that _____ density, by itself, has few negative effects.

density

55. While outside _____ appears to have few negative effects, inside

residence

density, the number of people within a _____, has been found in some studies to be related to higher rates of juvenile delinquency, homicide, and suicide.

inside

56. Thus, of the two measures, (*outside/inside*) density appears to have the greatest negative effects.

57. Investigators suggest that crowded conditions within the home may lead to *greater frustration* as one's daily routines are thwarted; and this greater

frustration

_____ leads to *aggression*.

inside

58. One explanation of the negative effects of _____ density is that frustra-

aggression

tion leads to _____.

negative

59. But even the conclusion that inside density has (*positive/negative*) effects on people may be true only for certain cultures. A study in Hong Kong, one of the world's most crowded cities, found no relationship between the size of each family's living space and measures of stress and strain among the family members. Thus, cultural factors (for example, social skills that make it possible to live harmoniously under

inside

crowded conditions) appear to influence the effects of _____ density.

60. Most of the studies we have been talking about used correlational methods to deter-

outside, inside
(either order)

mine the relationship between density (either _____ or _____) and such factors as happiness, suicide and homicide rates. But as we have learned, correlation does not establish cause and effect. A different approach to the study of crowding compared the attitudes and behavior of residents of large college dormitories (high-density environment) with those of students living in smaller residence units (low-density environment).

61. Residents of the large dormitories reported feeling more crowded and less satisfied with the quality of their social interactions; compared to residents of smaller living units they were also more withdrawn and less cooperative when participating in a

high

laboratory experiment. Thus the (*high/low*) density living environment did have negative effects.

high

62. The investigators suggest that the negative effects of _____-density living stem from the *inability to control* the number and quality of one's social interactions.

63. High-density living causes problems when people feel helpless in their ability to

control

_____ the number and quality of their social interactions. Note that this conclusion is revelant to our discussion of the effects of noise. Crowding and high noise levels by themselves may not have negative effects; what is important is

control

the real or perceived lack of personal _____.

noise

64. It is the unpredictable and uncontrollable n_____ and the uncontrollable social intrusions that cause us problems.

TERMS AND CONCEPTS

prejudice _____

_____

_____

_____

discrimination _____

_____

_____

_____

stereotype _____

_____

_____

_____

"contact hypothesis" _____

_____

_____

_____

scapegoat _____

_____

_____

_____

authoritarian personality _____

_____

_____

_____

social norms _____

_____

_____

_____

environmental psychology _____

_____

_____

_____

inside density _____

_____

_____

_____

outside density _____

_____

_____

_____

achievement motivation _____

_____

_____

_____

voir dire* _____

_____

_____

_____

*Indicates terms used in Critical Discussions

SELF-QUIZ

_____ 1. Perhaps the most significant finding from research on the psychological effects of noise is that the most important variable is whether the noise is
   a. loud or soft
   b. constant or varying in pitch
   c. predictable or not
   d. frequent or infrequent

_____ 2. The objectivity of science lies in
   a. the capability of scientists to avoid the prejudices of their society
   b. the choice of questions studied
   c. its methodology
   d. all of the above

_____ 3. Southern Americans were found by Pettigrew to express much more anti-black attitudes than northern Americans, but not more anti-Semitic ones. This finding _____ explanation of prejudice.
   a. tends to support an authoritarian-personality
   b. tends to reject an authoritarian-personality
   c. tends to reject a social-norms
   d. is not relevant to either

_____ 4. The concept of "working stereotype" refers to
   a. an overgeneralized view of lower-income people
   b. an inevitable process in our learning to deal with people
   c. any overgeneralized view of a group of people that is negative in content
   d. a deliberate attempt to discredit a group that one disagrees with

_____ 5. An unconscious bias may enter into behavioral scientists' work in several ways. For example, it can influence the
   a. questions they choose
   b. objectivity of their methods
   c. data they decide to publish
   d. all of the above

_____ 6. The mass media have been shown to be both effective and ineffective in changing behavior. Media are _not_ very effective, for example, in
   a. changing political opinions
   b. helping a small group of manufacturers dominate a market

   c. creating "name recognition" for an unknown political candidate
   d. creating demand for a new product

_____ 7. Studies based on the "contact hypothesis" for reducing intergroup hostility have found that interacting with members of another group
   a. can perpetuate stereotypes if participants are of unequal status
   b. can reduce prejudice if participants must cooperate in efforts toward a common goal
   c. can reduce prejudice if the participants are of equal status
   d. all of the above

_____ 8. Crowding has been considered as a potential cause of social problems. Some studies of _____ have, in fact, found correlations with indices of social pathology.
   a. inside density
   b. outside density
   c. population density per square mile
   d. all of the above

_____ 9. True "backlash" as a result of legislation to change discrimination
   a. has been found only with respect to the Equal Rights Amendment
   b. has been found only with respect to Supreme Court rulings on school desegregation
   c. is found fairly frequently with actions such as the above
   d. is almost never found

_____ 10. When the United States was considering limiting immigration in the early 1900s, psychologists boldly used their science to
   a. protest against such policies
   b. study completely different problems
   c. support society's prejudices
   d. none of the above

_____ 11. The word "discriminate," as defined in the text, means to _____ solely because of their group memberships.
   a. hold negative attitudes toward individuals
   b. treat individuals badly
   c. hold either positive or negative attitudes toward individuals
   d. treat individuals well or badly

12. Individuals who fit the description of the authoritarian personality do *not* tend to
   a. be submissive to their superiors
   b. project their own undesirable traits onto members of out-groups
   c. be contemptuous to their inferiors
   d. be introspective

13. Subjects exposed to a two-year media campaign to reduce risk factors for heart disease
   a. showed no reduction in risk factors
   b. reduced their risks but not significantly more than controls
   c. reduced their risks but not nearly as much as a group given individual counseling
   d. reduced their risks almost as much as the group given individual counseling

14. Knowing that one *can* control a noise
   a. is ineffective in reducing negative effects unless that control is actually used
   b. reduces the negative effects at the time of the noise, but not the aftereffects
   c. reduces both the negative effects at the time and the aftereffects
   d. is ineffective in reducing negative effects even if the control is used, as long as some noise remains

15. The text uses two Supreme Court decisions on racial relations, one from 1896 and one from 1954, to illustrate an important point about psychology and society. They show
   a. how much more favorable to minorities the 1954 decision was
   b. that little changed between 1896 and 1954
   c. that both decisions mirrored the psychology of the times
   d. that only recently have psychological theories been influential in court decisions

16. The "jigsaw puzzle" technique used in interracial classrooms is an example of arranging for the _____ necessary to reduce prejudice.
   a. equal status of participants
   b. cooperative effort

c. exposure to nonstereotypic individuals
d. potential for personal acquaintance

17. Studies of living arrangements in college dormitories have found long-corridor residents to be more pessimistic and less cooperative than short-corridor residents, apparently as a result of
   a. frustration from the inability to control social encounters
   b. greater noise level in such quarters
   c. a higher level of outside density
   d. all of the above

18. According to the concept of the authoritarian personality, such people relieve their own feelings of insecurity and frustration by blaming
   a. themselves
   b. members of minority groups
   c. those they consider their superiors
   d. those under their authority, for example, employees

19. In seeking to explain why the media were not more effective in changing behavior, it was found that people selectively bias their
   a. exposure to media
   b. attention to messages in the media
   c. interpretation of messages received from the media
   d. all of the above

20. The findings on the negative effects of noise and crowding are parallel; in both cases, what is most important is the individual's
   a. lack of perceived control
   b. personality
   c. cultural upbringing
   d. age and sex

KEY TO SELF-QUIZ

1. c p. 559	6. a p. 555	11. b p. 548	16. b p. 551
2. c p. 567	7. d p. 550	12. d p. 552	17. a p. 562
3. b p. 553	8. a p. 561	13. d p. 558	18. b p. 552
4. b p. 548	9. d p. 554	14. c p. 559	19. d p. 556
5. a p. 566	10. c p. 565	15. c p. 564	20. a p. 563

INDIVIDUAL EXERCISE

REVERSING SEXISM

Introduction

One of the major social concerns of our time is the achieving of true personal equality for all individuals—of different races, ages, and sexes. One of the difficulties in dealing with such problems is the difficulty many of us have in identifying sexism—in ourselves, in others, and in the institutions that shape and support us. Bem and Bem have called the result an "unconscious ideology" and have suggested the technique for learning to recognize it that forms the basis of this exercise.[1]

Procedure

1. First, review the two descriptions of a modern egalitarian marriage on page 549 of the text.

2. As you have seen, the marriage described is far from equal. The husband is simply generously sharing some of the tasks that are jointly produced—such as laundry—but which are by stereotype the wife's duties. The technique used by Bem and Bem for analyzing such questions is very simple. If you can substitute "he" for "she" and vice versa in any such description, it is truly nonsexist. This technique is a good general one for you to keep in mind. It allows you to spot and recognize sexist stereotypes that might otherwise slip by.

3. To use this technique, try substituting a male for a female, and vice versa, in thinking about situations. For example, the liberated women among you might consider the situation in which a male friend picks up a lunch tab for you. Would you accept the same from a female friend? If not, you're supporting sexism.

4. This procedure is so convincing that it makes a useful demonstration for others whose consciousness may not be as raised as yours. The next time you wish to convince someone that a procedure is sexist, try turning it around in this way.

Questions for Discussion

1. If one wishes to be egalitarian, why is it not easy simply to be so? Why do we have to use such tricks as this?

2. What would have to happen for such tricks to become unnecessary? Is it likely to? How soon, do you think? (Hint: are pink and blue blankets equal?)

[1] S. L. Bem and D. J. Bem, "Homogenizing the American woman: The power of unconscious ideology," in *Psychology for our times*, 2nd ed., eds. P. Zimbardo and C. Maslach (Glenview, Ill.: Scott, Foresman, 1977).

Appendix:
Statistical Methods
and Measurement

LEARNING OBJECTIVES

A-1.   Be familiar with the presentation of data in the form of frequency distributions, frequency histograms, and frequency polygons. Understand why such presentations are termed descriptive statistics.

A-2.   Be able to define the measures of central tendency termed mean, median, and mode. Understand how and why these differ from each other for a skewed distribution.

A-3.   Be familiar with the measures of variation termed range and standard deviation. Be able to state what further descriptive information such measures provide that measures of central tendency do not.

A-4.   Be able to explain the logical basis on which one makes a statistical inference about a population based on sample data.

A-5.   Be able to describe a normal curve. Know the approximate percentages of cases falling within ±1, 2, and 3 standard deviations of the mean.

A-6.   Know what is meant by scaling data and be familiar with scaling using standard scores.

A-7.   Understand why the specialized standard deviation termed the standard error of the mean is used.

A-8.   Be able to explain what a finding of statistical significance tells you about the difference between two means. Understand the use of the critical ratio and its relationship to the 5-percent level of significance.

A-9.   Be familiar with the computation of the product-moment and rank correlation coefficients and know how these are related. Be able to describe the general relationship between a scatter diagram and a computed r.

A-10.   Be able to interpret various values of a correlation coefficient, including the meaning of a positive vs. negative sign. Know the linear limitation on correlation and be able to demonstrate, with an original example, why correlation cannot show cause.

1. If we administer a test to 1,000 students and enter their scores in a notebook, we will be recording information about the test results in the form of *raw scores*. The

raw   scores are called _____ because these are the data as they were collected; they have not been changed in any way.

2. The number a person receives on any measure (height, weight, a test, and so on) is

raw   called a _____ score because it has not been manipulated in any way—it remains just as it was collected.

3. Raw data become comprehensible if they are presented in the form of a *frequency distribution*. If we follow a common procedure, we may list each possible score and record next to it the number of people who made that score. In this way the raw

distribution   data are rearranged as a frequency _____ .

4. Whenever we take raw data and arrange them so that we can tell how many people

frequency distribution   made each possible score, we have a _____ _____ .

5. Since we cannot keep 1,000 raw scores in mind at any one time, it would be convenient if we could *describe* these scores more simply. There are a number of ways to describe (or summarize) frequency distributions; all of them, so long as they merely *describe* the distribution, are classified as *descriptive statistics*. Whenever we use a number (for example, an average) to describe a distribution, we are using a

descriptive   _____ statistic.

6. A professor, who has given a test to a large class, wishes to compute the average score in order to describe how well her students as a whole have performed. The

descriptive statistic   professor is using a _____ _____ .

7. Anyone who describes a distribution of scores by the use of summarizing or simpli-

descriptive statistics   fying scores is using _____ .

8. One descriptive statistic, used often, is the *mean;* it is nothing more than the familiar arithmetic average. In order to determine the *mean* of a distribution of scores, one merely sums (that is, adds up) all the scores and *divides* by the *number* of scores. If you sum the raw scores and divide by the number of scores, you have

mean   computed the _____ .

9. John has taken eight tests during a semester, each of which counts equally toward his final grade. To get an idea of how well he has done, he sums the scores received

mean   on the tests and divides the sum by eight. He has computed a _____ grade.

10. In order to compute a mean, one sums all the raw scores and divides by the

number   _____ of scores.

11. Another descriptive statistic is called the *median*. The *median* is defined as the middle score of the distribution. This statistic is obtained by arranging all the scores from low to high and counting in to the middle from either end. The middle score

median is the _____ score. If the number of cases is even, one simply averages the

median cases on either side of the middle. For instance, with 10 cases, the _____ is the average of the fifth and sixth scores when they are arranged from low to high.

12. Put another way, if we find the score that divides the distribution in half, we have

median found the _____ .

13. The *mode* is the score that appears most *frequently* in the distribution. We find the mode by merely examining the distribution; it requires no computation. Whenever we are talking about the score that occurs most frequently, we are talking about the

mode _____ .

frequently 14. The mode, then, is the score that appears most _____ in the
(or synonym) distribution.

descriptive 15. The mean, the median, and the mode are all _____ statistics. They simply describe the distribution of scores.

16. Let us illustrate the way these three statistics may differ by using an example. Let us consider the salaries of five people. Assume that Jim earns $5,000 a year, Mary earns $10,000, Harry also earns $10,000, Bob earns $20,000, and June earns $155,000. First let us compute the *mean* salary. To make this computation, sum all

divide the salaries and _____ by the number of salaries. (Use a separate sheet for this computation and keep it in view.)

5 17. When we sum the salaries of the five people, and divide by ___, we arrive at a mean

$40,000 salary of $ _____ .

18. Next find the *median* salary. The median is the salary in the middle of the distribution. Arranging the five salaries in order from high to low and counting in to the

$10,000 middle yields a median of $ _____ .

19. Finally we examine the distribution to find the *modal* salary. It is obvious that the

$10,000 *mode* of the distribution is $ _____ , since this is the salary that appears most often in the distribution.

20. It now becomes clear that these three statistics may be very different from one an-

same other. In this particular example, the mode and median both take on the _____

larger value, but the mean is much _____ .

21. Once we have a mean, it is often helpful to know whether the scores are all very close to the mean or whether they are spread from very low to very high. In other words, we would like to have a *measure of variation* to describe whether the scores vary a lot or just a little. One measure of variation is the *range*, which is the spread

from the lowest to the highest score. For example, if the instructor says that the scores on a test went from a low of 32 to a high of 93, he or she is giving the

range

_____ of scores.

variation

22. The range is one measure of _____.

23. Joyce got a 63 on a test. Her roommate asked her how well the others in the class did, and she replied that the scores ran from 40 to 74. Joyce was describing the

range

variation of scores in terms of their _____ .

24. Most scores are not the same as the mean; that is, they deviate from the mean. The *standard deviation* is a frequently used measure of the amount by which scores

mean

deviate or depart from their _____. The standard deviation is thus another

variation

measure of _____ .

25. The lower-case Greek letter σ is frequently used as an abbreviation for the standard

deviation

_____ . The formula for computing the standard deviation is as follows:

$$\sigma = \sqrt{\frac{\text{Sum of } d^2}{N}}$$

The deviation, *d,* for each score is first computed by subtracting the score from the mean. Next, the *d* for each score is squared, and then the squared deviations for all the scores are summed.

26. Statisticians use *N* as a shorthand for the number of scores. When we divide the sum

deviations

of the squared _____ by *N,* we are dividing by the number of

scores

_____ .

27. In computing the *standard deviation,* then, the first step is to determine the devia-

square

tion of each raw score from the mean. The second step is to _____ each of these deviations.

28. In the third step, sum these squared deviations and then divide by *N.* To review:

deviation

The first step is to determine the _____ of each raw score from the

square

mean. The second step is to _____ each of these deviations. Third, sum

N

the squared deviations and divide by _____.

29. When we then take the *square root* of the result of step three, we arrive at the

standard deviation

_____ _____ .

mean

30. To recapitulate: First, determine the deviations of the raw scores from the _____;

deviations, sum

second, square each of these _____ ; third, _____ these squared

root

deviations and divide by *N.* Finally, take the square _____ of the result to

standard deviation

obtain the _____ _____ .

31. Let us consider the following example to show how a standard deviation is calculated. For the sake of simplicity, we will use only a few scores. Suppose a test is given to five people and the scores are as follows: 11, 13, 14, 15, 17. In this case

14   the mean would be _____ . (Use a separate sheet of paper.)

32. For the score of 11, the deviation from the mean (obtained by subtracting the

9   score from the mean) is 3. Squaring this we would arrive at the number _____ .

1,1   **33.** The deviation of the score of 13 would be _____ . Squaring this yields _____ .

0,0   **34.** The deviation of the score of 14 would be _____ . Squaring this yields _____ .

1   **35.** The deviation of the score of 15 would be –1 (14 – 15 = –1). Squaring –1 yields ___ .

–3, 9   **36.** The deviation of the score of 17 would be _____ . Squaring this yields _____ .

37. We now have the squared deviation of each of the scores. In other words, we have completed steps one and two in the sequence mentioned above and are ready to move on to step three in the computation of the standard deviation. In step three

sum, 5   we _____ the squared deviations and divide by N. In this case N equals _____ .

4   **38.** When the operations in step three are carried out, we arrive at ___ (*number*) as a result.

39. We now perform the final operation; we take the square root of the result of step

2   three. The square root of 4 is _____ .

2   **40.** Therefore the standard deviation of this distribution of scores is _____ .

standard   **41.** We have examined two *measures of variation:* the range and the _____ deviation.

variation **42.** The range and the standard deviation are both measures of _____ . Since these two statistics merely *describe* the distribution, they are classified as

descriptive   _____ statistics.

43. We often wish to say something about large groups of people, for example, the population of China, or the population of the United States, or all college students, or all students at a particular college. The group we wish to talk about is called the *population,* whether it contains 50,000,000 or 100 people. In research, the total

population   group we wish to make our statements about is called the _____ .

44. Professor Jones wishes to find out whether English males are taller than German males. Since he wants to say something about both English males and German

populations   males, these are his _____ s.

45. It is obvious that Professor Jones will not have enough time or money to test all English and German males. Therefore he will have to be satisfied to test fewer than all of them. In a way he has the same problem that customs inspectors have. Customs inspectors want to make sure that no one brings in contraband, but they haven't time to inspect everyone's luggage. Therefore they select some of the people and inspect their baggage thoroughly. They have drawn a *sample* of the total population. A _____, then, is a smaller number of cases that is drawn from the _____.

sample

population

46. Whenever we select and test a smaller number of cases from the total population we are interested in, we have drawn a _____ from the population.

sample

47. A sample should be selected in such a way that it is *representative* of the total population. Otherwise, we cannot make reasonable *inferences* about the total _____ based solely on information obtained from the sample.

population

48. A sample that is not representative of the population will not allow us to make reasonable _____ about the population.

inferences

49. One way of obtaining a representative sample is to select it at *random.* To do this, we can put the names of the members of the population in a hat and draw out the number we need, or use any other means of selection that will guarantee that *every person in the population has an equal chance of being chosen.* When we draw a sample in such a way that each individual in the population has an equal chance of being chosen, we have drawn a r_____ sample.

random

50. A key feature of a random sample is that each individual in the population has an _____ _____ of being chosen.

equal chance

51. If we collect data on a sample of 100 people in a town of 1,000 people and then make statements about the *entire* population of the town on the basis of these data, we cannot be *sure* our statements are correct. Only if we collect data on the entire _____ of the town can we be sure that any statements based on the data will be correct for the whole population.

population

52. When we make statements about a population on the basis of a sample, we *infer* that what is true about the sample will also be approximately true for the entire population. A statement about a population based on a sample of that population is called an _____ence. We can never be completely _____that such an inference is correct.

inference, sure
(or synonym)

53. Another way of putting this is to say that when we make an inference about a population from a sample, we have only a certain probability that our statement is correct for the population as a whole. The probability of our statement being true would be 100 percent only if we had data on the _____ population.

entire (or synonym)

54. The smaller the size of the sample, the smaller the probability of making a correct inference about the population. Since we are making inferences about the _____, based on *statistics* that are computed from only a _____ of the population, we call this process *statistical inference.*

population

sample

55. When the Gallup poll interviews a small number of people and makes a pre-

diction about who will be elected President of the United States, a statistical

inference

_____ is being made.

56. Suppose a researcher is interested in the population of a particular college with 10,000 students. She goes to the college directory and takes each hundredth name,

random

thus drawing a _____ sample of the population of students at that college.

57. She tests this sample of students and, on the basis of their scores alone, she makes

population

statements about the entire _____ of the college. When she does

statistical inference

this, she is making a _____ _____ .

58. Suppose we gave an intelligence test to all the people in the United States and then plotted on a graph the scores and the number of people who got each score. We plot

horizontal

the number of people on the vertical axis and their scores on the <u>hor</u>_____ axis. In schematic form the graph would look like the illustration below.

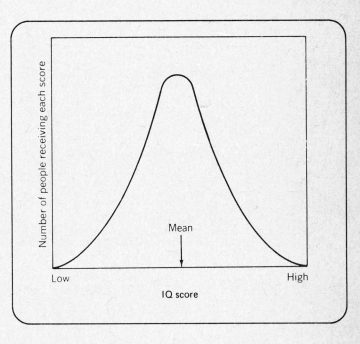

59. This graph represents a *frequency distribution* of scores. Looking at the graph, we find that there are relatively few people who got very low scores and that the num-

increases

ber of people who got any particular score (*increases/decreases*) as we move upward toward the mean. As we move past the mean to the right, there are fewer and fewer people getting the higher scores and very few getting the highest scores.

60. Note that the curve of the frequency distribution is *symmetrical* in form; that is,

above

the part of the curve below the mean is a mirror image of the part _____the mean. Symmetry implies that for every score a fixed distance above the mean there

below

is a corresponding score the same distance _____ the mean, so that the number of people receiving each score will be the same.

frequency

61. The curve of the _____ distribution shown above not only is symmetrical in form but also is shaped very much like a bell. A frequency-distribution curve that is symmetrical and also _____ -shaped is called a *normal curve.*

bell

distribution

normal

62. When we plot a frequency _____ and get a curve that is bell-shaped, we call this curve a _____ curve.

63. For a normal curve the mean, median, and mode all have the same value. There are the same number of cases below and above the middle of the distribution; for every score below the mean there is another score the same distance above the mean; and the number of cases receiving a score a given distance below the mean is matched by an equal number of cases receiving a score the same distance above the mean. In

symmetrical

other words, the two halves of the curve are _____ .

fifty

64. If fifty people have a score of 80 and the mean is 100, then _____ (*number*) people can be expected to have a score of 120 if the curve is a normal curve.

65. If we actually administered the Stanford-Binet intelligence test to all the people in the United States, we would find that the frequency distribution of scores would take the form of a normal curve. The *mean* of the scores would be 100 and the *standard deviation* would be 16. The standard deviation, as you will remember, is a

variation

measure of var_____ .

66. Statisticians often talk about a score as being one or more standard deviations away from the mean. If the mean of the scores on an intelligence test is 100 and the standard deviation is 16, a score of 84 would be said to be one standard deviation

below

_____ the mean.

67. One of the properties of the normal curve is that *68 percent* of all the cases in the distribution will have scores that lie between one standard deviation below and one above the mean. The normal curve is so defined that this will *always* be true. If a

68

distribution of intelligence test scores fits a normal curve, _____ percent of the cases

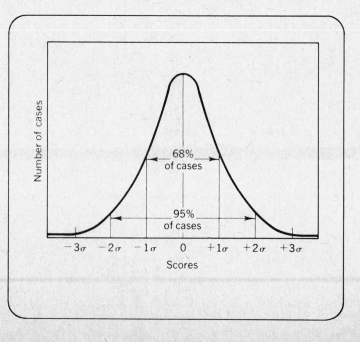

will have scores between one standard deviation below the mean and one standard

above deviation _____ the mean. This characteristic of the normal curve is shown in the illustration on page 286, in which new labels have been added to the normal curve with which you are already familiar.

68. As you already know, the Greek letter σ is the abbreviation for standard deviation.

below Thus -1σ means one standard deviation _____ the mean.

69. Referring again to the intelligence test with a mean of 100 and a standard deviation

84 of 16, the score that is one standard deviation below the mean is _____ (*number*).

116 70. The score that is one standard deviation above the mean would be _____.

71. Therefore, if we group all the people with scores between 84 and 116 on the intelli-

68 gence test, we will have _____ percent of the population.

72. If we look again at the new illustration of the normal curve, we see that 95 percent of the population have scores that lie between *two* standard deviations below the mean and two standard deviations above the mean. To go back to the intelligence test with a mean of 100 and a standard deviation of 16, 95 percent of the popula-

132 tion will have scores between 68 and _____ .

73. If 68 percent of the population have scores that lie between one standard deviation below the mean and one standard deviation above the mean on the normal curve,

34 then it follows that ____ percent of the population have scores between one standard deviation below the mean and the mean itself.

74. In other words, in our example, 34 percent of the population have scores between

100 84 and _____.

75. If 95 percent of the population have scores between two standard deviations below the mean and two standard deviations above the mean, then 47.5 percent of the population have scores between two standard deviations above the mean and the mean itself. In our example, then, 47.5 percent of the population have scores

132 between 100 and _____.

76. Again looking at our illustration of the normal curve, we can see that almost all of the people (over 99 percent) have scores that lie between three standard deviations

above below the mean and three standard deviations _____ the mean. Thus for

three practical purposes virtually all of the scores fall between minus and plus _____ standard deviations from the mean.

77. To use our example once more, we would expect that practically all the people who took the intelligence test (mean = 100, standard deviation = 16) would have scores

52, 148 between _____ and _____.

78. As a quick example of how one can use the concept of the standard deviation on the normal curve, let us suppose that Susan had a score of 148 on the intelligence test. Knowing the mean and the standard deviation of that test, Susan can be sure

three that she has earned one of the very highest scores, since her score is _____ standard deviations above the mean. In other words, she knows how her score compares with those from the population at large.

Note: The Appendix in the text can be only an introduction to the subject of statistics. In turn, this programmed unit can be only an introduction to that material. You have learned about some of the basic terms and techniques of statistical analysis, but several concepts that are treated in the text have not even been mentioned in this program. You should, however, find it easier to master the text treatment if you have understood the concepts presented here.

TERMS AND CONCEPTS

descriptive statistics _____

_____

_____

_____

frequency distribution _____

_____

_____

_____

mean _____

_____

_____

_____

median _____

_____

_____

_____

mode _____

_____

_____

_____

skewed distribution _____

_____

_____

_____

range _____

_____

_____

_____

standard deviation _____

_____

_____

_____

population _____

_____

_____

sample _____

_____

_____

_____

statistical inference _____

_____

_____

_____

normal distribution _____

_____

_____

_____

standard score _____

_____

_____

_____

standard error of the mean _____

_____

_____

_____

statistical significance _____

_____

_____

_____

critical ratio _____

_____

_____

_____

product-moment correlation (*r*) _____

_____

_____

_____

rank correlation (*rho*) _____

_____

_____

_____ 1. Descriptive statistics
   a. include the analysis of variance
   b. provide a shorthand notation for summarizing a large number of observations
   c. exclude measures of variation
   d. allow us to learn about a population by studying small samples

_____ 2. Suppose scores on test A have a mean of 20 and a standard error of the mean of 1, while scores on test B have a mean of 25 and also have a standard error of the mean of 1. Can we depend on the difference between the two means, that is, is it significant?
   a. Yes, since the critical ratio is high.
   b. No, the difference is not significant.
   c. Maybe, since the critical ratio is close to the significance level.
   d. We cannot tell from these data.

_____ 3. The curve that results from a large number of chance events occurring independently is a _____curve
   a. standard
   b. normal
   c. random
   d. chance

_____ 4. What two measures of central tendency are identical for this distribution: 1, 1, 3, 4, 6?
   a. mean and mode
   b. mode and median
   c. mean and median
   d. all of the above

_____ 5. Suppose you take a midterm and a final in this course. Will you be able to tell on which one you do better when there are different numbers of questions? If the midterm has a mean of 50 with a standard deviation of 10, the final has a mean of 120 with a standard deviation of 20, and your scores are 55 and 135, you will have
   a. done better on the final
   b. done worse on the final
   c. stayed the same on the final
   d. failed the course

_____ 6. It should always be remembered that correlation
   a. does not measure linear relationships
   b. cannot show statistical significance
   c. does not yield causal relationships
   d. all of the above

_____ 7. A measure of variation
   a. is the range
   b. tells us how representative the mean is
   c. is the standard deviation
   d. all of the above

_____ 8. A rank correlation
   a. is designated by r
   b. is a simpler method for determining correlations than is the product-moment correlation
   c. should probably be done on a computer, because of the complexity of the formula
   d. does not go below zero, because ranks are involved

_____ 9. If we wished to know whether the average of a distribution is typical of the scores within it, we would look at the _____ for a simple indicator but would compute the _____ if we wished a more sensitive measure.
   a. range, standard deviation
   b. range, standard score
   c. mean, standard deviation
   d. mode, critical ratio

_____ 10. The most widely used graph form for plotting data grouped into class intervals is the
   a. frequency distribution
   b. symmetrical distribution
   c. frequency histogram
   d. normal distribution

_____ 11. A standard score is
   a. based on the standard deviation
   b. offers a way of scaling the data
   c. tells us how one score compares to the others in a distribution
   d. all of the above

_____ 12. The conventional rule of thumb for an acceptable level of statistical significance is _____ percent, that is, we are willing to risk a chance result occurring _____ in 100 decisions.
   a. 1, once
   b. 2, twice
   c. 5, five times
   d. 10, ten times

13. If a normal distribution has a mean of 100 and a standard deviation of 5, we know that
   a. 68 percent of the scores fall between 95 and 105
   b. 95 percent of the scores fall between 85 and 115
   c. approximately half of the scores fall between 80 and 120
   d. the range of scores is 75 to 125

14. A correlation of $r = -.80$
   a. is significant
   b. means that increases in x are accompanied by decreases in y
   c. means that increases in x are accompanied by increases in y
   d. makes the relationship between x and y unclear

15. The median is
   a. obtained by adding the scores and dividing by the number of cases
   b. that part of the scale where most cases occur
   c. the score with the highest frequency
   d. the middle score in a distribution

16. We can have confidence in a statistical inference if the
   a. sample is significant
   b. effect is large relative to the sampling error
   c. population is normal
   d. all of the above

17. If a general round of wage increases were to be combined with a reduction of extremely high incomes, the
   a. mean income would tend to go up
   b. distribution of income would become more skewed

   c. median would tend to go down
   d. distribution of income would become less skewed

18. Since the standard error of the mean is a special case of the standard deviation, it tells us about the distribution of the *population* made up of *sample means.* For example, we know that if a sample has a mean of 50 and a standard error of the mean of 5, the population mean almost certainly falls in the range of
   a. 45–55
   b. 40–60
   c. 35–65
   d. 30–70

19. The _____ is very useful, in that it gives us a mathematical way of stating the degree of relationship between two variables.
   a. rank correlation (*rho*)
   b. coefficient of correlation
   c. product-moment correlation (*r*)
   d. all of the above

20. In order to make a judgment about a population without testing all members of it, we
   a. draw a random sample for testing
   b. examine the normal distribution
   c. develop a standard score
   d. examine the standard error of the scores

KEY TO SELF-QUIZ

INDIVIDUAL EXERCISES

Introduction

Although a mastery of statistical techniques requires time and training, the basic notions of statistics can be understood by those with a minimum of mathematical background. The following exercises use simple data in order to make computations easy. These exercises are designed to illustrate how the formulas work rather than to provide skill in their use; you should attempt the exercises only after you have read the Appendix in the textbook. (The

answers to these exercises are given in the Appendix of this book, page 298.)

FREQUENCY DISTRIBUTION

Eleven applicants for a job made the following scores on a test of relevant skills:

25 53 42 64 38 43 56 36 38 48 47

Complete the table below by counting the scores in each class interval; then plot the diagram.

Frequency Distribution

Scores on test	Number of applicants making these scores
20–29	_____
30–39	_____
40–49	_____
50–59	_____
60–69	_____

FREQUENCY DIAGRAM

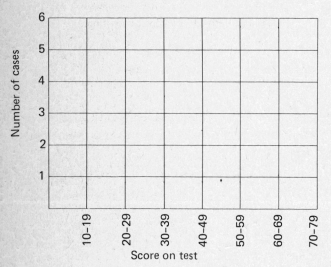

Questions

1. What is the class interval?

2. Is the distribution symmetrical?

MEASURES OF CENTRAL TENDENCY

Questions

3. Determine the *median* score for the above data by arranging the scores in order and finding the *middle* case (that is, the 6th from either end of 11).

    Median = _____

4. Calculate the *mean* for the above data by adding the *raw scores* and dividing by the number of scores.

    Mean = _____

5. Under what circumstances do the mean and median differ?

6. If the person getting the high score of 64 had in fact gotten a score of 75, how would it have affected the mean and the median?

MEASURES OF VARIATION

Consider the following weekly earnings reported by five part-time taxicab drivers:

Driver	Weekly earnings
A	$50
B	$60
C	$70
D	$80
E	$90

Questions

7. What is the *range* of weekly earnings? _____

    The *mean?* _____

8. Compute the *standard deviation* by completing the following table.

Driver	Weekly earnings	Deviation from mean (d)	Deviation squared (d^2)
A			
B			
C			
D			
E			

Sum of d^2 = _____

$\dfrac{\text{Sum of } d^2}{N}$ = _____

Standard deviation = $\sqrt{\dfrac{\text{Sum of } d^2}{N}}$ = _____

STANDARD ERROR OF THE MEAN

The more cases that enter into the computation of a mean, the more confidence we have that our obtained mean represents the total group from which our sample has been drawn.

Suppose that we draw successive samples of increasing size in order to measure some psychological characteristic, such as speed of reaction, among college students. How does our confidence increase with the size of the sample?

Suppose that the means of our reaction-time measurement fluctuate around 150 milliseconds (0.150 seconds), with standard deviations around 15 milliseconds. Where does the true mean reaction time fall?

These problems will be dealt with as you answer Questions 9 and 10.

Questions

9. Let us compute the *standard error of the mean,* assuming different numbers of cases (persons) in our sample. Complete the following table, using the formula:

$$\text{Standard error of the mean } (\sigma_M) = \frac{\text{Standard deviation } (\sigma)}{\sqrt{N}}$$

Number of cases (N)	$\sqrt{N}$	Standard deviation (σ)	Standard error of mean (σ_M)
25	5	15	
100	10	15	
400	20	15	

Note that the standard error of the mean decreases as N increases. How can we convert this into some kind of statement about the true mean?

10. *Confidence limits.* We can state that with repeated measurements we can expect our means to fall within the range from -2.0σ to $+2.0\sigma$ in 95 percent of the cases. Using the table at the top of the right-hand column, determine the confidence limits for the mean reaction times of the three different sample sizes.

Sample size	Mean reaction time (milliseconds)	95 percent confidence limits	
		Lower limit (mean less 2.0 × standard error)	Upper limit (mean plus 2.0 × standard error)
25	150		
100	150		
400	150		

Thus far nothing has been said about the true mean of the population. Setting the confidence limits as we have, we may infer that the true mean lies within our confidence limits 95 percent of the time.

SIGNIFICANCE OF A DIFFERENCE

Suppose that we are comparing the mathematics scores of boys and girls in the fourth grade, with the following results:

	Number of cases (N)	Mean	Standard error of mean (σ_M)
Girls	50	72.0	0.4
Boys	50	70.5	0.3

Questions

Do the girls score significantly higher than the boys? To find out, we compute a *critical ratio,* but first we have to find the *standard error of difference,* according to the following formula.

11. The formula for the standard error of difference is

$$\sigma_D = \sqrt{\sigma_{M_1}^2 + \sigma_{M_2}^2}$$

where σ_{M_1} and σ_{M_2} are the standard errors of the means for girls and boys. Work out this formula using the data above.

$$\sigma_D = \sqrt{(\qquad)^2 + (\qquad)^2} = \sqrt{(\qquad)} = \underline{\qquad}$$

12. Compute the critical ratio, using this formula:

$$\text{Critical ratio} = \frac{\text{Difference between means}}{\sigma_D} =$$

$$\frac{(\quad) - (\quad)}{(\quad)} = \underline{\hspace{1.5cm}}$$

13. If the absolute size of the critical ratio is over 2.0, we usually call the difference *significant.* In our example, is there a significant difference between the mathematic scores of boys and girls?

COEFFICIENT OF CORRELATION

Job applicants were given a test of sales ability before being hired. Then their scores were compared with subsequent performance on the job (as shown in first table below).

Questions

The degree of relationship between scores and sales is expressed by the *coefficient of correlation.* This index may be computed from two different formulas.

14. The most frequently used method yields the *product-moment correlation, r.* What is the product-moment correlation between the applicants' test scores and earnings? Complete the computations indicated in the table on page 295 and copy your result here:

$r = \underline{\hspace{3cm}}$.

15. When there are few cases, an approximate method, known as *rank correlation,* yielding *rho* instead of *r,* is useful. The data are converted to ranks and then the following formula is used:

$$rho = 1 - \frac{6(\text{Sum } D^2)}{N(N^2 - 1)}$$

where *D* is difference in ranks for the measures and *N* the number of cases. Compute the rank correlation, using the table below.

16. On the basis of this correlation, what can be said about the cause-and-effect relations between test scores and sales performance?

Applicant:	Anderson	Brown	Cook	Dodge	East
Test score:	50	60	70	80	90
Sales (in thousands of dollars):	$60	$80	$90	$70	$100

COMPUTATION OF RANK CORRELATION

Applicant	(1) Sales test score rank	(2) Earnings score rank	Difference in rank D = (1) – (2)	Squared difference (D^2)
Anderson				
Brown				
Cook				
Dodge				
East				

$$rho = 1 - \frac{6(\quad)}{(\quad)(\quad)} = 1 - \frac{(\quad)}{(\quad)} = \underline{\hspace{2cm}}$$

COMPUTATION OF PRODUCT-MOMENT CORRELATION (r)

Correlation between a sales test and later sales in thousands of dollars

Applicant	Scores on the sales test and computation of σ_x			Sales success and computation of σ_y			Cross-products used in computing r
	Test score (x)	Deviation from mean (dx)* (mean = 70)	$(dx)^2$	Sales score (y)	Deviation from mean (dy)* (mean = $80)	$(dy)^2$	Product of deviations (dx) (dy)
Anderson							
Brown							
Cook							
Dodge							
East							
	Sum $(dx)^2$ =			Sum $(dy)^2$ =			Sum (dx) (dy) =
	$\dfrac{\text{Sum } (dx)^2}{N}$ =			$\dfrac{\text{Sum } (dy)^2}{N}$ =			
	$\sigma_x = \sqrt{\dfrac{\text{Sum } (dx)^2}{N}}$ =			$\sigma_y = \sqrt{\dfrac{\text{Sum } (dy)^2}{N}}$ =			

*Subtract mean from score: respect the sign of the difference.

$$\text{Coefficient of correlation, } r = \frac{\text{Sum } (dx)\,(dy)}{N\,\sigma_x\,\sigma_y} = \frac{(\qquad)}{(\quad) \times (\quad) \times (\quad)} = \frac{(\quad)}{(\quad)} = \underline{\qquad\qquad}$$

Appendix

Note. This Appendix includes answers to exercises and problems presented in the *Study Guide.* The student should not read this material until reference is made to it in the text of the *Guide.*

CHAPTER 11 (PAGE 174) MEASURING MOTIVATION

Score your completed sentences as follows:

P . . . . if your response indicates a positive, humorous, or hopeful attitude

C . . . . if your response indicates conflict, antagonism, pessimism, emotional disturbance

N . . . . if your response is neutral, that is, not clearly positive or conflictful

Examples of how your responses should be scored:

Men _____.

P . . . . are friendly, are easy to get along with, are nice, are good sports, are considerate, are fun at a party, are good friends, are O.K.

C . . . . are a pain in the neck, get on my nerves, can't be trusted, bother me, give me a headache, think they are superior, are rude, are stupid.

N . . . . are human beings, are taller than women, are stronger than women, are the opposite sex, are the same sex.

Count the total number of P, C, and N scores. Your instructor may ask you to write these on a slip of paper so that he or she can determine the distribution of results for the entire class. (You may then complete the table below and determine the median score.) You need not identify yourself. Compute your score by adding fifty to the number of C responses and subtracting the number of P responses. Any omissions (incompleted sentences) are not scored.

Score	Number of students	Score	Number of students
96–100		46–50	
91–95		41–45	
86–90		36–40	
81–85		31–35	
76–80		26–30	
71–75		21–25	
66–70		16–20	
61–65		11–15	
56–60		6–10	
51–55		1–5	

Median score

CHAPTER 12 (PAGE 189) INDIVIDUAL DIFFERENCES

The unscrambled sentences are as follows:

1. The good that men do lives after them.
2. Don't shoot until you see the whites of their eyes.
3. The most valuable thing in the world is the free human mind.
4. Tell your yarn and let your style go to the devil.
5. It is only at rare moments that we live.
6. Do not blame me too much for not knowing all the answers.
7. The greatest of faults is to be conscious of none.
8. It is better to understand a little than to misunderstand a lot.
9. The worst use that can be made of success is boasting of it.
10. Better a witty fool than a foolish wit.
11. First love is only a little foolishness and a lot of curiosity.
12. The power of laughter is astonishing.
13. Money cannot cure unhappiness.
14. Your reputation grows with every failure.
15. Talk to a man about himself and he will listen for hours.
16. The truth is the one thing nobody will believe.
17. My way of joking is to tell the truth.
18. It is not pleasure that makes life worth living.
19. I had rather be right than President.
20. Very simple ideas lie within the reach only of complex minds.

CHAPTER 15 (PAGE 235) CLASSIFYING ABNORMAL BEHAVIOR

The cases are designed to illustrate the following disorders:

Case 1 Psychosis—manic-depressive reaction, manic state

Case 2 Psychosis—schizophrenia

Case 3 Neurosis—conversion reaction

Case 4 Neurosis—anxiety reaction

Case 5 Neurosis—phobia

Case 6 Neurosis—compulsive reaction

Case 7 Psychopathic personality

Case 8 Neurotic depression

APPENDIX: STATISTICAL METHODS AND MEASUREMENT (PAGE 291)

Answers to the *Individual Exercises.*

1. 10
2. No
3. Median = 43
4. Mean = 44.55
5. When the frequency distribution is not perfectly symmetrical about the mean
6. Increased the mean, no effect on the median
7. Range from $50 to $90, or $40; Mean = $70
8. Standard deviation = 14.14
9. Standard errors: for 25 cases, 3.0; for 100 cases, 1.5; for 400 cases, 0.75
10. Confidence limits: for 25 cases, 144–156; for 100 cases, 147–153; for 400 cases, 148.5–151.5
11. Standard error of difference = 0.5
12. Critical ratio = 3.0
13. Yes
14. $r = .70$
15. $rho = .70$
16. No definite conclusions about cause-and-effect relations can be drawn from correlational evidence. See discussion of this topic in text.